Learner English

SECOND EDITION

A teacher's guide to interference and other problems

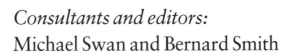

Consultants and editors:
Michael Swan and Bernard Smith

CAMBRIDGE
UNIVERSITY PRESS

CAMBRIDGE UNIVERSITY PRESS
Cambridge, New York, Melbourne, Madrid, Cape Town, Singapore,
São Paulo, Delhi, Dubai, Tokyo

Cambridge University Press
The Edinburgh Building, Cambridge CB2 8RU, UK

www.cambridge.org
Information on this title: www.cambridge.org/9780521779395

First published 1987
Second edition 2001
13th printing 2010

Printed in the United Kingdom at the University Press, Cambridge

A catalogue record for this publication is available from the British Library

Library of Congress Cataloguing-in-Publication Data
Learner English: a teacher's guide to interference and other problems / [edited by]
Michael Swan and Bernard Smith. – 2nd ed.
   p. cm. – (Cambridge handbooks for language teachers)
Includes bibliographical references and index.
ISBN 978-0-521-77939-5 (pb) – ISBN 978-0-521-00024-6 (audio cd) – ISBN 978-0-521-77497-0 (cassette)
1. English language – Study and teaching – Foreign speakers. 2. Interference (Linguistics)
I. Swan, Michael.   II. Smith, Bernard, 1937– .   III. Series.

PE1128.A2 L36 2001   00-046785
428'.0071–dc21

ISBN 978-0-521-77939-5 Paperback
ISBN 978-0-521-00024-6 Audio CD

Learner English

Cambridge Handbooks for Language Teachers

This is a series of practical guides for teachers of English and other languages. Illustrative examples are usually drawn from the field of English as a foreign or second language, but the ideas and techniques described can equally well be used in the teaching of any language.

Recent titles in this series:

Ways of Doing
Students explore their everyday and classroom processes
PAUL DAVIS, BARBARA GARSIDE *and*
MARIO RINVOLUCRI

Using Newspapers in the Classroom
PAUL SANDERSON

Teaching Adult Second Language Learners
HEATHER MCKAY *and* ABIGAIL TOM

Teaching English Spelling
A practical guide
RUTH SHEMESH *and* SHEILA WALLER

Using Folktales
ERIC TAYLOR

Personalizing Language Learning
Personalized language learning activities
GRIFF GRIFFITHS *and* KATHRYN KEOHANE

Teach Business English
A comprehensive introduction to Business English
SYLVIE DONNA

Learner Autonomy
A guide to activities which encourage learner responsibility
ÁGOTA SCHARLE *and* ANITA SZABÓ

The Internet and the Language Classroom
Practical classroom activities and projects
GAVIN DUDENEY

Planning Lessons and Courses
Designing sequences of work for the language classroom
TESSA WOODWARD

Using the Board in the Language Classroom
JEANNINE DOBBS

Teaching Large Multilevel Classes
NATALIE HESS

Writing Simple Poems
Pattern poetry for language acquisition
VICKI L. HOLMES *and* MARGARET R. MOULTON

Laughing Matters
Humour in the language classroom
PÉTER MEDGYES

Using Authentic Video in the Language Classroom
JANE SHERMAN

Stories
Narrative activities for the language classroom
RUTH WAJNRYB

Language Activities for Teenagers
edited by SETH LINDSTROMBERG

Pronunciation Practice Activities
A resource book for teaching English pronunciation
MARTIN HEWINGS

Five-Minute Activities for Business English
PAUL EMMERSON *and* NICK HAMILTON

Contents

Notes on contributors

Alexander Burak (Russian) is an Associate Professor at Lomonosov Moscow State University, where he is Head of the Lexicography and Translation Department in the Faculty of Foreign Languages.

Jung Chang (Chinese) is a former lecturer at the School of Oriental and African Studies, University of London, and is now a full-time writer.

Norman Coe (Spanish and Catalan) is Coordinator of English at the Open University of Catalonia (ncoe@campus.uoc.es).

Niels Davidsen-Nielsen (Scandinavian) is Professor of English at the Copenhagen Business School, and Vice-Chairman of the Danish Language Council.

Xavier Dekeyser (Dutch) is Professor Emeritus at the University of Antwerp.

Betty Devriendt (Dutch) teaches English language and linguistics at the University of Antwerp.

Alison Duguid (Italian) has worked as a teacher and teacher trainer in Italy and elsewhere.

Steven Geukens (Dutch) teaches English language and linguistics at the University of Antwerp.

Lucyna Gołębiowska (Polish) teaches English at the Polish Academy of Sciences and writes EFL reference books.

Neville Grant (Swahili) is a writer, educational consultant and teacher trainer. He has written textbooks for students of English in Africa, the Caribbean and China.

Peter Harder (Scandinavian) is a Professor of English at the University of Copenhagen.

Jung-Ae Lee (Korean) is a Professor of Comparative Literature, French and Korean at Josai International University in Japan, and is a Visiting Fellow of Lucy Cavendish College at the University of Cambridge. She has written a number of books and papers on cultural and linguistic topics.

Bruce Monk (Russian) taught at Moscow State University for nine years. He is now a Professor at Nagoya University of Commerce and Business Administration, Japan.

Sita Narasimhan (Tamil) is a retired fellow of Newnham College, Cambridge, and an affiliated member of the Faculty of Divinity, Cambridge.

Sophia Papaefthymiou-Lytra (Greek) is Professor of Applied Linguistics and a teacher trainer at the University of Athens.

Christopher Shackle FBA (South Asian) is Professor of Modern Languages of South Asia at the School of Oriental and African Studies, University of London.

David Shepherd (Portuguese) has extensive experience of EFL teaching, lecturing and teacher training in Brazil.

Bernard Smith (Arabic) was an Arabic teacher and interpreter for the Ministry of Defence, and is now an EFL teacher and writer who has written three courses for the Arab world.

David Smyth (Thai) is a lecturer in Thai and Cambodian at the School of Oriental and African Studies, University of London.

Grzegorz Śpiewak (Polish) is a teacher trainer and a lecturer in applied linguistics at the University of Warsaw Institute of English Studies.

Michael Swan (German) writes English-language teaching and reference books.

Ian Thompson (Japanese, Turkish) has taught English in Britain, Japan, Turkey and South America, and has a special interest in contrastive studies.

Guy Tops (Dutch) teaches English language and linguistics at the University of Antwerp. He is joint editor-in-chief of the Van Dale English-Dutch/Dutch-English dictionary.

The late **Philip Tregidgo** (West African) was a specialist in the practical description of English grammar, and wrote English textbooks for schools in various parts of Africa.

Catherine Walter (French) has taught English in France and carried out research on French learners' acquisition of reading skills in English. She is the author and co-author of several English language textbooks.

Lili Wilson (Farsi) taught English in Iran and is currently a lecturer at the University of Brighton, specialising in Computer Assisted Language Learning.

Martin Wilson (Farsi) taught English in Iran and is now a senior lecturer at the University of Brighton, involved in teaching English as a foreign language and training EFL teachers.

Janet Yong (Malay/Indonesian) is a lecturer at the Faculty of Bahasa and Linguistics of the University of Malaya at Kuala Lumpur.

Introduction

Purpose and scope of the book

This book is a practical reference guide for teachers of English as a foreign language. It is meant to help teachers to anticipate the characteristic difficulties of learners of English who speak particular mother tongues, and to understand how these difficulties arise.

It is obviously only possible, in a work of this kind, to give an outline account of the problems of the speakers of a few of the world's many languages. We hope, however, that in the twenty-two chapters that follow many teachers will find information that is useful to them. Since the book is designed primarily for teachers of British English, the selection is biased slightly towards the problems of those students that British teachers most often find themselves teaching. Teachers of other varieties should, however, also find much that is relevant to their purposes.

Most of the chapters discuss the typical 'interlanguage' of speakers of a particular mother tongue. (By 'interlanguage' we mean the variety of a language that is produced by non-native learners.) In some cases (Swahili, Hindi, Tamil), the language focused on can be taken as broadly representative of a whole group, in that speakers of related languages are likely to share a number of the problems described. In two chapters (those on West African and Scandinavian learners), the description relates to the English of speakers of a whole group of languages.

A CD with recordings of learners, illustrating some of the pronunciation problems described in the various chapters, is also available.

Approach

The book is written especially for the practising non-specialist teacher who needs an introduction to the characteristic problems of a particular group of learners. Technical linguistic terminology has been kept to a minimum, and contributors have in general aimed at producing clear simple descriptions of usage rather than detailed scholarly studies. This is particularly the case in the area of pronunciation, where excessive technical detail can be confusing and counterproductive for the non-specialist. Within these limits, however, we believe that the descriptions given here are valid and reasonably comprehensive.

British and other varieties of English

Learners' problems are described in terms of the way their typical 'interlanguages' deviate from a standard British variety of English. (This choice implies no value judgement.) Not all the comparisons are valid for other types of English, especially those relating to pronunciation, and forms that are 'incorrect' in one variety may be correct in another. Teachers of American, Australian or other non-British varieties will therefore need to be selective in their use of the information given here. (There is a note on pages xii–xiii for teachers of American English.) Teachers working in regions which have their own established forms of second-language English, such as India, West Africa or Singapore, need to be especially careful in this respect. A particular 'typical mistake' (seen through British eyes) may be a perfectly normal and acceptable form in the local standard, and the question of whether to correct it may not be a straightforward one for a teacher.

Editorial conventions

In the 'distribution' sections, capitals are used for the names of countries in which the language concerned has official or quasi-official status at the time of publication. Lower case letters are used for other countries in which substantial numbers of native speakers of the language may be found. Thus the distribution of Italian is given as: ITALY, REPUBLIC OF SAN MARINO, VATICAN, SWITZERLAND, Malta, Somalia.

Pronunciation is shown by the use of common phonetic symbols between slashes, thus: /ðʌs/. These necessarily provide rough guides only; the context should make it clear whether the transcription is intended to represent a correct English pronunciation, a characteristic learner's mistake, or a sound in a foreign language.

Except in the sections on pronunciation, an unacceptable or doubtfully acceptable form or usage is preceded by an asterisk (*).

All foreign words are printed in a different typeface: e.g. autorzy.

Errors and the mother tongue

There is less disagreement than there used to be about how far interlanguages are influenced by learners' native languages, and most linguists would probably now agree that the mother tongue can affect learners' English in several ways.

1. Where the mother tongue has no close equivalent for a feature, learners are likely to have particular problems in the relevant area. Japanese or Russian students, for example, whose languages have no article systems, have a great deal of difficulty with English articles.
2. Where the mother tongue does have an equivalent feature, learning is in general facilitated. French- or German-speaking students, for instance, find English articles relatively easy in most respects, despite the complexity of the system.
3. However, equivalences are rarely exact, and so-called 'interference' or 'transfer' mistakes are common where students assume a more complete correspondence than exists, so that they carry over mother-tongue patterns in cases where English forms or uses are not in fact parallel. French- or German-speaking students typically make certain mistakes in English (e.g. *The life is hard*, *My sister is hairdresser*) precisely because their languages do have article systems.
4. Since transfer mistakes arise where the systems of two languages are similar but not identical, they are most common (at least as far as grammar and vocabulary are concerned) in the interlanguage of students who speak languages closely related to English. Speakers of unrelated languages such as Chinese or Arabic have fewer problems with transfer, and correspondingly more which arise from the intrinsic difficulty of the English structures themselves.

A learner's English is therefore likely to carry the signature of his/her mother tongue, by virtue both of what goes wrong and of what does not. This is most striking in the case of pronunciation, where the phonological structure of a speaker's first language and the associated 'articulatory setting' of the lips, tongue, jaw, etc. usually affect his or her English speech quite strongly, giving rise to what we call, for example, a Dutch, Turkish or Chinese 'accent'. But vocabulary, syntax, discourse structure, handwriting and all other aspects of language use are also likely to some extent to carry a mother-tongue 'accent'. While not all of a learner's problems, by any means, are attributable to direct mother-tongue 'interference', the overall patterns of error do therefore tend to be language-specific – so that it makes sense to talk about 'Thai English', 'Japanese English', 'Greek English' and so on. To characterise these various kinds of English is the concern of the contributors to this book.

Note for teachers of American English[1]

Pronunciation

The British vowel charts given in some of the chapters will appear complicated to Americans. This is mainly because of the diphthongs (/eə/, /ɪə/ etc.) which have replaced vowel + *r* in standard British English.

British English also has an 'extra' pure vowel as compared with American English. This is the rounded short *o* (/ɒ/) used in words like *dog*, *cot*, *gone*. (*Cot* and *cart* have quite different vowels in British English, whereas in American English the main difference is the absence or presence of an *r* sound.)

Many words written with *a* + consonant (e.g. *fast*, *after*) are pronounced with /ɑː/ (as in *father*) in standard southern British English, while American and most other varieties of English have /æ/.

Because of differences between British and American pronunciation, some of the 'mistakes' described in the various chapters may not be mistakes if American English is the target variety. Note in particular:

1. The standard British vowel /əʊ/ (as in *boat*, *home*) is rather different from the American equivalent. Some learners' approximations are wrong in British English but acceptable in American English.
2. Faulty pronunciations of British /ɒ/ (as in *dog*, *cot*, see above) may sound all right in American English.
3. Pronunciation of *r* after a vowel (as in *turn*, *before*, *car*) is a common mistake among learners of British English. It is of course perfectly correct in American English if the *r* is correctly articulated.
4. Some learners pronounce a flapped intervocalic /t/ (close to a /d/) in words like *better*, *matter*. Again, this produces a mistake in British English but an acceptable American pronunciation.

---

[1] In compiling these notes, we have been greatly helped by information supplied by Professor J. Donald Bowen and Professor Randall L. Jones.

Grammar

There are few differences between British and American English grammar, and almost all of the descriptions of learners' grammar problems are valid for both varieties. Note, however:

1. The present perfect is used in British English in some cases where Americans prefer a past tense (e.g. *He's just gone out / He just went out*; *I've already paid / I already paid*). This can lead to differences in the acceptability of learner usage depending on which is the target variety.

2. Pre-verb adverbs are often placed later in the verb phrase in British English than in American English (e.g. *He would probably have agreed / He probably would have agreed*). Again, this can mean that a 'mistake' in British English is a correct American form.

Spelling, punctuation and vocabulary

The problems described in these areas, with very few exceptions, are common to learners of both varieties of English.

List of phonetic symbols

The following symbols are used in the book to represent either the English sounds shown, or reasonably close equivalents in other languages.

vowels

/iː/	as in 'peat' /piːt/		/eɪ/	as in 'bay' /beɪ/
/ɪ/	as in 'pit' /pɪt/		/aɪ/	as in 'buy' /baɪ/
/e/	as in 'pet' /pet/		/ɔɪ/	as in 'boy' /bɔɪ/
/æ/	as in 'pat' /pæt/		/əʊ/	as in 'go' /gəʊ/
/ɑː/	as in 'part' /pɑːt/		/aʊ/	as in 'cow' /kaʊ/
/ɒ/	as in 'pot' /pɒt/			
/ɔː/	as in 'port' /pɔːt/		/ɪə/	as in 'hear' /hɪə/
/ʊ/	as in 'put' /pʊt/		/eə/	as in 'hair' /heə/
/uː/	as in 'poodle' /puːdl/		/ʊə/	as in 'tour' /tʊə/
/ʌ/	as in 'putt' /pʌt/			
/ɜː/	as in 'pert' /pɜːt/			
/ə/	as in 'about', 'upper' /əbaʊt/, /ʌpə/			

consonants

/p/	as in 'pea' /piː/		/m/	as in 'map' /mæp/
/b/	as in 'bee' /biː/		/n/	as in 'nap' /næp/
/t/	as in 'toe' /təʊ/		/ŋ/	as in 'hang' /hæŋ/
/d/	as in 'doe' /dəʊ/		/l/	as in 'led' /led/
/tʃ/	as in 'chin' /tʃɪn/		/r/	as in 'red' /red/
/dʒ/	as in 'gin' /dʒɪn/		/j/	as in 'yes' /jes/
/k/	as in 'cap' /kæp/		/w/	as in 'west' /west/
/g/	as in 'gap' /gæp/		/h/	as in 'head' /hed/
/f/	as in 'fat' /fæt/			
/v/	as in 'vat' /væt/			
/θ/	as in 'thing' /θɪŋ/			
/ð/	as in 'this' /ðɪs/			
/s/	as in 'sip' /sɪp/			
/z/	as in 'zip' /zɪp/			
/ʃ/	as in 'ship' /ʃɪp/			
/ʒ/	as in 'measure' /meʒə/			

stress

/'/ /,/   primary and secondary stress, as in 'entertainment'
              /ˌentəˈteɪnmənt/

other symbols

/ɸ/   an *f* made with both lips instead of teeth and lip
/β/   a *v* made with both lips instead of teeth and lip
/ç/   like the *h* in *huge*, or the *ch* in German *ich*
/x/   like the *ch* in Scottish *loch* or German *ach*
/ɣ/   like /x/, but voiced.
/ʔ/   glottal stop (like a light cough, or the cockney *t* in *butter*)
/ʉ/   like the vowel in *too*, but with no lip-rounding
/o/   a pure 'o', as in Scottish or Irish *rose*
/~/   nasalisation of a vowel

Some other symbols used in particular chapters are explained in the
text.

Acknowledgements

Our most grateful thanks are due to the following, who have given valuable help in the preparation of this new edition: Valerie Bevan, Jan Borsbey, Joris de Roy, John Moorcroft, Alexandra Morais, Ninik Poedjianto, Ruth Swan, Rosey Wilson.

We would also like to thank the many people who gave generously of their time and efforts in the production of the accompanying cassette and CD. Without the co-operation of the students, schools and colleges involved, this project could not have been attempted. In addition to the fifty or so people who were actually recorded, special thanks must go to the following institutions.

In the Eastbourne area: The Eastbourne School of English; ECAT; LTC International College; St Bede's School, The Dicker; St Giles College; SLC.

In the Brighton and Hove area: Bellerby's College; University of Brighton English Department.

Special thanks to Tim Douglass of Forum Productions for the recording and editing of all the material.

The authors and publishers are grateful to the authors, publishers and others who have given permission for the use of copyright material identified in the text. In the cases where it has not been possible to identify the source of material used the publishers would welcome information from copyright owners.

Dutch speakers

Guy A. J. Tops, Xavier Dekeyser, Betty Devriendt
and Steven Geukens

Distribution

THE NETHERLANDS, BELGIUM, Surinam, Dutch Antilles; about 20
million people. (Its mutually intelligible descendant Afrikaans, spoken
by about 6 million native speakers and used as a *lingua franca* by about
15 million people in South Africa and Namibia, is now officially
considered a separate language.)

Introduction

Dutch is a member of the (West) Germanic branch of Indo-European,
and as such is closely related to Frisian, English, German and the
Scandinavian languages. It is the standard language in the Netherlands
and in Flanders, the northern part of Belgium, where it is often but
unofficially called 'Flemish'. The use of the standard language as the
first language is far more widespread in the Netherlands than in
Flanders. There most people habitually use one of the many local
dialects or an approximation of the standard language. The variation,
though diminishing, is still very great. The standard language is understood almost everywhere, but dialects tend to be mutually unintelligible,
both in the Netherlands and in Flanders.

Dutch and English being so closely related, they have many similarities in all areas of their grammars, and Dutch speakers regard
English as easy to learn, at least initially, when they make rapid
progress.

Phonology

General

The Dutch and English phonological systems are broadly similar, so
that speakers of Dutch do not normally have serious difficulties in
recognising or pronouncing most English sounds.

Many learners may use strong regional accents in their Dutch, and

1

Dutch speakers

their problems with English tend to vary accordingly. Universal features of Dutch giving rise to a Dutch accent in English are:
- Devoicing of final consonants and a corresponding shortening in the length of preceding vowels: *dock* for *dog*, *leaf* for *leave*, etc.
- A much narrower intonation range, not reaching the same low pitch areas as English.
- Pronunciation of *r* whenever it occurs in the spelling.

Vowels

iː	ɪ	e	æ	eɪ	aɪ	ɔɪ
ɑː	ɒ	ɔː	ʊ	aʊ	əʊ	ɪə
uː	ʌ	ɜː	ə	eə	ʊə	aɪə / aʊə

Shaded phonemes have equivalents or near equivalents in Dutch, and should therefore be perceived and articulated without serious difficulty, although some confusions may still arise. Unshaded phonemes may cause problems. For detailed comments, see below.

1. Depending on the learners' region of origin, /ɪ/ may be pronounced too close (leading to confusion between pairs like *sit* and *seat*), or too open (with confusion between pairs like *sit* and *set*).
2. Standard Dutch /e/ is somewhere between English /e/ and /æ/. This results in confusion of the latter two (in pairs like *set* and *sat* or *then* and *than*), especially since Dutch has no vowel corresponding to /æ/.
3. Many learners pronounce English /ɑː/ very far back; it may sound similar to /ɔː/ (which is often very open), leading to confusion between pairs like *part* and *port*.
4. /ɒ/ and /ʌ/ may not be distinguished, leading to confusion in pairs like *not* and *nut*. Some learners may also pronounce /ʌ/ rather like /ə/.
5. Dutch speakers find English /ɔː/ and /əʊ/ difficult, and may confuse pairs like *caught* and *coat*.
6. Dutch has no equivalent of /ʊ/, as in *book*. It may be pronounced rather like /ʌ/ (with confusion between *look* and *luck*, for example), or like /uː/ (making *pool* similar to *pull*).
7. /ɜː/ (as in *heard, turn*) is usually pronounced with lip-rounding by Dutch learners.

2

Consonants

p	b	f	v	θ	ð	t	d
s	z	ʃ	ʒ	tʃ	dʒ	k	g
m	n	ŋ	l	r	j	w	h

Shaded phonemes have equivalents or near equivalents in Dutch, and should therefore be perceived and articulated without serious difficulty, although some confusions may still arise. Unshaded phonemes may cause problems. For detailed comments, see below.

1. The lenis ('voiced') consonants /b/, /d/, /v/, /ð/, /z/, /ʒ/ and /dʒ/ do not occur at the ends of words in Dutch. Learners will replace them by their fortis ('unvoiced') counterparts: *Bop* for *Bob*; *set* for *said*; *leaf* for *leave*; *cloth* for *clothe*; *rice* for *rise*; *'beish'* for *beige*; *larch* for *large*. (Most learners also fail to make the English distinction in the length of vowels before voiced and unvoiced consonants.)
2. In other positions in words, too, many Northern Dutch learners pronounce /f/ instead of /v/, /s/ instead of /z/, and /ʃ/ instead of /ʒ/: *file* for *vile*; *sue* for *zoo*; *'mesher'* for *measure*.
3. Dutch lacks the phoneme /g/ as in *get*. Learners will use either /k/, the fricative /x/ (as in Scottish *loch*), or its voiced equivalent /ɣ/.
4. /p/, /t/ and /k/ are not aspirated at the beginning of a word in Dutch; this can make them sound rather like /b/, /d/ and /g/: *bay* for *pay*; *den* for *ten*; *goat* for *coat*.
5. /tʃ/ is often reduced to /ʃ/ and /dʒ/ to /ʒ/ (or /ʃ/): *shop* for *chop*; /ʒæm/ or *sham* for *jam*.
6. /θ/ is usually pronounced /s/ or /t/: *sank* or *tank* for *thank*. /ð/ is usually pronounced /z/ or /d/: *zen* or *den* for *then*.
7. Northern Dutch speakers may make /s/ rather like /ʃ/: *sheet* for *seat*.
8. Learners may make /w/ with teeth and lip, leading to confusion with /v/: *vile* for *while*.
9. Dutch /r/ exhibits a lot of variety; none of the versions are like English /r/.
10. Dutch postvocalic 'dark' /l/ is very 'dark', with the tongue further back in the mouth than in English, especially after /iː/, /ɪ/ and /e/. Some Dutch accents have 'dark' /l/ before vowels, where English has 'clear' /l/.

3

Dutch speakers

11. /h/ can be a problem for learners with a dialect background from the coastal provinces of Belgium: they produce a /x/-like fricative.

Consonant clusters

English clusters are not in general difficult for Dutch speakers. Students may insert /ə/ between /l/ and certain other consonants: *'fillum'* for *film*; *'millock'* for *milk*.

Influence of spelling on pronunciation

1. The Dutch system for spelling vowels and diphthongs is fairly simple and consistent. Learners have great difficulty therefore in dissociating a word's spelling from its pronunciation.
2. Learners tend to pronounce the letter *r* wherever it occurs, leading to mistakes if they are aiming at standard British English.
3. Dutch lacking a /g/, the combination *ng* is always pronounced /ŋ/ in Dutch. This leads to problems with words like *finger, hunger*, etc.
4. Even very advanced learners will pronounce the letter *o* in words like *front* and *mother* as /ɒ/ instead of /ʌ/.
5. The letters *u* and *w* in words like *caught* and *saw* lead many speakers to use an /əʊ/-like sound instead of /ɔː/.
6. Final -*w* is often pronounced as /w/: *how* pronounced /haʊw/; *saw* pronounced /sɔːw/; *draw* pronounced /drɔːw/, etc.
7. Learners will tend to pronounce the silent letters in words like *knot, gnaw, comb, bomb, half, sword, psychiatrist*, etc.

Stress

Dutch and English stress patterns in words and sentences are quite similar. There are some problems, though.
1. Dutch compounds regularly have stress on the first element, leading to problems where an English compound does not. Hence **'appletart* for *apple 'tart* (Dutch 'appeltaart).
2. Dutch stress patterns are not susceptible to variation depending on grammatical category, as in *con'vict* (verb) vs *'convict* (noun). This leaves learners very uncertain about the stress patterns of many words.
3. Dutch does not have as many weak forms as English, nor does it use them so consistently. Many speakers will overstress words like *and, but, than*, etc., using strong forms throughout.

Intonation

Dutch intonation moves within a much narrower range than English. The Dutch intonation range is on the whole relatively high and does not reach the same low pitches as English. Learners trying to widen their voice range tend to move it upwards rather than downwards.

Juncture and assimilation

1. Dutch does not have final voiced stop or fricative consonants. Learners who have acquired final /b/, /d/, /g/, /v/, /ð/, /z/, /ʒ/ and /dʒ/ will still tend to make them unvoiced if the next word begins with an unvoiced sound. Conversely, Dutch word-final unvoiced sounds will often become voiced before a word beginning with a voiced stop or a vowel. This leads to problems in English. For example:
   Dad comes pronounced '*Dat comess*'
   if it is Tom pronounced '*iv id iss Tom*'
   this is Kate pronounced '*thiz iss Kate*'
   back door pronounced '*bag door*'
2. In Dutch, a sequence of two identical or similar stop consonants is usually reduced to one:
   sharp pins pronounced '*sharpins*'
   hard times pronounced '*hartimes*'

Punctuation

Dutch puts a comma after restrictive relative clauses; hence mistakes like:
   *The concern they show, is by no means exaggerated.
Commas may be used between unlinked clauses:
   *This is somewhat surprising, as they are forbidden in Dutch too, they nevertheless occur regularly.
Quotation marks are written like this:
   * „I am thirsty," he said.
Abbreviations entirely in lower case or ending in lower case are normally followed by periods: hence *Mr.* and *Mrs.*, even in texts that try to write British English. And *ie* for traditional *i.e.* may be found confusing.

With some exceptions, Dutch compounds are written as one word, no matter how long they are, even when they are borrowed from or inspired by English (e.g. *marketinginformatiesysteem*). This leads to spellings like **marathonrunner, *satellitechannel.*

Dutch speakers

Grammar

General

Typologically speaking, the Dutch language occupies a position midway between English and German. Word order is virtually the same as in German; Dutch still has grammatical gender, and a high percentage of its vocabulary betrays its Germanic origin.

However, Dutch is not a variety of German. Apart from a fair number of language-specific differences, its morphology comes close to the English system. The inflectional system is relatively simple; neither verbs nor prepositions govern 'cases'; there are only a few relics of the old subjunctive.

Interrogative and negative structures

1. Dutch has no *do*-support. Interrogatives are formed by simple inversion; negatives by placing niet (= *not*) after the verb or before the first non-finite verbal element:
   * *What mean you?*
   * *Thank you, I smoke not.*
   * *I have her yesterday not seen.*
2. Preposition-stranding in questions is unknown in Dutch (see however section 3 and 'Relative pronouns', section 5), and has to be taught explicitly. It takes a while before Dutch speakers will naturally produce *Who are you talking to?* instead of *To whom are you talking?*, a stilted construction that is liable to persist in their speech.
3. Dutch uses interrogative adverbials beginning with the equivalent of *where* to ask questions about things (see also 'Relative pronouns'). They are separable and thus might inspire preposition-stranding, but the substitution of *where* for the pronoun is a real danger:
   * *Where are you thinking of?* (for *What are you thinking of?*)
   * *Where do you need that for?*
4. Questions with inversion can have falling intonation in Dutch. This is sometimes transferred to English, which can make a simple, innocuous enquiry like *Are there no theatres open in London?* sound almost belligerent.

Tags, short answers and reply questions

Dutch has no construction comparable with the English question tag; instead it uses particles and adverbs:

She is your best friend, eh? / or not? (for *She is your best friend, isn't she?*)

Unlike Dutch, English has quite a number of fixed subject-plus-auxiliary patterns which are frequent in conversational exchange. The over-short answers of a Dutch speaker may sometimes give an impression of abruptness, aggressiveness or rudeness.

'*Are you coming with us?*' '*Yes.*' (for '*Yes, I am.*')

'*Your glass is empty.*' '*Oh, yes.*' (for '*So it is.*')

'*They never listen to good advice.*' '*No.*' (for '*No, they don't.*' or '*No, they don't, do they?*')

'*You can't speak without a regional accent.*' '*Yes!*' (for '*Yes, I can.*' or '*But I can.*')

Auxiliaries

The general perfective aspect-marker, in Dutch as in English, is hebben (= *have*). However, zijn (= *be*) is used to form the perfect tenses of zijn, of blijven (= *remain, stay*) and of common intransitive change-of-state verbs:

*He is been here, but he isn't stayed long.

*He is left ten minutes ago.

The Dutch marker of the passive voice is worden (= *become*) in the simple tenses; however, in the perfect tenses Dutch uses the simple forms of zijn (= *be*). Speakers of Dutch tend to translate this zijn as a present tense, all the while thinking that the English verb in, e.g., *the report is published*, is a perfect tense and that they will be understood as having said *the report has been published*. Their problem is compounded by the existence, in English, of constructions like *the article is written in a racy style*, which seems to provide a model for *the article is translated by John*. This type of mistake is very persistent, even in the English of fairly advanced learners.

Time, tense and aspect

A. Past time

To refer to a past event Dutch can use both a past tense and a perfect tense, without much difference in meaning. The latter is the more usual form. Conversely, Dutch can use a past tense where English would use a present perfect:

*I have seen him yesterday.

*All my nineteenth-century ancestors have lived here.

> *Since I made my report last year, there was a steady improve-ment in the company's trading position.*

B. Present time

To express how long a present state of affairs has been going on, Dutch normally uses a present tense, not a present perfect:
> *I know him for five years.*
> *I live in Amsterdam since I was a child.*

C. Future time

1. Even though Dutch has a future tense formed with an auxiliary (roughly equivalent to the *shall/will* future of English), it often uses the present tense to refer to the future:
   > *I promise I give it to him tomorrow.*
2. To express how long a future state of affairs will have lasted, Dutch often uses a simple future or even a simple present:
   > *In 2015 I will work here for 17 years.*
   > *Tomorrow I work here for five years already.*
3. Dutch can freely use the future in a subclause of time:
   > *He'll be an old man when he'll get out of jail.*

D. Aspect

Dutch does not have progressive verb forms:
> *I lived in London at that point in my life.*
> *I have a lot of trouble with John at the moment.*

'Progressive' meanings can however be expressed, if necessary, by the use of certain adjectives and adverbs:
> *What were you busy with yesterday?* (for *What were you doing yesterday?*)
> *You've worked on this non-stop this last week, eh?*

Some beginners overgeneralise the English progressive:
> *The house is belonging to my father.*

Conditionals

1. There are no such sharp distinctions between the use of verbal forms in the Dutch subclause and main clause as there are in English; apart from the equivalents of the normal English forms, Dutch allows those of *shall/should/would* in the subclause, and past tenses of full lexical verbs in the main clause. Hence mistakes like:

*If I shall see him, I shall tell him.
*If you would know him, you wouldn't (or even *didn't*) *say such things.*
*If he would have worked harder, he had succeeded.

2. It is common in Dutch to use the adverb dan (= *then*) in the main clause of a conditional construction:

?**If you see him tomorrow, will you then tell him I won't be at home next week?*
?**Had I known in time, then I would have come along.*

Modal verbs

On the whole, the Dutch and English systems of modal verbs are similar. But:

1. English *must* is deceptively like Dutch moeten (= *must, have to, be to*); hence the frequent use of *must* when this is not the appropriate modal:

*When must you take up your new appointment? (for *When are you to . . .?*)
*In Venice people must go everywhere by boat. (for *. . . have to . . .*)

The negative moest niet means *should not, ought not to*:

*You mustn't smoke too much, if I may say so.

2. More specifically, learners may take *must* to be the equivalent of the Dutch past tense moest (= *had to* or *was to*).

*I must go to London yesterday.
*The wedding must have taken place yesterday, but it was postponed.

3. In Southern Dutch moet niet means *don't have to, needn't,* and is therefore completely different from *must not*:

*Parking here is free today so you mustn't pay.

4. Dutch kan (infinitive kunnen) denotes all types of possibility; there is no equivalent of English *may/might* used in this sense:

*It can rain tonight: don't forget your umbrella.
*I can have told you already.

5. The past tense of Dutch kunnen, kon (sg) / konden (pl), when denoting ability, usually implies more than mere ability: it almost invariably suggests that the action expressed by the main verb was actually carried out. Even advanced Dutch speakers may be misled by this:

*Yesterday he could just catch the 7 o'clock train. (for *. . . was able to catch . . .*)

6. Permission is mostly sought and granted in Dutch by means of the

modal mag (infinitive mogen), even in informal registers, leading students to overuse *may* and avoid *can*. English *might* looks like the past tense of mag, which is mocht (= *could, was allowed to*):
  **She might go out every night when she was sixteen.*
7. Dutch zou has several different meanings, only a few of which can be expressed by 2nd or 3rd person *should*:
  **They did not know they should never see each other again.* (for . . . *would never see* . . . or . . . *were never to see* . . .: destiny)
  **He should leave on Sunday, but there was a problem with his visa.* (for . . . *was going to leave* . . .: unfulfilled intention)
  **Andrew should be ill.* (for *Andrew is said to be ill.*: rumour)

Non-finite forms

Dutch uses considerably fewer non-finite forms than English. This causes various problems, especially in the area of verbal complementation. This varies from word to word, both in English and in Dutch, and a Dutch speaker must pay special attention to learn the English complementation of a word if it differs from its Dutch equivalent.

1. Dutch speakers will substitute *that*-clauses or adjectival or adverbial constructions for infinitives and gerunds after verbs:
  **He wants that I go.*
  **I've always gladly gone there* or **I have always been glad to go there* (for *I've always loved going there.*)
  **This entails that the whole configuration changes.*
2. Dutch has no equivalent of the English gerund, and will often substitute a *to*-infinitive for one. A few very typical examples:
  **I don't mind to do it.*
  **If you can't avoid to go, you risk to upset your dad.*
  **I suggest to go to the pictures instead.*
  **It's no use to ask her.*
  **I am used to do this.*
  **I look forward to hear from you.*
Incidentally, the absence of a gerund equivalent will also lead to the occurrence of *to*-infinitives after prepositions: **Instead of to fight, they laughed.*
3. There is no equivalent of the structure 'verb + object + past participle', whose meanings are expressed in a number of different structures:
  **I hear my name call.*
  **I like that it is done quickly.*
  **Try to make yourself understandable.*

Finally, present participle clauses are rare in Dutch. Dutch learners are liable to replace postmodifying participle structures, like *the girl sitting in the corner*, by relative clauses (*the girl who is sitting in the corner*). Also, it takes a while to get them to use adverbial present participle clauses, like *Realising that she was pregnant, she panicked.* Making them write present perfective participle clauses, like *Having secured his position, he did not fail to proceed* (which has no Dutch equivalent at all) will take even longer.

Word order

Word order in Dutch is less simple than in English. Some of the most striking differences will only interfere at an elementary level, but other Dutchisms may be so deeply rooted that they will yield problems at a more intermediate or even advanced level.

A. Main clause

1. In Dutch, the subject and the finite form of the verb are not separable:
    He works sometimes on Sundays.
2. The Dutch finite verb group tends to be separated from the rest of the verbal group (infinitives, past participles):
    I must at once my sister see.
    They were of everything robbed.
3. In contrast to English, Dutch can have its verb and (simple) objects or complements separated by adverbials:
    I hear every day the bells ring from my bedroom.
    Bill loved passionately his wife.
    She kept fortunately her mouth shut.
4. Inversion always occurs in Dutch if the sentence opens with a constituent other than the subject or a conjunction:
    Tomorrow shall I see him.
    Incredible is that!
    This have we already examined.
5. The internal order of adverbials is also different, time adverbials tending to precede those of place:
    She has already been living for two years in London.
6. The adverb particle tends to come at the end of the clause:
    He got quickly up.
7. In Dutch, the article can be separated from its noun by a complex participial clause or by an adjective and its complement:

11

Dutch speakers

> *The by the Senate with unanimity voted down proposal.*
> *He is a hard to convince man.*

8. For word order in interrogative clauses, see the section 'Interrogative and negative structures'.
9. Dutch often begins sentences with the equivalent of *also* and *already*:
   > *We told the Smiths. Also they were shocked.* (for *They too were shocked.*)
   > *Already in 1992 I went there.*

B. Subclause

A verb or verbal group comes at the end of a subordinate clause:
> *He asked whether we John had seen.* (or even *. . . seen had*)

Constructions with it and there

1. Clauses identifying people and things begin with het, the Dutch equivalent of *it*. But het is followed by a plural verb form when a plural noun follows. Even advanced students will persist in producing sentences like:
   > *It are the Joneses.*
   > *It were the soldiers that shot first.*
2. Dutch also uses het in initial position of *be*-sentences to introduce information about persons mentioned previously.
   > 'Is Ralph a friend of yours?' *'No, it's just a colleague.'*
3. Dutch er is used in far more constructions than its English equivalent *there* /ðə/, which is almost invariably followed by a form of *be*. Dutch speakers will overuse *there* and say and write things like:
   > *There lay twelve books on his night table.*
   > *There were made many mistakes.* (sometimes *There were many mistakes made.*)
   > *There happened a lot of accidents that night.*
   > *There is said in the paper that the government will not survive.*

Articles

The Dutch system of definite and indefinite articles is basically the same as in English. Apart from a number of differences of an idiomatic nature, the main points to note are:
1. Dutch sometimes uses a definite article with uncountable and plural nouns referring to something/things/people in general:

    The wages have been rising recently.
    the life in modern Britain
2. Dutch has no indefinite article in a subject complement with a countable noun denoting a profession, occupation or status, a religion or a nationality; nor after the equivalents of *as* and *without*:
    She is professor, Buddhist and Swede. She's also widow.
    As basketball player he is hopeless; as friend he's wonderful.
    She came to the party without friend.
3. There are many words in English (like *bed, church, prison*) which are preceded by the article when they denote what seems to be their primary meaning, a place, but which lack the article when the sentence is rather about the activity for which that place is typically used. Though Dutch has some parallel phrases without the article, like naar bed/school gaan (= *go to bed/school*), they are far fewer; hence mistakes like:
    to go to the church (for *to go to church*)
    be sent to the prison
4. Names of meals and seasons are normally preceded by an article. This leads to a reluctance to use *in winter* rather than (rarer) *in the winter* and leads to mistakes like:
    Let's talk about that during the lunch.
5. The numerals 100 and 1,000 have no article in Dutch; hence *hundred* and *thousand*.

Adjectives and adverbs

Adverbs are identical with the uninflected form of the corresponding adjective. This use of unmarked adverbial forms is so deeply rooted in the Dutch speaker's competence that even advanced learners tend to make mistakes like:
    She drives very careful.
    You speak English very good.
or in noun phrases:
    an economic weak theory

Quantifiers and determiners

1. Dutch does not use different quantifiers with countable and uncountable nouns; hence mistakes like *much books* and, less often, *little persons* (for *few persons*).
2. The distinction between *some* and *any* will have to be taught

explicitly, as there is nothing that comes close to these quantifiers in Dutch. The same holds for *either/each/every*. Some typical mistakes:
> *I don't have some books. (beginners only)
> *. . . too expensive to buy some
> *Can I have any more cake?
> *Take a ball in every hand.

Interrogative pronouns

Here the only problem is the appropriate use of *which*, there being no exact equivalent for this in Dutch; hence:
> *What is your second language, English or French?

Relative pronouns

1. Dutch does not have different relative pronouns for people and things. The use of *which* with a personal antecedent (*A person which . . .*) is difficult to eradicate.
2. There being no distinction between restrictive and non-restrictive clauses as far as the choice of pronouns is concerned, beginners often do not understand why structures like *My parents, that were born in France* or *My father, you met in Amsterdam* are ungrammatical.
3. Wat has a much wider coverage than English *what*: it is used with clause antecedents, with quantifier antecedents, and in very recent usage also with neuter nouns. This explains the use of *what* in a number of cases where English requires *which*:
> *John went to Brussels, what explains everything.
> *This is all what I know.

   Occasionally also:
> *The picture what I was drawing . . .
4. Contact clauses (clauses without overt relative pronouns) and pre-position stranding are totally unknown in Dutch syntax; therefore beginners tend to make excessive use of structures like:
> the woman whom I met in Glasgow the other day
> the pen with which Jane was writing yesterday
5. Instead of relative pronouns + stranded prepositions, Dutch often uses compound relative adverbials of a type that is now generally obsolete in English, viz. *where-* + preposition. In informal Dutch they are even used after human antecedents. They are optionally separable, which would be a great help in teaching preposition stranding, except that it leaves *where* instead of (zero) relative:

> *The technology where he had relied on proved to be untrust-
> worthy.*
> *The man whereof I speak is a good friend of mine.*

6. For commas with relative clauses, see 'Punctuation'.

Reflexive pronouns

Dutch does not inflect the second half of reflexive pronouns for number, hence mistakes like *ourself*, *yourself* and *themself* (for *themselves*; *theirself* and *theirselves* also occur). And they are overused, in combination with what are normally middle verbs (simple intransitive verbs referring to things that people do to themselves) in English, which have no Dutch equivalent:

> *He never shaves himself after he has washed himself.*

The indefinite pronoun one

Men is not nearly as formal as its English equivalent *one*, and Dutch speakers should be told that it has a range of stylistic equivalents:

> *In the Middle Ages one actually believed that.* (for . . . *it was actually believed that* or . . . *people actually believed that*)
> *One could just as well claim* . . . (for less formal *You could just as well claim* . . .)
> *One intends to build a skyscraper here.* (for *They intend* . . .)

Gender

The natural gender system of English has no match in Dutch: Southern Dutch speakers have mostly preserved the tripartite Germanic system (just like the Germans), while speakers of Northern Dutch now use a binary system (masculine and neuter) with a limited and shrinking number of feminine nouns. Whichever system is adhered to, Belgian and Dutch students are often inclined to treat certain inanimate nouns as either masculine or feminine, in agreement with their Dutch equivalents:

> *The English language . . . she . . .*
> *The state . . . he . . .*

Countability and number

1. In Dutch, collective nouns are always followed by singular verbs. It takes a while before students are willing to let English ones be followed by plurals when appropriate; they will go for *the entire family has decided* rather than *the family have all decided*. A collective that requires a plural verb will keep trapping speakers into errors like:
   > **The police has arrested him.*
2. Pair-plurals are unknown; *jeans* has been re-interpreted as a singular in the borrowing process, leading to:
   > **Where's my jeans? I can't find it.* (or *him*; see 'Gender')
   A more common type of error involves the plural formation: **two pyjamas* instead of *two pairs of pyjamas*.
3. Dutch also distinguishes countable and uncountable nouns, but not all equivalents belong in the same category; hence mistakes like **an information, *an advice, *give me two breads, please*.
4. If the first element of a noun + noun compound denotes a plural, it is mostly singular in English. In Dutch the number can vary, leading to mistakes like **a books shop* and **a ten-miles trip*.
5. Students need to be told the difference between, for example, *They'll all go to another university* and *They'll all go to other universities*, for in Dutch the singular phrase would be used in both cases. Hence mistakes like
   > **They fell on their face.*

Conjunctions

The only real problem here is the common confusion between *if* and *when*:
> **When it rains the trip will have to be cancelled.*

Prepositions

Though it is possible to indicate rough equivalences between Dutch and English prepositions, there are so many instances where there is no match that students will have to learn many prepositions in their collocations. A few common mistakes, by way of example:
> **on the party*
> **He lives on number 9.*
> **with/by my aunt* (for *at my aunt's*)
> **good in games*

on the meadow
on sea
That is typical for him.
There's no proof for that.
to discriminate women (for *to discriminate against women*)
The list is endless. However, a few systematic remarks can be made:
1. Sinds translates as either *for* or *since*; students tend to use *since* only:
    I've lived here since four years.
2. Achter translates as either *after* or *behind*; students confuse them:
    He stood after me.
3. In translates as either *in* or *into*; students tend to use *in* only:
    Go in the room.

Vocabulary

Dutch and English share the same basic Germanic vocabulary (e.g. voet = *foot*, groet = *great*, zien = *see*, mij = *me*, in = *in*), which greatly facilitates learning, in spite of the numerous false friends. Learning the Romance part of the vocabulary is facilitated by the fact that Dutch has borrowed fairly extensively from Romance and that many educated people know French (especially in Belgium) and even some Latin.

False friends

The close genetic relationship and the geographical proximity between Dutch and English plus the fact that both have borrowed extensively from Romance necessarily results in the existence of numerous false friends. Many of those mentioned in the chapters on related languages and on French apply to Dutch as well, as do the following:

English word used like	Dutch	to mean
dramatic	dramatisch	tragic
solicit	solliciteren	apply (for a job), go job-hunting
become	bekomen	get, acquire
mark	merk	brand, make
bring	brengen	take
camping	camping	camping-site
parking	parking	car park, parking lot
smoking	smoking	dinner jacket, tuxedo
chance	chance	luck
technique	techniek	technology

17

Dutch speakers

concurrence	concurrentie	competition
control	controleren	check (up on)
nephew	neef	cousin
niece	nicht	cousin
actual	actueel	current
actually	actueel	at present, currently
defect	defect	defective
ride	rijden	drive (a car)
amuse oneself	zich amuseren	enjoy oneself
eventual	eventueel	possible
learn	leren	teach
miss	missen	do without
fault	fout	error
novel	novelle	short story
stage	stage	traineeship
backside	achterkant	back

Some typical mistakes with high-frequency words

make vs *do*	*I still must make my homework.
what vs *how*	*How do you call that?
own	*She has an own room.
please	'Can I have your book?' (handing it over:) *'Please.'
already vs *yet*	*Have you finished already? (for *Have you finished yet?*)
though vs *however*	*Though, he was still in trouble.
a(n) half	*a(n) half hour ago
just now ≠ *just*	*I have seen him just now.
once	*I must once talk to her. (for *I must go and talk to her.*)

Compounding

English compounds less frequently than Dutch and students will make such odd compounds as *life-habits*.

Multi-word verbs

They exist in Dutch, too, but they are used far less than in English, and it will often be necessary explicitly to draw the students' attention to everyday prepositional verbs that they will otherwise fail to notice and use:

Dutch	Simple verb	Multi-word verb
zoeken	*seek, search for*	*look for*
beschouwen	*consider*	*look on*
verdragen	*bear*	*put up with*

(Many multi-word verbs fortunately pose no problem, as they are matched by similar or compound but separable verbs in Dutch.)

A sample of written Dutch with a word-for-word translation

Vele   malen heb ik al   meegemaakt, als   in een gezelschap
Many times have I already experienced, when/if in a   company

iemand   zo onhandig   is te verklappen dat ik taalkundige
someone so unhandy [clumsy] is to betray   that I linguist

ben, dat men reageert met: 'Oei,   dan mag ik wel   op
am, that one reacts   with: 'Oops, then may I   well [I'd better] on

mijn woorden letten!'. Misschien dat een politiecommissaris   dat
my words   watch!'. Maybe   that a   police commissioner that

wel herkent,   maar de wijnkoper,   de hondenfokker of de
well recognises, but   the wine buyer, the dog raiser   or the

leraar   wiskunde heeft zoiets   niet. Hoe komt het
teacher (of) maths   has   so something not. How comes it

toch   dat de taalkundige of de leraar   Nederlands in
yet [on earth] that the linguist   or the teacher (of) Dutch   in

hetzelfde schuitje   zit als de politiecommissaris?   Ik weet
the same boat [diminutive] sits as the police commissioner? I know

het niet, maar Nederlandstaligen, aan beide zijden van de grens, zijn,
it not, but Dutchophones,   on both sides of the border, are,

als   het om hun taal   gaat, vóór   alles onzeker, voorzichtig,
when it   about their language goes, before [above] all   unsure, careful,

bang. Bang gemáákt, lijkt   me. Terwijl   de meesten
scared. Scared <u>made</u>,   (it) seems (to) me. Whereas the most [most people]

Dutch speakers

toch minder reden tot schrik   hebben dan in de
yet less   reason to fear *[noun]* have   than in the

nabijheid van de politiecommissaris.   Vreemd   genoeg zijn het
nearness of the police commissioner. Strange(ly) enough are it

juist de leraren   Nederlands en de taalkundigen die
just the teachers (of) Dutch   and the linguists   who

in taalkwesties   veelal het meest tolerant zijn. Veel
in language questions mostly the most tolerant are. Much

toleranter   dan vele   anderen buiten hun kring. Niet
more tolerant than many others outside their circle. Not

vreemd wegens hun opleiding, maar wel   vreemd
strange owing to their education, but   well [yet] strange

omdat   het ijzeren schrikbewind   dus uit   andere
because the iron   fear government [tyranny] thus out (of) other

bron   moet voorkomen. Lag het aan   de doorsnee-
source must forthcome. Lay it on [Were it up to] the average

taalgebruiker, men zou   onze taal   onmiddellijk tot kerntaak
language user, one would our   language immediately to core task

uitroepen van een minister tot   Bevordering van de
proclaim of a   minister to [for] (the) Furthering of   the

deugdzaamheid en Preventie   van het kwaad.
virtue   and Prevention of the evil.

('Joops column' by Joop van der Horst, in *Over taal* 37 (1998) p. 62.)

Speakers of Scandinavian languages: Danish, Norwegian, Swedish

Niels Davidsen-Nielsen and Peter Harder

Distribution

DENMARK, NORWAY, SWEDEN, FINLAND (Swedish), Germany (Danish).

Introduction

The Scandinavian languages are Indo-European languages belonging, like English, to the Germanic branch. Considerable contact in past and present between the English and Scandinavian languages, as well as common outside influences, have served to keep up and reinforce the close relationship between the languages. English is therefore relatively easy for Scandinavians to learn.

For the sake of simplicity, the following description concentrates on the major problems which Danish, Norwegian and Swedish learners of English have in common. Less attention has been paid to issues which require cross-Scandinavian comparisons (though it has been necessary to deal with some points of this kind in the sections on phonology). And, for reasons of space, it has not been possible to include the difficulties of Icelandic and Faroese learners.

Phonology

General

All three Scandinavian languages are phonologically broadly similar to English, and most features of English pronunciation do not present serious difficulty to speakers of these languages. The phonological systems of Danish, Norwegian and Swedish are characterised by considerable similarity, both with respect to sound segments (for example the rounded front vowels) and to prosody, and, as will appear below, there are many common Scandinavian errors in English. Nevertheless, several pronunciation features do exist which separate the Scandinavian languages from each other, and it is therefore only from a

21

bird's-eye view that it makes sense to speak about English pronounced with a 'Scandinavian accent'. In the vowel and consonant charts below inter-Scandinavian differences have not been marked, but some differences of this type are described in the text.

Vowels

iː	ɪ	e	æ	eɪ	aɪ	ɔɪ
ɑː	ɒ	ɔː	ʊ	aʊ	əʊ	ɪə
uː	ʌ	ɜː	ə	eə	ʊə	aɪə / aʊə

Shaded phonemes have equivalents or near equivalents in all three Scandinavian languages and are perceived and articulated without serious difficulty, although some confusions may still arise. Unshaded phonemes may cause problems to speakers of Danish, Swedish and/or Norwegian. For detailed comments, see below.

1. /ɪ/ is often pronounced as a close vowel /iː/: *seat* for *sit*.
2. /æ/ is often pronounced by Swedish speakers as /e/: *bed* for *bad*. Conversely, some Norwegians tend to pronounce /e/ as /æ/: *bad* for *bed*.
3. /ʊ/ (as in *book*) is often pronounced as a close and clearly rounded vowel by Danes and Swedes. Norwegians tend to substitute a more advanced, less closely rounded vowel.
4. /uː/ (as in *too*) is often pronounced as a central vowel by Norwegians, and as a strongly advanced and somewhat lower vowel by Swedes.
5. Swedes and Norwegians frequently replace /ʌ/ (as in *duck*) by a more rounded front vowel.
6. Danes characteristically replace /ʌ/ by a vowel intermediate between English /ʌ/ and /ɒ/. They also tend to partly unround /ɒ/, and consequently find it very difficult to keep *hut* apart from *hot*, *luck* from *lock*, etc.
7. /ɜː/ (as in *turn*) is typically rounded and advanced by Swedes and Danes.
8. /ə/ is not always sufficiently reduced ('unstressed').
9. Norwegians may pronounce /eɪ/ (as in *take*) too open: /æɪ/.
10. /əʊ/ is often pronounced by Swedes as /uː/ (*soup* for *soap*), by Danes as /ɔu/ or /œu/, and by Norwegians as /au/ or /ɒu/. Norwegians

typically find it difficult to distinguish between English /əʊ/ and /aʊ/ (as in *load* and *loud*) and, at a more advanced level, to distribute them correctly.

11. /ɪə/, /eə/and /ʊə/ (as in *here*, *there* and *tour*) are usually pronounced with /r/ instead of /ə/ by Norwegians and Swedes. Danes typically replace them with the diphthongs /iɒ/, /eɒ/ and /uɒ/ respectively.

Consonants

p	b	f	v	θ	ð	t	d
s	z	ʃ	ʒ	tʃ	dʒ	k	g
m	n	ŋ	l	r	j	w	h

Shaded phonemes have equivalents or near equivalents in all three Scandinavian languages and are perceived and articulated without serious difficulty, although some confusions may still arise. Unshaded phonemes may cause problems to speakers of Danish, Swedish and/or Norwegian. For detailed comments, see below.

1. /θ/ does not occur and is typically pronounced as /t/ or (by Danes) as /s/: *tank*, *sank* for *thank*; *tree* for *three*.
2. /ð/ does not occur in Norwegian and Swedish and is often pronounced as /d/: *den* for *then*; *udder* for *other*; Danes tend to replace it with a much more loosely articulated /ð/.
3. /z/ does not occur and is typically replaced by /s/: *racer* for *razor*. Once they master /z/, some learners tend to overuse it and to 'buzz' too much.
4. /ʒ/ does not occur and is typically replaced by /ʃ/: 'mesher' for *measure*.
5. /tʃ/ does not occur and is often pronounced as /tj/.
6. /dʒ/ does not occur. It is often pronounced as /dj/ by Danes and Norwegians, and as /j/ by Swedes: *year* for *jeer*.
7. /r/ is pronounced with the back of the tongue by Danes and some (southern) Swedes. Norwegians and most Swedes replace it by other non-English tip-of-the-tongue *r*-sounds.
8. /w/ does not occur and tends to be replaced by a lax /v/: *vine* for *wine*.
9. 'Dark' /l/, as in *full*, *fill*, occurs only in some Swedish and Norwegian dialects; students tend to replace it by 'clear' /l/, as in *light*.

10. Danes tend to replace word-final /b/, /d/ and /g/ with /p/, /t/ and /k/: *pup* for *pub*; *set* for *said*; *dock* for *dog*. Between vowels, the opposite may happen: *rabid* for *rapid*; *ladder* for *latter*; *bigger* for *bicker*.
11. In Swedish and Norwegian, consonants are pronounced very long after short vowels; this may be carried over into English words like *coffee, letter, cuff*.

Influence of spelling on pronunciation

Spelling and pronunciation are more closely related in the Scandinavian languages (especially Swedish and Norwegian) than in English, and there are fewer ambiguities. Mistakes may be made in cases where a letter has different values in English and the mother tongue; or where English orthography lets the learner down after he or she has worked out the basic rules for correspondences between letters and sounds in English. Note particularly:

1. Beginners may pronounce the letter *i* as /iː/, *y* as /y/ (like German *ü* or French *u*), *a* as /ɑː/, and (depending on nationality) *u* as /ʊ/ and *au* as /aʊ/, leading to mistakes in words like *ride, symbol, parade, rush, automatic*. (For example, Danish beginners sometimes use pronunciations like /ˈriːðə/and /pɑˈrɑːðə/.)
2. /ə/ is always spelt *e* in Scandinavian languages. When /ə/ is spelt with another letter in English, students may use an unreduced vowel, pronouncing for example /ɒ/ in *commercial*, /æ/ in *alliance* and /ɑː/ in *particular*.
3. Even after Scandinavian students have learnt to pronounce English /z/, they commonly mispronounce the letter *s* as /s/ in words such as *cousin, trousers, reserve, president*.
4. Even after Scandinavian students have learnt to pronounce English /ð/ (as well as /θ/), they may mispronounce *th* as /θ/ in *smooth, with*, etc.
5. The *r* may be pronounced in words like *mattered, bothered, wondered*, leading to mistakes in British English.

Rhythm and stress

Patterns of word and sentence stress are quite similar in English and the Scandinavian languages, so there are relatively few problems in this area.

Note, however:

1. Scandinavian compound nouns are usually stressed on the first element. Mistakes are common in English compounds which do not follow this pattern:

    *'prime minister (cf. 'statsminister)

    *'town hall

    Conversely, compound nouns made up of 'verb + adverb' combinations tend to be stressed on the second element:

    *break'down

    *come-'back

    *hang'over

    *hold-'up

2. The Scandinavian languages have fewer 'weak forms' than English, so students often wrongly use the stressed forms of words like *and, but, a(n), the, than, as, have, was*, giving them their 'strong' pronunciations in too many cases. This prevents learners from acquiring a natural sentence rhythm. Beginners may have difficulty in perceiving weak forms.

Intonation

1. Unstressed syllables in Danish (and very often in Norwegian and Swedish) are pronounced on a higher pitch than a preceding stressed syllable. This is often transferred to English, together with a tendency to pronounce the first stressed syllable of a tone unit on too low a pitch:

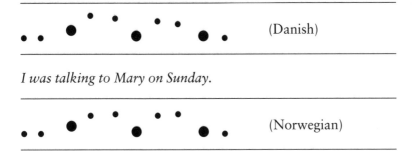

I was talking to Mary on Sunday.

2. Danes are inclined to use a pitch range which is too narrow, and to a lesser extent this also applies to Swedes and some Norwegians.
3. The fall-rise tone is difficult for Scandinavian learners.
4. Norwegians (and some Swedes) tend to use too many rising tone units and to make their upglides too long and too high.

Orthography and punctuation

Spelling

Those who have become aware of the distinction between /v/ and /w/ but do not fully control it tend to replace *v* by *w* (**wery, *wolley ball*), probably because this spelling is assumed to be the more 'English'. Influence from German may make some students write *sch* instead of *sh* (**schoot, *schut up*). The letter *k* is used much more frequently than *c* in the Scandinavian languages, and this may lead to errors like **kapitalism, *kannibal*.

Punctuation

1. As most Scandinavian compounds are written as one word, the use of the hyphen in words like *fire-alarm* (brandalarm), and of spacing in words like *front door* (ytterdør) create difficulty.
2. Scandinavian students sometimes use a comma instead of a semi-colon between main clauses which are not separated by a co-ordinating conjunction, but are felt to be closely related:
   *That's the way it had to be, he was not ashamed of it.
3. Danes tend to use commas before object clauses and restrictive relative clauses:
   *I think, there has been a mistake.
   *What's the worst thing, that could happen to you in that minefield?
4. Apostrophes are not used in the same way as in English. This leads to confusion, especially when there is a minimal contrast (*ones/one's*; *its/it's*).

Grammar

Order of constituents

In the Scandinavian languages, it is easy to begin a sentence with something other than the subject – which is then placed after the verb. In English, only adverbials are regularly 'fronted', and this does not generally cause subject–verb inversion. To give prominence to objects, complements, etc., English tends to use intonation. Typical mistake:
   *That have I not seen.

Position of adverbs

In the Scandinavian languages, mid-sentence adverbs are generally placed after the finite verb. This leads to mistakes in English sentences with one-word verbs:

> *Children leave often home nowadays.

However, in subordinate clauses adverbs are placed *before* finite verbs in Scandinavian languages. This leads to mistakes in English sentences with complex verb phrases:

> *. . . that children often will leave home nowadays.

This can happen with quite long adverbials:

> *He said that they in the northern part of Jutland speak a special dialect.

Constructions with it and there

1. In Norwegian and Swedish, the equivalent of the *there is* construction uses the pronoun det, which also means *it*. Beginners tend to overuse *it* as a consequence:

> *It is somebody at the door.

2. In all three languages, the *there* construction is used with a wide range of verbs (whereas in English it is only common with *be* used as a main verb). This results in mistakes like:

> *It/There was shot a man here yesterday.
> *It/There happens something strange here quite often.
> *It/There left a lot of tourists because of the epidemic.

3. Scandinavian languages tend, more often than English, to avoid having indefinite noun phrases in subject position. This may result in overuse of *there*-cleft sentences like *There was someone who told me that* ... instead of the less cumbersome *Someone told me that . . .*

Nouns: countability and number

1. The countable/uncountable distinction is found in Scandinavian languages, but there are some differences of distribution which give rise to problems:

> *informations   *an advice   *a work (for *a job*)   *a progress

2. The Scandinavian counterparts of *money* are plural:

> *How many money have you got?

3. Collective nouns as a special group do not exist in the Scandinavian languages. Pronominal reference like *The government . . . they . . .* occurs, but is felt to be colloquial.

4. In some cases where English nouns are in the plural, singular nouns are used in the Scandinavian languages. Possible mistakes:
   *a pyjama   *a scissor   *the custom* (for *the customs*)
   the Middle Age (for *the Middle Ages*)
   The police is on its way.
5. In some cases it is the other way round, leading to errors like:
   Public expenditures are too high.
   There were many frictions between them.
6. Difference of usage in some numerical expressions causes mistakes like:
   in the 2nd and 3rd chapter
   in one and a half hour

Articles

1. The definite article occurs in Scandinavian languages before uncountable and plural nouns used in a general sense. In English it is normal to use no article in these cases. This leads to errors like:
   Some people always blame the society for everything.
   The horses were introduced into America by Spanish soldiers.
2. In subject or object complement function, and similarly after *as*, the Scandinavian languages do not use the indefinite article when reference is non-specific, which leads to errors like:
   He has been teacher for many years.
   As member of the family he wanted to come.
3. In a large number of more or less idiomatic cases the same tendency is found, particularly when the noun is in object position and can be seen as forming a semantic whole together with the verb. Thus phrases like *get an answer, take a seat, drive a car* would have no article in the Scandinavian languages. Articles are also commonly left out after the words for *with* and *without*:
   *a man with hat   *a cat without tail*

Premodification

1. The *'s* genitive (without an apostrophe) is found in the Scandinavian languages, and is not subject to the restrictions that limit its use in English. This may lead to errors:
   *the car's driver   *the water's temperature*
2. Nouns can be used to modify other nouns, as in English. However, in the Scandinavian languages the two nouns form a compound, written as one word and stressed on the first element (see earlier sections on stress and punctuation).

3. In official styles, attributive adjectives or participles can have sentence elements attached to them, as in Danish:

   den i de gamle regler beskrevne måde (= *the in the old rules described manner*)

   Learners may occasionally try to transfer this type of construction to English.
4. The rules for using adjectives without a head noun in the Scandinavian languages are considerably less restrictive than in English, which leads to errors like:

   A poor never gets the chance to have a good life.

Postmodification

1. The Scandinavian languages often use full relative clauses (e.g. *the house which was built to accommodate the library* or *a man who is waiting to join*) in cases where English prefers less cumbersome participle constructions (e.g. *the house built to accommodate the library* or *a man waiting to join*).
2. In some cases English uses a prepositional phrase with *of* as a postmodifier, where the Scandinavian languages use an apposition. This leads to a common mistake in the use of the words *sort* and *kind*:

   this sort cheese

Adjective or adverb?

1. Scandinavian adverbs of manner tend to be similar in form to adjectives, which leads to frequent mistakes:

   She spoke to me quite polite.
   You don't sing very good.
2. The opposite mistake can occur in sentences with the verbs *look, sound, smell, taste, feel*, which in most cases take adverbs, not adjectives, in Scandinavian languages:

   I feel terribly.

Pronouns and determiners

1. The *who/which* distinction has no counterpart in Scandinavian languages:

   the man which I told you about
2. *Some* and *any* have a single equivalent:

   Sorry, I haven't got some.

3. In front of a noun followed by a relative clause, Scandinavian languages use a type of demonstrative determiner:
   That man we're talking about is sitting in the next room.
4. The Scandinavian languages have a completely unspecific personal pronoun man, which corresponds to the English 'general' use of *you*, *they* and *one*, and may be used where English has a passive in cases like *It isn't done.* Many learners tend to use *you* as an equivalent in all cases.
5. In some cases where the possessive determiner is obligatory in English, but where it is clear from the context who is the possessor, the Scandinavian languages use the definite article: *He put the hand in the pocket.*

Verb forms

There is no inflection for person or number in Scandinavian languages. Consequently learners tend to drop the third-person -s; even very advanced speakers slip up in their speech on this point occasionally:
   He fly to Copenhagen twice a week.
Are (the form of *to be* most similar to the single Scandinavian present tense verb form er/är) tends to be used for *am, are* and *is*:
   I don't know if she are ready yet.

Do

Scandinavians have the same problems with the *do* construction as other types of learners, and need practice to get used to the formation of questions and negatives. Negatives are especially difficult in subordinate clauses:
   They asked why he not came.
Note the common use of 'double' past/present forms:
   He didn't came.
   She do(es)n't listens.

-ing forms

1. The Scandinavian present participle plays a very limited role as compared with English, being used mainly as an attributive adjective (as in *a sleeping child*), and with certain verbs (as in *he came running*). Consequently learners have problems with the present participle in a number of cases, for example in adverbial clauses (as

in *Going home that evening, I called at the chemist's for some razor blades.*).

2. The absence of the gerund in their own language tends to make Scandinavians use the infinitive in cases like:
    I really must stop to smoke. (Meaning '. . . stop smoking.')
    Instead of (to) get on with his work he slept all afternoon.

Progressive aspect

Scandinavian languages have no progressive verb forms. Elementary students often generalise the English 'simple' forms:
    The band plays now.
Intermediate students may overwork progressive forms as the result of intensive practice in their use:
    In Scandinavia we're putting people in prison if they have struck another person.

Tense

1. In Danish, perfect tenses are commonly formed not only with the auxiliary *have* but also with the equivalent of *be*. Transfer of the *be*-perfect, which is used to express change from one state to another, is not uncommon among elementary Danish learners:
    The prisoner is escaped.
    They are become famous.
2. The Scandinavian present perfect can be used with definite past reference, leading to mistakes like:
    Dickens has written many novels.
    He has left school in 1982.
3. In Swedish, the present tense is often used in sentences constructed with sedan (= *since/for*):
    I know him since a long time.
4. In the Scandinavian languages, future tenses are not used when the sense of the verb, or accompanying adverbs, already makes it clear that the reference is to the future. This leads students to use the simple present instead of the *will* future (and the present perfect instead of the future perfect):
    She doesn't come anyway.
    I don't tell you. You only forget it.
    We talk about it next week.
    By this time tomorrow I've finished sorting out the replies.

The simple present is also used with future reference instead of the present progressive or *going-to* form:
> *Jane moves to the States.*
> *I think I faint.*

Voice

In the Scandinavian languages the passive voice is expressed in either of two ways: with the suffix -s or with the auxiliary blive/bli (which can also mean *become*). Both of these structures result in occasional transfer mistakes:
> *It finds not. (for It is not found.)*
> *He became killed.*

The passive may also be under-used in favour of the impersonal structure with *you* (see the section 'Pronouns').

Modal verbs

Although a number of the English modals have rough Scandinavian equivalents, there are various differences in the use of modals, with consequent learning problems. Some of the most important are as follows:

1. Kan, unlike *can*, is used in affirmative sentences to talk about whether things are the case, or may happen in the future:
   > *Peter can be in London now.*
   > *The time can come when the educational system is mixed.*
2. Skal is used to express compulsion or command (like English *must, have to, is to*). The similarity with *shall* leads to confusion:
   > *You shall lie down quietly now.*
3. Skal can also express the idea of report or rumour (like English *is said to* or *is supposed to*):
   > *He shall be a poor researcher.*
4. Another use of skal is to talk about arrangements (English *is to* or *is going to*):
   > *My daughter shall start school in August.*
   > *John shall play football tonight.*
5. In Swedish and Norwegian, the past tense form skulle corresponds to a number of English verbs besides the apparent equivalent *should*. This leads to mistakes:
   > *She said she should do it. (for She said she would. . .)*
   > *She looks as if she should be ill. (for . . . might . . .)*

Complementation

1. Problems arise where a Scandinavian verb is used in different patterns from its English equivalent. Indirect objects are sometimes differently distributed:
   She told that she was fed up with her job.
   He explained me what he meant.
2. Verbs with obligatory reflexive pronouns are much more common in the Scandinavian languages than in English:
   Hurry yourself!
3. The 'object + infinitive' structure is rare in Scandinavian languages, and students will tend to avoid it:
   *He caused that the prisoners were put to death. (for *He caused the prisoners to be . . .*)
   I don't want that there is any misunderstanding.

Prepositions

1. In the Scandinavian languages a preposition can be followed by an att/at-clause (the equivalent of an English *that*-clause). This may lead to errors like:
   He convinced me of that he was innocent.
   They insisted on that they knew nothing about it.
2. A preposition may also be followed by an infinitive construction. Possible mistakes:
   They dreamed of to emigrate.
   I long for/after to see the mountains again.
3. In passive sentences the agent is introduced by the preposition af/at, resulting in errors like:
   The bone was eaten of the dog.
4. The highly frequent preposition i is often used where English uses other prepositions than *in*. The leads to errors like:
   *the floor in the house   *go in school

Vocabulary

The close relationship between the Scandinavian languages and English makes a large proportion of English vocabulary easily accessible to Scandinavians. Words like *can, have, good, man* are virtually 'the same'; and in a number of cases the spelling, which reflects older stages of the language, helps to establish familiarity where the pronunciation differs markedly, e.g. in cases like *side*. Some of the similarities, of course, are deceptive; below will be found a list of English 'false friends' that are problematic for speakers of all three languages.

False friends

In the following list, common meanings of Scandinavian cognate words are shown in brackets. For instance '*announce* (S = *advertise*)' means that there are Scandinavian words that look like *announce* but which actually mean *advertise*. (The words in this case are Danish annoncere, Norwegian annonsere and Swedish annonsera.) In some cases, Scandinavian words listed may have not only the 'false friend' meaning but also, in some contexts, the same meaning as the English cognate. For instance, komme/komma corresponds to *come* as well as to *get* (*somewhere*) and *arrive*.

actual (S = *of current interest, topical*)
announce (S = *advertise*)
bear (S = *carry, wear*)
blank (S = *shiny*)
branch (S = *trade, line of business*)
come (S = *arrive, get (somewhere)* as well as *come*)
cook (S = *boil*)
control (S = *check*)
critic (S = *criticism*)
delicate (S = *delicious*)
eventual(ly) (S = *possible, if any, if the situation arises*)
fabric (S = *factory*)
first (S can mean *not until*, as in Danish Han kom først kl. 10 = *He didn't arrive until 10.*)
genial (S = *brilliant*)
gift (S = *poison*)
history (S = *story*)
lame (S = *paralysed*)
luck (S = *happiness*)
lucky (S = *happy*)
mean (S = *think, be of the opinion*)
meaning (S = *opinion*)
motion (S = *physical exercise*)
novel (S = *short story*)
offer (S = *sacrifice, offering*)
overtake (S = *take over*)
place (S = *room, space, square, job*)
public (S = *audience, spectators*)
rent (S = *(rate of) interest*)

see (S = *look*)
spare (S = *save*)
sympathetic (S = *likeable*)
take place (S = *sit down*)
will, will have (S = *want*)

Some problems involving grammatical words

1. *As* and *like*, in many of their uses, have one Scandinavian equivalent. This may create problems with the distinction between, for instance, *Like a cabinet minister . . .* and *As a cabinet minister . . .*, as well as mistakes such as **I speak as my mother* and problems of style as in *He did like he had chosen to do.*
2. Scandinavians have one word covering *very, much* and (in affirmative sentences) *a great deal / a lot*. This may tend to produce some overuse of *much* as the most 'similar' word.
3. The word *også/också* covers the area of English *also, too, as well* in their main uses, as well as some uses of *so*. Apart from problems of choice this leads to considerable difficulties of word order, for example:
   *I teach also/too evening classes.
4. The demonstrative adverb *there* corresponds to a Danish and Swedish word which can also be used as a relative. This occasionally leads to the use of *there* in place of a relative. Danes use it in substantival function, as in **The man there was present* (for . . . *who was present*); Swedes use it in adverbial function, as in **The place there I was born* . . ., reflecting the usage in their respective languages.
5. The word *om* functions both as a conjunction (= *if, whether*) and a preposition (= *about, on*). Following verbs where both types of word are possible, mistakes like **Do you know about he has come?* can be found.

A sample of written Danish with a word-for-word translation

Der holdt mindst hundrede taxaer med dørene på klem,
There stood still least hundred taxis with the doors ajar,

og han havde aldrig set så mange biler på en gang. Havde det
and he had never seen so many cars at one time. Had it

stået til ham, var han styrtet
stood to him [= if it had been left to him], was he rushed

fra   den ene vogn til den anden, indtil han havde fundet en
from the one car to the other, until he had   found a

chauffør med et ansigt, han kunne lide.   Men hans
driver with a face, he could suffer [= he liked]. But his

far   løftede blot en finger, en mand med kasket på hovedet så
father lifted just a finger, a man with cap   on the head saw

det, stødte øjeblikkelig i en fløjte   og straks blev der
it, blew immediately in a whistle and at once was there

bevægelse i den yderste   bilrække.
movement in the outermost car-row.

(From 'Johnny' by Bent William Rasmussen in *Jeanne Moreau i Middelfart*)

Acknowledgements

The authors' thanks are due to Stig Johansson, Moira Linnarud, Tom Lundskær-Nielsen, Thor Sigurd Nilsen, Stig Ørjan Ohlsson, Nils Røttingen and Brit Ulseth for advice.

German speakers

Michael Swan

Distribution

GERMANY, AUSTRIA, SWITZERLAND, LIECHTENSTEIN, LUXEMBOURG, France, Italy, Denmark, Belgium, Holland, Poland, Czech Republic, Slovakia, Hungary, Romania, United States.

Introduction

German is an Indo-European language, closely related to Dutch, English and the Scandinavian languages. It exists in a wide variety of dialects, some so different from each other as to be more or less mutually unintelligible. The standard language of Germany (Hoch-deutsch, or 'High German') is used for written communication throughout the German-speaking area, with a few small regional differences. It is spoken by most Germans, Austrians and German-Swiss either as their first language or as a second dialect (often with strong regional colouring).

Because of the close family relationship between English and German, there are many similarities between the two languages as regards phonology, vocabulary and syntax. German speakers therefore find English easy to learn initially, and tend to make relatively rapid progress.

Phonology

General

The German and English phonological systems are broadly similar, and German speakers do not have serious difficulty in perceiving or pronouncing most English sounds. Among the features of German which can give rise to a 'German accent' in English are:

- More energetic articulation than English, often with tenser vowels, more explosive stop consonants (/p/, /t/, /k/); and more lip-rounding and spreading.

- Different intonation patterns.
- Frequent use of glottal stops before initial vowels, giving a staccato effect.
- Tendency of some speakers to use a generally lower or higher pitch than most British people.

Vowels

iː	ɪ	e	æ	eɪ	aɪ	ɔɪ
ɑː	ɒ	ɔː	ʊ	aʊ	əʊ	ɪə
uː	ʌ	ɜː	ə	eə	ʊə	aɪə / aʊə

Shaded phonemes have equivalents or near equivalents in German, and should therefore be perceived and articulated without great difficulty, although some confusions may still arise. Unshaded phonemes may cause problems. For detailed comments, see below.

1. /e/ and /æ/ are often confused: *set* and *sat*.
2. /ɔː/ and /əʊ/ are often confused: *caught* and *coat*. Both may be pronounced as a close pure vowel /oː/.
3. /ʌ/ may be pronounced like /ɑ/.
4. /eɪ/ is sometimes pronounced as a close monophthong /eː/.
5. Stressed vowels may be pronounced over-long before unvoiced consonants (as in *shape*, *hot*, *like*).
6. Swiss speakers may nasalise certain vowels.

Consonants

p	b	f	v	θ	ð	t	d
s	z	ʃ	ʒ	tʃ	dʒ	k	g
m	n	ŋ	l	r	j	w	h

Shaded phonemes have equivalents or near equivalents in German, and should therefore be perceived and articulated without great difficulty, although some confusions may still arise. Unshaded phonemes may cause problems. For detailed comments, see below.

1. /ʒ/ and /dʒ/ are rare in German. German speakers often realise them as /ʃ/ and /tʃ/ in English: *'mesher'* for *measure*; *chain* for *Jane*.
2. The voiced sounds /ʒ/, /dʒ/, /z/, /v/, /b/, /d/ and /g/ do not occur at the ends of words in German. Students tend to confuse them with or replace them by their unvoiced equivalents in this position: *'beish'* for *'beige'*; *etch* for *edge*; *rice* for *rise*; *leaf* for *leave*; *pup* for *pub*; *set* for *said*; *dock* for *dog*.
3. /θ/ and /ð/ do not occur in German; students may replace them by /s/ and /z/: *useful* for *youthful*; *wizard* for *withered*.
4. There is only one German phoneme in the area of /v/ and /w/: *vine* for *wine* or (less often) *wine* for *vine*.
5. /r/ may be pronounced with the back of the tongue (as in French) or as a flap (like English /r/, but more energetic, depending on the variety of German).
6. 'Dark' /l/ (as in *fill, full*) does not exist in standard German. Students may replace it by 'clear' /l/ (as in *light*).

Stress

Patterns of word and sentence stress are quite similar in English and German, so there are few problems in this area. Note, however:
1. German compound expressions are generally stressed on the first element; those English compounds which are not may be mispronounced (e.g. **'front door*; **'chocolate cake*).
2. German has few 'weak forms', so German speakers may overstress words like *and, but, than, as, have, were*, giving them their strong (written) pronunciations in all contexts. Beginners may have difficulty in perceiving weak forms.

Intonation

This varies widely over the German-speaking area. North German intonation is quite like English. South German and Austrian intonation often has long rising glides in mid-sentence:

When I arrived at the house I found that Mary was out.

Swiss speakers may end sentences with a rise followed by a slight fall (*I don't know*): this sounds odd in English.

German speakers

Certain features of German intonation transferred to English (together with the more energetic articulation which is common) can make speakers sound peremptory. It is worth giving special practice in *wh*-questions (which German speakers may produce with a rising intonation which can sound hectoring to the English ear), and in requests.

Juncture

A German word or syllable beginning with a vowel is often separated from what comes before by a glottal stop (instead of being linked, as is usual in English). This can create a very foreign-sounding staccato effect:

ʔ*in* ʔ*and* ʔ*out* (German ʔaus ʔund ʔein).

Orthography and punctuation

Spelling

German speakers do not have more trouble than other learners with English spelling. Beginners may tend to represent English sounds by the appropriate German letters, making mistakes like *raund abaut, *schopping, *wery much*. Note that German nouns are written with initial capital letters, leading to mistakes like *I bought my Car from a Friend*.

Punctuation

Punctuation conventions are roughly the same in German and English. The main difference is that commas are used before all subordinate clauses, as well as infinitive complements of verbs, nouns and adjectives.

I think, that there has been a mistake.
She knew exactly, what he meant.
I hope, to see you soon.
He felt the need, to explain everything.
She was very anxious, to get there as early as possible.

Semi-colons are used less than in English. Quotation marks are written differently:

„How can I help you?" she asked.

Grammar

The German and English grammatical systems are very similar in most ways. There are the same 'part of speech' categories, and German has, for instance, singular and plural forms, definite and indefinite articles, regular and irregular verbs, auxiliary and modal verbs, and active and passive verbal structures. Time relations are signalled by the verb phrase much as in English, though the form which resembles the English present perfect is not used in the same way; there are no progressive forms.

German is a highly inflected language, in which words change their form (especially their endings) according to their grammatical function – articles, adjectives and nouns, for example, have different forms ('cases') according to whether the noun phrase is subject, direct object, indirect object or possessor. This means that word order is somewhat freer than in English, where the grammatical function of a word is principally indicated by its position. German has grammatical gender: nouns and pronouns are masculine, feminine or neuter. (There is little relationship between gender and meaning.) The lack of any systematic inflectional system in English often leads German-speaking students to feel that English has 'no grammar'.

Questions and negatives; auxiliaries

1. The auxiliary *do* has no equivalent in German; interrogatives are made by simple inversion, and one-word verbs are made negative by putting nicht (= *not*) after the verb:
     * *When started you to play the piano?*
     * *Thank you, I smoke not.*
2. Perfect tenses are generally formed with haben (= *have*) + past participle, as in English. However, some verbs (mostly common intransitive verbs referring to change of state) form their perfects with sein (= *be*):
     * *She is gone out.*
3. Because of the similarity of form, English *had* is often misused as an equivalent of German hat (= *has*) or hätte (which can mean *would have* – see below):
     * *Do you know if Andrew had telephoned yet?*
4. German has nothing corresponding to the complicated English system of question tags: agreement is normally solicited by a single invariable word or phrase such as nicht wahr? (= *not true?*). Learners may use English *no?* or *yes?* as an equivalent:
     * *It's getting late, no?*

Time, tense and aspect

A. Past time

1. German has forms similar to the English simple past, simple present perfect and simple past perfect, but there are no progressive forms:
   I realised that somebody came slowly up the stairs.
   I'm sorry I'm late. Have you waited long?
2. The German form which resembles the present perfect is not used in exactly the same way: it often functions just as a conversational past tense:
   I have seen Mary yesterday.
3. Conversely, the German past may be used where we would use a present perfect:
   The German prison system improved a lot in recent years.
4. In indirect speech, German tends to use a present subjunctive where English uses a past tense after past reporting verbs:
   I didn't know if she is at home.

B. Present time

1. The German lack of a present progressive causes mistakes:
   What do you look at?
2. To say how long a present state of affairs has been going on, German often uses a present tense where English uses a present perfect:
   How long are you in Germany? (meaning *How long have you been . . .?*)
   I know her since we were children.

C. Future time

German has no equivalent of the *going to* future. There is a future tense formed with an auxiliary (roughly equivalent to the *shall/will* future). The present tense is used extensively to refer to the future:
   I promise I bring it back tomorrow.

Conditionals

In spoken German conditional sentences, the auxiliary würde (which corresponds roughly to *would*) may be used in both clauses:
   If he would ask me, I wouldn't tell him anything.
   (Wenn er mich fragen würde, würde ich ihm nichts sagen.)
The opposite can also happen. With certain common verbs, German

may use the past subjunctive (a one-word form) instead of the conditional (compare older English *It were better if . . .*). Since German subjunctives often resemble the related English past tenses (e.g. käme/ came, wäre/were, hätte/had), confusion is especially likely:

> *If she had more time, she came more often.*
> *If I had known, I had told you.*
> *Tuesday were better for the meeting.*

Conditional meanings are expressed by inversion more freely in German than in English:

> *Were I in charge, I had changed the times.*

And German so is often used before the main clause:

> *If he would come at six, so could we eat earlier.*

Modal verbs

The English modals *can*, *must*, *may*, etc. have rough German equivalents. Inevitably there are differences of use which lead to mistakes. Some examples of common problems:

1. Ich kann (= *I can*) can be used with the name of a language to mean *I can speak*:
   > *I can Russian.*
2. English *must* looks like the German past tense musste (= *had to*):
   > *Yesterday I must go to London.*

   Must be may be used instead of *must have been*:
   > *Did you? That must be interesting.*
3. Muss nicht = *don't have to* or *needn't*; it is not the same as *must not*:
   > *I mustn't show my passport as my identity card is enough.*
4. German will means *want(s)*, not *will*:
   > *She doesn't know what she will.*

   This can lead to confusion between *would* and *wanted* (German wollte):
   > *I told her I would a coffee.*
5. German soll (= *is supposed to, is to, should*) is sometimes mistranslated as *shall*, and sollte (= *was supposed to, was to*) as *should*:
   > *He shall be a brilliant musician. (for He is supposed to be. . .)*
   > *I took my first look at the building which should be my school for seven years.*
6. German modals form questions and negatives in the same way as other verbs. This can lead to English modals being treated in the same way:
   > *Do you can swim?*
   > *You didn't must say that.*

43

Passivisation

German often uses an active sentence with the subject man (= *one*) where English prefers a passive.
> *One speaks English here.
> *One has never beaten his record.

There is . . .

A common German equivalent of *there is* is es ist (literally *it is*):
> *It is a man in the garden.

German can also use es before plural verbs in this case; and the structure is common with verbs other than sein (= *be*):
> *It were some problems with the financing.
> *There happened something very strange.

German also uses es gibt (literally *it gives*) as an equivalent of *there is/are*.
> *It gives a swimming pool behind the town hall.

Non-finite forms

German has no equivalent of the English noun-like use of the -*ing* form ('gerund'). Lachen, for instance, can correspond to English *to laugh*, *laughing* or in some cases to the bare infinitive *laugh*, according to the context and structure. These are all therefore often confused.
> *Instead of fight / to fight, they decided on talking / to talk.
> *I want start / starting work at once.
> *I came here with the hope to find a job.
> *I really must stop to smoke.

Like most other learners, German speakers have difficulty with the English 'object + infinitive' construction:
> *I wanted, that she came to my house.

Word order

1. Infinitives and past participles tend to come at the ends of clauses in German. The English word order is quickly learnt, but beginners sometimes make mistakes:
> *I must at once my sister telephone.
> *He was in a road accident killed.

2. Main verbs generally come at the ends of German subordinate clauses, leading beginners to make mistakes:
   Did I tell you, that my mother English speaks?
3. German has a basic 'verb second' word order. If the subject of a main clause is preceded by anything other than a conjunction, the subject and verb are inverted:
   On Tuesday have we a holiday.
4. A sentence may begin with the direct object or complement:
   This car have I very cheap bought.
   Fantastic is that!
5. Adverbs may separate a verb from its object or complement; this is unusual in English:
   You speak very well German.
   He became finally President.
6. Adverb particles tend to come at the ends of clauses:
   He walked quickly in.
7. German does not, however, strand prepositions at the ends of clauses, so students have trouble with structures like *That's the woman I was talking about* or *Who did you buy that for?*
8. In German, an article may be separated from its noun by quite a complex participle phrase:
   The in Britain with unusual excitement awaited budget . . .
9. Vor (= *ago*) precedes an expression of time. Entlang (= *along*) follows its noun:
   I bought it ago three years.
   I met her for/before six months.
   She was walking the road along.

Articles

1. In German, the definite article often accompanies nouns which are used in a general sense:
   The human beings are strange animals.
   We all have to live in the society.
2. The indefinite article is not used when defining people's professions:
   My sister is doctor.
3. The indefinite article is often omitted after the equivalents of *with*, *without* and *as*:
   You can't get there without car.
   I am telling you this as friend, not as boss.

Gender

Nouns are masculine, feminine or neuter. Nouns with a 'diminutive' ending are neuter. Pronouns are used accordingly:
> *My watch is broken. Can you mend her?*
> *The girl* (das Mädchen – diminutive) *was lost. It didn't know where it was.*

Number and countability

1. German nouns form their plurals in various ways. Common plural endings are -en and -er; beginners sometimes drop the -s from the plurals of English nouns that end in these letters:
   > *I have three brother.*
2. Some English uncountable nouns have countable German equivalents – for instance *news, hair, furniture, damage, advice, English, weather.*
   > *All the news are terrible today.*
   > *He speaks a wonderful English.*
   > *Can you give me an advice?*
3. Some English plural nouns have singular German equivalents: for example *trousers, scissors, the Middle Ages, the police.*
   > *Can you lend me a scissor?*
   > *The police is looking for him.*

Possessive 's

German has an equivalent of the English possessive *'s* structure, but it is mostly used with names. In other cases von (= *of*) is generally used:
> *I went skiing with the husband of my sister.*

Adjectives and adverbs

1. A German adverb of manner is usually identical in form with the uninflected adjective. For example, gut = *good/well*; schrecklich = *terrible/terribly*:
   > *She can drive very good.*
   > *He is very good-educated.*
   > *I was terrible impressed.*
2. A noun may sometimes be dropped if it can be 'understood' after an adjective:
   > *The most important is, to tell everybody at once.*

Relative pronouns

1. German *was* corresponds not only to *what*, but also to *that* (in certain cases) and to *which* when the antecedent is a clause. This leads to misuse of *what*:
    The only thing what he could do . . .
    All what we want . . .
    His offer was rejected, what took him by surprise.
2. German does not distinguish relative *who* and *which*:
    I know the people which came to see you this morning.
3. Since there is no grammatical distinction in German between restrictive and non-restrictive relative clauses, beginners may not understand why structures like *Her mother, that lives in Paris* or *My uncle, you met yesterday* are ungrammatical.
4. German cannot drop object relative pronouns, so students tend to overuse structures like:
    the girl whom I am going to marry

Conjunctions

1. German has the same word for *as* and *like* (referring to similarity):
    You look as your sister.
2. The German word *falls* (literally *in case*) is used to mean *if* in certain contexts. This can lead to uses of *in case* which are not correct in British English:
    Phone me in case you can't come.

Prepositions

Most German prepositions have rough English equivalents. Problems arise in cases (too many to list) where a fixed English expression or collocation is not constructed with the 'same' preposition as is used in German. Typical mistakes in this area:
    dressed with a dark suit
    You remind me at/on your father.
    That's typical for him.
    full with water
Other problems (easier to predict) occur when a German preposition has more than one regular English equivalent. Some common difficulties:
1. Nach (= *after*) can also mean *according to*:
    After my teacher, this is correct.

2. Seit can mean *since* or *for*:
   I've known her since three years.
3. Von = *of* or *from*; also *by* when talking about authorship:
   Can I have a piece from that cake?
   a photo from my mother
   a symphony from Beethoven
4. Zu = *to* or *at*:
   *to Easter   *He was a student to Heidelberg.*
5. An = *at* or *on*:
   *at Monday   *on a party*
6. Vor = *before* or *in front of*; also *ago*:
   The bus stop is before our house.
   I arrived before/for ten minutes.
   I married for ten years. (Meaning *I got married ten years ago.*)
7. Mit (= *with*) is used with ages:
   With 16 you can ride a motorbike.
8. Während = *during* or *while*:
   She phoned during you were out.
9. Bei corresponds to a large number of prepositions in English, depending on the context – but rarely to *by*:
   I spent the evening by John and Alice. (for . . . at John and Alice's)
   By this weather no planes can fly.

Vocabulary

Very many German and English words are derived from the same roots (e.g. Haus = *house*; Schuh = *shoe*; jung – *young*; singen = *to sing*). This facilitates learning on the whole, though there are a certain number of 'false friends' (see below). German-speaking Swiss generally know some French, which helps them with that part of English vocabulary which is of French or Latin origin (though it may also lead them to make typically French mistakes of spelling or vocabulary use).

False friends

A large number of German words have meanings or uses which are slightly or completely different from those of their English cognates. Students may misuse the following words (among others):

come   (German kommen = *come* or *go* according to context)
go   (German gehen = *go* or *walk* according to context)

bring	(German bringen = *bring* or *take* according to context)
mean	(German meinen usually = *think* or *say*)
actual(ly)	(German aktuell = *present, current, topical, at present*)
eventual(ly)	(German eventuell = *possible/possibly/perhaps*)
sympathetic	(German sympathisch = *nice*)
thank you	(German danke can mean No, *thank you*)
when	(German wenn = *if* or *whenever*)
become	(German bekommen = *obtain, get*)
control	(German kontrollieren = *check*)
while	(German weil = *because*)
cook	(German kochen = *boil* or *cook*)
lucky	(German glücklich = *happy* or *lucky*)
rentable	(German rentabel = *profitable*)

Note also that *who* (German wer) and *where* (German wo) are easily confused by beginners.

Other confusions

Apart from difficulties caused by misleading cognates, problems arise more generally where one German word has more than one English equivalent, or where a pair of contrasting words are not distributed in quite the same way as their apparent English equivalents. A few examples:

say and *tell*
so and *such*
yet, still and *again*
this and *that*
as and *how*
as and *than*
as and *when*
to and *too*
miss and *lose*
leave and *let*
leave and *forget*

Phonetically motivated confusions:

man and *men*
prize and *price*
save and *safe*

The German word for *please* (bitte) is used when offering something, and also as a formulaic reply to thanks (rather like *not at all*, but used much more widely). This leads students to misuse *Please* in English.

49

German speakers

Swiss speakers sometimes use *Why not?* inappropriately where a polite response to an invitation is required:
> '*Would you like to join us for a week touring the Mediterranean on Lord Canterville's yacht?*' *'Why not?'*

Word formation

Complex nouns are common in German (Dorfschullehrer = *village school teacher*), and students may try to make similar one-word compounds in English.

A sample of written German with a word-for-word translation

Eines Abends   saß ich im   Dorfwirtshaus
One   evening [genitive] sat I   in the village pub

vor   (genauer   gesagt, hinter)   einem Glas
in front of (more exactly said,   behind) a   glass

Bier, als   ein Mann gewöhnlichen Aussehens
beer, when a   man [of] ordinary   appearance [genitive]

sich   neben mich setzte   und   mich mit   vertraulicher
himself beside me   placed and me   with confidential

Stimme fragte, ob   ich eine Lokomotive   kaufen wolle.
voice   asked, whether I   a   locomotive to buy want [present subjunctive].

Nun   ist es zwar   ziemlich leicht,   mir   etwas   zu verkaufen,
Now is it   indeed rather   easy,   to me something to sell,

denn ich kann schlecht nein sagen,   aber bei   einer
for   I   can   badly   no   say [I find it difficult to say no], but   with a

größeren Anschaffung dieser Art   schien   mir   doch
bigger   purchase   of this kind seemed to me however

Vorsicht am   Platze.
caution at the place [caution seemed to me to be indicated].

Obgleich   ich wenig von Lokomotiven verstehe,   erkundigte
Although I   little   of   locomotives understand, informed

ich mich   nach Typ   und Bauart,   um   bei
I   myself [I enquired] after type and construction kind, in order in

dem Mann den Anschein   zu erwecken, als   habe er es hier
the man the impression to awake,   as [if] have he it here

mit   einem Experten zu tun, der nicht gewillt sei, die Katz'
with an   expert   to do, who not willing be, the cat

im   Sack zu kaufen, wie man so schön   sagt.
in the sack to buy,   as one so beautiful(ly) says.

('Eine größere Anschaffung' by Wolfgang Hildesheimer from *Lieblose Legenden*)

French speakers

Catherine Walter

Distribution

FRANCE (including French West Indies), BELGIUM, SWITZERLAND, CANADA, HAITI; some parts of northwestern Italy and Luxembourg; official or widespread second language in many former French and Belgian colonies in north, west and central Africa, Asia, the Pacific, and South America.

Introduction

French belongs to the Romance group of Indo-European languages, and is closely related to Italian, Spanish, Portuguese, Romanian and other Romance tongues. There are some differences between standard Belgian or Canadian French, for example, and the standard French of France, but the differences are not greater than those between British and American English; the different standard French dialects are certainly mutually comprehensible.

Because French is an Indo-European language, and because the Norman contribution to English was so great, there are some similarities between French and English, both in syntax and vocabulary. The phonological systems exhibit some important differences, however, and this usually presents French speakers with problems in understanding and producing spoken English, and in making links between spelling and pronunciation.

Phonology

General

French shares many phonological characteristics with English. French speakers do not have great difficulty in perceiving or pronouncing most English consonants, but some of the vowel sounds present problems. Perhaps most importantly, the French and English systems of word stress and rhythm are very different, and this can lead to serious difficulties both in understanding and in producing spoken English. Among the features of French which lead to a 'French accent' in English are:

- All French words of two syllables or more are stressed in a regular way (see below), unlike the English system where the stress pattern for each word or word-type must be learnt. This can lead to problems of comprehension and comprehensibility.
- Unstressing a syllable in French does not involve reducing the time given to its pronunciation, as it does in English. In addition, there is little of the vowel reduction that occurs in unstressed English syllables. These two factors make it seem to French speakers that English speakers 'swallow' their words, and can make the English spoken by French speakers sound monotonous or staccato.
- French uses tenser, more rounded lips and more frequent jaw opening; the tip of the tongue is not used, and there is more use of the blade (the part behind the tip) of the tongue, giving 'softer' sounds to some consonants.

Vowels

iː	ɪ	e	æ	eɪ	aɪ	ɔɪ
ɑː	ɒ	ɔː	ʊ	aʊ	əʊ	ɪə
uː	ʌ	ɜː	ə	eə	ʊə	aɪə
						aʊə

Shaded phonemes have equivalents or near equivalents in French, and should therefore be perceived and articulated without serious difficulty, although some confusions may still arise. Unshaded phonemes may cause problems. For detailed comments, see below.

1. French has only one sound in the area of /iː/ and /ɪ/, leading to confusions between pairs like *leave* and *live*.
2. /ʌ/ is sometimes pronounced almost like /ə/, so that *much* becomes '*mirch*'.
3. French has only one sound in the area of /ʊ/ and /uː/, leading to confusion between pairs like *pull* and *pool*.
4. /ɒ/ is often unrounded, so that, for instance, *not* is realised something like *nut*.
5. Both /ɔː/ and /əʊ/ are moved towards the French /o/, leading to confusion between pairs like *naught* and *note*.

6. /æ/ often creates difficulty. Depending on how it is perceived by the French speaker, it may be realised:
   - very like an English /ʌ/, so that words like *bank* and *bunk* are confused;
   - rather like /ɑː/, so that, for instance, *hand* sounds like 'hahnd';
   - as /e/, causing confusion between pairs like *pat* and *pet*.
7. /eɪ/ sometimes becomes /e/, so that, for example, *paper* sounds like *pepper*. Since /æ/ can also be realised as /e/, this can lead to confusion in pairs like *mad* and *made*.
8. Other diphthongs are not usually too problematic, but they may be pronounced with equal force and length on the two elements: *I see now* becomes 'Ahee see nah-oo'.

Consonants

p	b	f	v	θ	ð	t	d
s	z	ʃ	ʒ	tʃ	dʒ	k	g
m	n	ŋ	l	r	j	w	h

Shaded phonemes have equivalents or near equivalents in French, and should therefore be perceived and articulated without serious difficulty, although some confusions may still arise. Unshaded phonemes may cause problems. For detailed comments, see below.

1. /θ/ and /ð/ do not exist in French, and the fact that spoken French does not require the tip of the tongue makes these sounds difficult to learn. /s/, /z/, /f/, /v/, /t/ and /d/ are common realisations of these phonemes. *Think* may be realised as *sink, fink* or 'tink'; and *that* as 'zat', *vat* or 'dat'.
2. /tʃ/ is often realised as /ʃ/ and /dʒ/ as /ʒ/. So *church* becomes 'shursh' and *joke* becomes 'zhoke'.
3. /h/ (which does not exist in French) is often dropped: 'I 'aven't seen 'enry today'.
4. /r/ is pronounced with the back of the tongue in French, and so is likely to be pronounced the same way in English.
5. 'Dark' /l/, as in *will*, does not occur in French, and students may replace it by 'clear' /l/, as in *lay*.
6. English lengthens vowels in stressed syllables before final voiced consonants. In fact, the main way an English speaker hears the

difference between words like *sat* and *sad* is by hearing the longer vowel before the *d* of the second word (the voiced/devoiced contrast between *d* and *t* is much less important for perception). French speakers do not typically lengthen these vowels, leading to confusion between pairs of words like *sat* and *sad*, *pick* and *pig*, and so on.

Consonant clusters

1. In words ending in consonant + *le*, the French speaker may re-interpret the 'dark' /l/ as /əl/. Combined with the tendency to stress multisyllabic words on the last syllable, this gives pronunciations like *'terri'bull' 'lit'tull'*.
2. At the end of words like *realism*, French speakers may pronounce /s/ plus devoiced /m/. An English speaker may hear *'realiss'*.
3. One does not normally find a consonant followed by /z/ at the end of a French word. So in pronouncing English plurals, French speakers tend to drop the *-s* after voiced consonants, making mistakes like **two tin*.

Stress

1. In French words of more than one syllable, the word stress (which is somewhat weaker than in English) is on the last pronounced syllable. With the exception of /ə/, which is sometimes elided, vowels which are not stressed retain their pronunciation, rather than being shortened, or weakened to /ə/ or /ɪ/ as in English. So French speakers have great difficulty in perceiving shortened or weakened syllables when English speakers pronounce them.

   This shortening and weakening also produces problems for French speakers trying to produce spoken English, as does moving from the very regular French system of word stress to English, where the stress pattern of each word or word-type must be learnt as part of its pronunciation.
2. Where English uses stress to mark contrast, French often uses a grammatical construction. Compare French and English answers to *'Didn't you go to the grocer's?'*:

English: *No, I went to the **baker's**.*
French: Non, c'est à la boulangerie que je suis allée.
   (= *No, it's to the baker's that I went.*)

Intonation

The French and English intonation systems are similar in many respects. But movements in French tend to be steplike and avoid glides, which can in some situations give an impression of vehemence where none is intended.

Influence of spelling on pronunciation

Although French spelling is complex, a French speaker can tell how to pronounce a word (with very rare exceptions) from the way it is spelt. French learners may therefore expect to be able to do the same in English. Additionally, mistakes may be made, especially by beginners, in cases where a letter or combination of letters has a different value in English and in French. Note particularly:

1. In syllables ending with the letter *r*, this letter is pronounced in French; interference here may cause problems for students of British English with words like *hard, early, garden*. In words like *sister*, French speakers may pronounce the final *e* as /e/: '*sistair*'.
2. *ou* may be pronounced /uː/, and *au* may be pronounced /o/: '*pronoonce*', '*otomatic*'.
3. In regular past endings, students may pronounce final /ɪd/ or /ed/ after all consonants, or after all unvoiced consonants: *warnèd, jumpèd*.
4. Final written consonants in French (e.g. plural -*s*) are often not pronounced. This tends to be carried over into English and lead to mistakes like **differen, *She stay, *four apple*.
5. There are a large number of cognates in English and French. It is very common for French students to transfer French stress patterns to these words.

Orthography and punctuation

French speakers do not have more trouble than other learners with English spelling. Note that days of the week, months, languages and national adjectives are not capitalised in French and may lead to mistakes like **I will begin german classes on the first tuesday of january*.

Punctuation conventions are roughly the same in French and English. Commas can be used in French in some cases where they would not be used in English, and may lead to mistakes like **Consonants that are doubled in writing, are usually pronounced like single consonants*.

Quotation marks are written slightly differently in French: «. . .» rather than '. . .' or ". . .".

Grammar

General

The French and English grammatical systems are very similar in most ways: there are the same 'part of speech' categories; word order is broadly similar; French has singular and plural verb forms, definite and indefinite articles, regular and irregular verbs, auxiliary verbs, active and passive forms, and past, present and future tenses. There are perfect verb forms (though the tense which is constructed like the English present perfect is not used in the same way).

There are some important differences, though. French verbs are inflected, so that the ending of a verb indicates both its tense and the person and number of the subject of the clause (though some of the inflections have disappeared from speech). French has no equivalent of the English progressive forms. The verbs in French which express modality are inflected and form questions and negatives in the same way as other verbs. There is nothing corresponding to phrasal/prepositional verbs in French. There are no inflected question tags. French has grammatical gender: nouns, pronouns, adjectives, articles and some determiners are masculine or feminine (though only a few nouns show a relationship between gender and meaning); the same words also inflect for plurality (at least in writing). 'Heads' of phrases typically come before their modifiers in French: so, for example, nouns typically come before attributive adjectives and verbs before adverbs.

Verbs

French speakers tend to have trouble learning to pronounce the -s endings on third person singular present tense verbs. There are many reasons for this. English is perceived as a non-inflected language compared to French, so the one sign of inflection tends to be forgotten. Final written -s in any French word is virtually never pronounced. And although there are differences in the spellings of first, second and third person singular present tense endings of regular verbs in French, all three forms are pronounced the same.

Questions and negatives; auxiliaries

1. The auxiliary *do* has no equivalent in French. French speakers can run into problems in English trying to form interrogatives as they do in French:
   - Simply by adding a question mark or by using question intonation:
     *You are coming this evening?
   - By inversion:
     *When think you to leave England?
2. Negatives in French are formed by putting ne . . . pas around a one-word verb, or around the auxiliary of a longer verb. This can lead to omission of *do/did* and/or incorrect placement of *not*:
   *She lives not in Paris.
   The ne also precedes the verb when another negative follows it, so:
   *I have not said nothing.
3. French has tenses which are formed like the English perfect tenses, generally with the verb avoir (= *have*). However, some verbs (including many common verbs of movement) form these tenses with être (= *be*):
   *Claude is come yesterday.
4. Conjugated question tags do not exist in French; whereas in English the question tag agrees with the main verb, French uses n'est-ce pas? (= *isn't it?* or *isn't that?*), or more casually non?, after all verbs:
   *You're American, isn't it?
   *Emma is with Simon, no?

Time, tense and aspect

A. Past time

1. There is a French tense that is formed much like the English present perfect, but it functions as a simple past in speech and informal writing:
   *I have been to Japan last month.
2. In French the present tense is used to talk about actions or states that began in the past and are continuing in the present:
   *I work in Paris since August / for six months.
   *She is going out with Marc since they were sixteen.
3. In writing, and sometimes in speech (especially when reporting conversations), the present tense may be used to talk about the past. In French this gives an effect of fast-moving action to a narrative:
   *On 24 July 1769, General O'Reilly arrives and takes official possession of Louisiana for Spain.

> *I phoned Eric last night. When I ask him 'Are you coming?', he says he can't.*

4. French has a tense which is used in the same way as the English past progressive, to talk about an action in progress at a given point in the past. But this same French tense is also used to talk about habits or repeated actions in the past, so French speakers may use the past progressive in place of a simple past tense, *used to*, or *would . . .* (in the sense of *was/were in the habit of*):

> *We were often going to the seaside when I was a child.*
> *I was eating here every day when I was working for IBM.*
> *Every Christmas my father was pretending to be Father Christmas, and we were pretending to believe him.*

This tense is also used in cases where the past perfect progressive would be used in English with *for* and *since*:

> *When I arrived, they were waiting for half an hour.*

Note that all verbs including 'state' verbs, can be put into this tense in French:

> *I was knowing him when he got his first big part.*

5. There is a tense in French which is formed like the English past perfect, and its usage corresponds generally to the English tense. But it can also be used when the action spoken about is separated from the present by facts that are common knowledge to the speakers – even though they may not be mentioned:

> *'Here we are. Room 232.'* *'But I had asked for a room with a view!'*

B. Present time

1. French has no present progressive form:

> *Julie can't come to the phone now. She has/takes a bath.*

2. French uses the present tense after expressions like *This is the first time . . .*:

> *This is the first time I come to London.*

C. Future time

French has the same three ways of expressing future time as English: a present tense, a *going to* structure, and a future tense. In general, French and English usage of these is similar, but there are some differences.

1. Since French has no present progressive tense, the simple present may be incorrectly used for the future:

> *I eat with Christine this evening.*

2. In French, the present tense is used to express a decision at the moment it is taken:

(the doorbell rings) **I answer it!*
The present is also used to express a promise:
*I'm doing/I do it this evening.
3. French uses the future tense for future time after the equivalents of *when* and *as soon as*:
*I'll phone you when she will arrive.
*Will you tell me as soon as he will have finished?

Modal verbs

The English modals *can, must, should*, etc. have French equivalents. But these verbs in French do not form a separate class: unlike their English counterparts, they do not behave differently from other inflected verbs, and have no special rules about questions, negatives or following infinitives. This leads to mistakes, especially for beginners, like **He cans . . .* and **Do you must . . . .*

There are other differences of use which lead to mistakes. Some common problems:
1. Since French speakers are taught that their infinitive form corresponds to the English *to*-infinitive, it is common for them to use the *to*-infinitive with English modals:
*I can to swim.
*You must to enter your password first.
*You should to try this new shampoo.
2. French uses forms of the single verb devoir to cover the notions of obligation and deduction expressed in English by *must* and *should*. This can lead to students saying *must* when they mean *should* and vice versa:
*You must (to) ask Eleanor if she has any ideas.
*You should (to) have a permit to work in America.
3. There is no structure in French corresponding to the English use of *shall* for making and asking for suggestions. Instead, other structures are used: the present tense, or the 'imperfect' with *if*:
*I set the table?
*Where do we go?
*If I lent you part of the money?
4. French present and past conditional tenses are used in the same way as their English equivalents. However, conditionals are also used (for example, in newspaper articles or news broadcasts) to indicate that the information given is not absolutely certain:
*The hijackers would be members of the extremist group. (instead of *The hijackers are thought to be / are allegedly . . .*)

According to Opposition leaders, the decision would have been taken. (instead of . . . *the decision was taken.*)
5. The French equivalents of modal perfects are constructed differently: the equivalent of *I ought to have gone*, for example, is j'aurais dû aller – literally '*I would have oughted to go*'. This can lead French speakers to use an English infinitive instead of a past participle:
   * *I ought to have go.*

Imperatives

1. In spoken French, the future is often used for instructions and directions, leading to mistakes in English:
   * *You will go straight until the lights, and then you will turn left . . .*
2. In written French, the infinitive is often used as an imperative form:
   * *To wipe your feet, please.*
   * *To break the eggs into a bowl and to beat lightly.*

Clause structure and complementation

1. French often prefers a relative clause where English uses an *-ing* form adjectivally:
   * *I love the feel of soft warm rain that falls on my face.*
2. French uses an infinitive, and not a gerund, when a verb form is needed to fill the place of a noun:
   * *To drive the children to school is a nightmare.*
   * *David is thinking to change his job.*
   * *I'm tired to tell her the same thing every day.*
   * *I want to talk to Susan about to change my job.*
   * *He can't start the day without to have a cup of tea.*
3. In cases where English uses an infinitive after a verb to express purpose, French uses the equivalent of *for*. So sentences like these occur:
   * *He is going to London for buy some books.*
   * *. . . for buying some books.*
   * *. . . for to buy some books.*
4. While English has both 'bare' and '*to-*' infinitives, French has only one sort. This leads to mistakes like:
   * *I want go.* * *I hope go.*
5. Spoken French allows an 'extraposed' subject or object in a sentence:
   * *Your sister she came.*
   * *The telephone they repaired it?*

French speakers

　　She is there, your mother?
6. Relative pronouns are never omitted in French, so French speakers can have trouble understanding, and may avoid producing, sentences like:
　　That's the man my sister interviewed.

Complementation with certain verbs

French verbs that have close equivalents in English often have a different complementation pattern. Some of the more common cases:
1. French uses a (subjunctive) clause, rather than an infinitive structure, after the equivalents of *want* and *would like*:
　　She wants that you come right away.
2. The equivalent of *know* in French can be followed by an infinitive:
　　I know to make pancakes.
3. With expressions of locomotion (*walk, run, dance,* etc.), French tends to specify the type of movement by a participle phrase, not by the choice of main verb as happens in English:
　　She left the room running. (for *She ran out of the room.*)
　　They went down the street dancing. (for *They danced down the street.*)
4. In both English and French, certain verbs can be immediately followed by indirect objects which say who is affected by the verb's action, but the list is not quite the same in the two languages:
　　I explained her the situation.
　　He suggested me another solution.

It *and* there

The French expression corresponding to *there is* is an idiomatic phrase beginning with the equivalent of *it*. This can lead to mistakes:
　　It's a problem with the steering.
The French equivalent of *there is (. . . that)* can also be used with a time expression to mean *ago* or *It's . . . since*:
　　I met here there are five years.
　　There are six weeks that she hasn't written.

Passivisation

1. French uses either a reflexive pronoun or the equivalent of *one* in many cases where English uses the passive:

*That does not do itself. (for That is not done.)
*One speaks English here.

2. In French, the beneficiary of a transitive verb (indirect object in an active construction) cannot be the subject of a passive sentence. For:

    We were given two days to finish the work.

    a French speaker will tend to say:

    *One gave us two days (for) to finish the work.

3. Like other learners, French speakers have trouble with complex passives:

    *The house is building. (for . . . being built.)
    *A lot of books have written on this subject.

Word order: influence of French

In French, heads of phrases typically come before modifiers. This is the opposite of what happens in English and has repercussions in more than one area.

1. Most attributive adjectives in French are placed after the noun. Some problems in English may arise from this:

    *a dress red
    *a lecture rather long
    *a request quite reasonable
    *She is the woman the most beautiful that I know.

2. Noun–noun compounds in French are less frequent than in English; when they do occur, the main noun is first and the modifying noun follows:

    *an article of newspaper
    *a shop shoe

3. There is no structure corresponding to the *'s* genitive structure in French. This, and French head-first word order, can lead to mistakes like:

    *the car of my brother
    *her blouse's friend

4. In French, an adverb often comes between the verb and the direct object:

    *I forget always the way to his house.
    *I like very much your dress.
    *Solange speaks very well English.
    *He offers never to help.

There are several other common sorts of mistake which reproduce French word order.

French speakers

1. French can use inversion in an object clause or relative clause if the subject of the clause is a noun:
    *I told her what wanted the directors.
    *Do you know how is coming John?
    *The song that was singing my mother when she was putting us to bed . . .
    *The house where lived my grandparents . . .
2. If the subject of the subordinate clause is a pronoun, normal sentence order is used in French, as in English; but overgeneralisation from English question forms may still lead to mistakes in reported speech:
    *They asked us where were we going.
    *I wonder which department does she work for.
3. French uses inversion after *see, hear, let,* and *perhaps*:
    *I saw go out a short plump man.
    *I heard open the living room door.
    *Ms Hadley let play the children a bit longer than usual.
    *Perhaps will they be late.
The (active) infinitive in the equivalent French structure can have an active or passive meaning, leading to English sentences like *I have never seen kill an animal.*
4. In French, expressions of quantity used as direct objects come before the past participle of a two-part verb:
    *I have too much eaten.
    *She has everything read, but she hasn't found the answer.
    *I have them all counted.
    *He's a lot done for both the children.
5. Many expressions with infinitives in French are preceded by de or à, which French speakers sometimes translate as *to*. This has an effect on their realisation of negative infinitives:
    *I asked him to not tell his sister.
6. Exclamations with the French equivalent of *how* + adjective/adverb do not use inversion:
    *How he runs fast!
7. Other typical mistakes arising from French word order are:
    *a such charming woman
    *ago ten minutes
    *Is your coffee enough sweet?
    *three days, about
    *the four last days (for the last four days)
    *the three next months
    *Has been your sister to France?

Word order: particles and prepositions

There is no verb category corresponding to phrasal/prepositional verbs in French. French speakers have difficulty learning how to use these verbs in English; word order with pronoun objects is a particular problem.

> *John phoned. Can you call back him?*

French cannot 'strand' a preposition at the end of a clause. When the question word is the object of a preposition in French, the preposition always comes before the question word. This can sound odd in spoken English:

> *From where are you?*

Note too that this leads to the unidiomatic usage:

> (*)*At what time . . .?*

Learners also avoid, and may have difficulty understanding, relative and passive structures like:

> *There's the girl I was talking to you about.*
> *He's just been operated on.*

Articles

1. In French, the definite article accompanies nouns which are used in a general sense:
   > *I like the Baroque music.*
   > *The whisky is a stronger drink than the sherry.*
2. French uses no article before the names of professions in complement position:
   > *Sarah is teacher.*
3. French uses a definite article before possessive pronouns and some determiners:
   > *This is the mine and that is the hers.*
   > *The most people think the euro is a good thing.*
4. In French, the indefinite article can sometimes be omitted after the equivalents of *as* and *without*:
   > *I used my spoon as shovel.*
   > *Did Tom go out without hat?*
5. Other typical mistakes arising from French use of articles are:
   > *the Mike's book*
   > *What time do you have the dinner?*
   > *The English is a difficult language.*
   > *He's coming the next week.*
   > *the Cambridge University*
   > *the Princess Caroline*

> * *I'm not in the office the Thursday.*
> * *What pretty jacket!*

Gender

1. Nouns are masculine or feminine. Pronouns are used accordingly:
   > * *I can't find my book – he was on the table a minute ago.*
   > * *This cooker doesn't work as well as she used to.*
2. The possessive determiners corresponding to *his* and *her* are identical; they agree in gender with the noun they modify:
   > * *I had dinner with John and her sister last night.*
   > * *Janet lent me his knife to open the parcel.*

Number

1. A number of nouns are countable in French and uncountable (mass) nouns in English. Common mistakes:
   > * *my hairs*   * *your luggages*
   > * *informations*   * *advices*
   > * *The news are good.*
2. Some things that are designated by plural nouns in English are designated by singular nouns in French. Possible mistakes:
   > * *a jean*   * *a trouser*   * *a short*   * *a pyjama*
   > * *the middle age* (for *the Middle Ages*)
   > * *the custom* (for *customs*)
   > * *The police is on the phone.*
3. Quantities of money and measures of liquids, solids, and distances typically take a plural verb and are followed by plural pronouns in French:
   > * *I need another five pence, but I haven't got them.*
   > * *Fifteen litres are more than I can carry.*
   > * *Six miles aren't far to walk if you're fit.*
4. When several people possess the same sort of thing, French often puts the noun referring to the thing in the singular:
   > * *We all put our coat on and went out.*
5. English noun–noun compounds may lead to problems, where one of the nouns has a plural meaning and a singular form:
   > * *a teethbrush*   * *a shoes shop*   * *a books publisher*

Adjectives and adverbs

(See also the section on 'Word order'.)

1. In a series of two or more adjectives, French usually puts et (= *and*) before the last one. This can lead to mistakes with English attributive adjectives:
     *a short and red dress
2. There are a number of adjectives that can be used as singular nouns in French:
     *The poor! (meaning *The poor man/woman!*)
     *The essential is to get the timing right.
   and any adjective can be used anaphorically without the equivalent of English proform *one*:
     'Which one is your brother?' *'The tall.'
3. Present and past participles used as adjectives (like *interesting* and *interested*, *boring* and *bored*) are often confused:
     *I am very boring in the lesson.
4. Comparatives and superlatives are always formed with the equivalents of *more* and *most*:
     *I thought she was much more old.
     *I am the most short person of the class. / the person the most short of the class.
5. With comparative adjectives and adverbs in French, the word que, (whose most common English equivalent is *that*) is used:
     *I am taller that two of my brothers.
     *She doesn't drive as fast that you.

Reflexive pronouns

French does not express a distinction in the first and second persons between reflexive pronouns and ordinary object pronouns. Nor does French have a distinction between the ideas 'oneself' and 'each other':
     *I hurt me with the hammer.
     *We just sat there looking at us.

Relative pronouns

1. In French there is one subject relative pronoun (qui, which as an interrogative pronoun means *who*); and one object relative pronoun (que, which as an interrogative pronoun means *what*). This can lead to problems in English:

French speakers

> *The book who made the biggest impression on me ...*
> *The man what I saw yesterday ...*

2. The article is not omitted after the French pronoun that corresponds to *whose*:
   > *The man whose the car was parked in front of mine ...*
3. French uses the word corresponding to *where* as a relative after some time expressions:
   > *There was a terrific storm the day where he was born.*

Conjunctions

1. French has the same word (comme) for *as* and *like* (referring to similarity):
   > *We're from the same family and went to the same school, but he isn't at all as me.*
2. French often does not use ellipsis after *and* and *or*:
   > *Have you got a knife and a fork?*
   > *In Germany or in Austria ...*

Prepositions

Most French prepositions have rough English equivalents. Problems arise in cases (too many to list) where an English expression is not constructed with the 'same' preposition as is used in French; or where one of the languages uses a preposition and the other does not. Typical mistakes in this area:

> *responsible of the whole project*
> *made in plastic*
> *married with my sister*
> *listen a record*
> *discuss of a solution*

Other problems (easier to predict) occur when a French preposition has more than one regular English equivalent. Some common difficulties:

1. Depuis can mean *since* or *for*:
   > *I have lived here since ten years.*
2. De can mean *of* or *from*, and is also used when talking about authorship:
   > *He is of Cannes.*
   > *a novel of Zola*
3. English place prepositions depend on whether one is speaking of movement or position (e.g. *at/in/to*). French place prepositions depend to some extent on the word class of the object of the

68

preposition. A city, for example, will be preceded by à, whether this means *at*, *in* or *to* in English:

> *She went at London last year.
> *There are hundreds of cinemas at Paris.
> *I went in Germany last year.

4. French uses articles, not prepositions, in common adverbials of time referring to days or parts of days:

> *It's very quiet here the night.
> *I usually work in the office the morning and make visits the afternoon.
> *I usually see Nick the Tuesday.

Vocabulary

Very many French and English words are derived from the same roots. The more intellectual or technical a word is, the more this is likely to occur. This facilitates learning on the whole, especially at the intermediate stage and beyond. However, it often means that French learners are inclined to use a less common, more erudite-sounding, cognate Romance item instead of a more common Germanic one, which may sound odd to native speakers: *liberate* instead of *set free*, *extinguish* rather than *put out*, *enter* rather than *go in*. The overuse of Romance items is sometimes a conscious avoidance strategy to get round the difficulty of using phrasal/prepositional verbs.

In addition, there are a number of 'false friends', which have different meanings in the two languages; and – perhaps worse – 'unreliable friends': words that mean almost the same in the two languages, or mean the same in one context and not in another.

'Bleached verbs'

Groups of multi-purpose 'bleached verbs' exist both in English and in French, but these groups are structured differently in each language:

1. Many of the concepts expressed in English with the verb *to be* are expressed in French with the verb corresponding to *to have*. This can lead to mistakes like:

> *I have hunger.
> *She has heat.
> *You have reason. (for *You are right.*)

Conversely, French uses the equivalent of *be* in Je suis d'accord (= *I agree*, literally *I am of agreement*), leading to the common mistake *I am agree.

2. French uses the equivalent of *take* in expressions where English speakers would use *have*, leading to mistakes like **Let's take a drink*.
3. Many everyday actions that are expressed with the verb *get* in English are expressed with reflexive verbs in French:
   *I woke me and dressed me early in case she arrived.

False and unreliable friends

An immense number of French words have meanings which are slightly or completely different in use from their English cognates. Here is a very small sample of the words that French speakers may misuse in English:

actual, actually (French actuel = *current, present*; actuellement = *now*)

advice (French avis = *opinion*)

chance (French chance = [*bit of*] *luck*)

command (French commander = *order* [*food, merchandise*, etc.])

corpse (French corps = *body*)

cry (French crier = *shout*)

demand (French demander = *ask*)

education (French éducation = *upbringing*)

engaged (French engagé = *committed*)

essence (French essence = *petrol*)

eventual (French éventuel = *potential, possible*)

evident (French évident = *obvious*)

experience (French expérience = *experience* or *experiment*)

fault (French faute = *mistake*)

gentle (French gentil = *kind, nice*)

ignore (French ignorer = *not to know*)

important (French important = *important* or *big, extensive*)

interesting (French intéressant = *interesting* or *lucrative, profitable, financially advantageous*)

large (French large = *wide*)

library (French librairie = *bookshop*)

occasion (French occasion = *opportunity, bargain*)

pass (an exam) (French passer un examen = *take, sit an exam*)

politics (French politique = *politics* or *policy*)

professor (French professeur = *teacher*)

savage (French sauvage = *wild*)

sensible (French sensible = *sensitive*)

sympathetic (French sympathique = *nice, easy to get on with*)

A sample of written French with a word-for-word translation

Le printemps était venu. Un dimanche, après avoir   nettoyé
The spring was come. One Sunday,   after to-have cleaned

sa boutique à grande eau, Lecouvreur, sentant les chaleurs
his shop at big   water, Lecouvreur, feeling the heats

proches, décide de sortir   la terrasse   : quatre
near,   decides to take out the pavement café : four

tables rondes et huit chaises de jardin, qu'on aligne   sur
tables round and eight chairs of garden, that one lines-up on

le trottoir,   sous un grand store   où on lit   en lettres
the pavement, under a big awning where one reads in letters

rouges: HOTEL- VINS-   LIQUEURS.
red: HOTEL-WINES-SPIRITS.

Lecouvreur aime musarder dans le quartier,   la cigarette
Lecouvreur likes to-stroll in   the neighbourhood, the cigarette

au   coin   des   lèvres . . . Toujours la même
at-the corner of-the lips . . . Always the same

promenade, tranquille, apaisante. Il longe
walk,   quiet,   calming. He walks-along-the-side-of

l'hôpital   Saint-Louis, puis il regagne le quai
the hospital Saint-Louis, then he regains the embankment

de Jemmapes. Des   pêcheurs sont installés sur le bord du
of Jemmapes. Some fishermen are installed on the bank of-the

canal, au   bon endroit. [. . .] Lecouvreur s'arrête.   Il
canal, at-the good place. [. . .] Lecouvreur himself stops. It

fait   beau . . .
makes fine . . .

Partout   les marronniers   fleurissent,
Everywhere the horse-chestnut-trees blossom,

de   grands arbres qui semblent plantés là
[indefinite number of] big   trees that seem   planted there

pour saluer les péniches. Des   bateliers
for to-greet the barges. [Indefinite number of] boatmen

French speakers

se   démènent . . .   Un peu plus   haut,
[themselves] work with frantic energy . . . A little more high,

des   montagnes de sable ou de pierre,
[indefinite number of] mountains of sand or of stone,

des   tas   de charbon, des
[indefinite number of] piles of coal,   [indefinite number of]

sacs de ciment,   encombrent le quai.
bags of cement, encumber   the embankment.

Des   voitures traversent le   pont   tournant.
[indefinite number of] cars   cross   the bridge turning. [= the swing
bridge].

(From *Hôtel du Nord* by Eugène Dabit, © Éditions Denoël)

Italian speakers

Alison Duguid

Distribution

ITALY, REPUBLIC OF SAN MARINO, VATICAN, SWITZERLAND, Malta, Somalia.

Introduction

Italian is an Indo-European language, directly descended from Latin and closely related to Spanish, Portuguese and French. There is a wide variety of regional dialects, many of which are mutually unintelligible, and some of which have a literary tradition of their own.

Most Italians are very conscious of their regional origins, and are quick to point out that they are Neapolitan, or Tuscan, or Sardinian, as well as Italian. Especially in the industrialised north, most educated Italians use the standard language, which evolved from a variety of Tuscan; but many can adopt the local dialect, and do so when speaking to dialect users, or in particular situations. In rural areas and in the south, dialect may be the first language for many.

Italian language is a compulsory subject throughout primary and secondary school, and this is likely to have an effect on the way English will be learned. Italian speakers have some assistance in learning English through their awareness of the Latin origins of much English lexis and syntax. The Anglo-Saxon elements in English, however, can cause difficulties, and basic and colloquial English usage often causes more trouble than more formal or academic registers.

Italian learners are often very worried about grammatical accuracy; this may reflect the insistence on 'correct Italian' that is common in mother-tongue teaching. They usually have a high level of grammatical awareness, which can be exploited in foreign language learning situations.

Phonology

General

Although there are differences between English and Italian in the inventory and distribution of individual sounds, the main difficulties for Italian learners lie in the areas of stress and rhythm, and it is here that learners have most problems in understanding and in making themselves understood. In addition, the relatively regular match between spelling and pronunciation in Italian and the strict rules for word stress sometimes cause learners to become quite indignant about the inconsistency of English.

Vowels

iː	ɪ	e	æ	eɪ	aɪ	ɔɪ
ɑː	ɒ	ɔː	ʊ	aʊ	əʊ	ɪə
uː	ʌ	ɜː	ə	eə	ʊə	aɪə / aʊə

Shaded phonemes have equivalents or near equivalents in Italian, and should therefore be perceived and articulated without great difficulty, although some confusions may still arise. Unshaded phonemes may cause problems. For detailed comments see below.

1. /ɪ/ is frequently realised or perceived as /iː/: *leave* for *live*.
2. /æ/ is frequently realised or perceived as /e/: *met* for *mat*.
3. /ʌ/ is also sometimes pronounced /æ/: *bat* for *but*.
4. Some loan words from English have adopted an Italian pronunciation: *flesh* for *flash*; 'creck' for *crack*.
5. There are no diphthongs in Italian, though the combinations of vowels which make up many English diphthongs appear together in Italian as separate contiguous vowels. If diphthongs are pronounced, students may give equal weight to the two elements, as in Italian, rather than stressing the first element.
6. Some English diphthongs may not be accurately perceived. Confusion is common between /əʊ/ and /ɔː/ or /ɒ/, all three vowels being realised as the Italian /o/; this leads to difficulty in distinguishing words like *coat*, *caught* and *cot*. A similar confusion may arise

between /e/ and /eɪ/ as in *get* and *gate*, both being realised as the Italian /e/.

7. The pronunciation of an Italian vowel is not affected by stress or its position in a word. So neutral vowels resulting from English stress-timing cause problems, particularly in the comprehension and production of normal colloquial speech. Unstressed vowels are often pronounced as they are written rather than being weakened or reduced (e.g. /ˈfotogræfer/ instead of /fətˈɒgrəfə/ for *photographer*) and weak forms of familiar words such as *can, have, are, must* may not be recognised.

Consonants

p	b	f	v	θ	ð	t	d
s	z	ʃ	ʒ	tʃ	dʒ	k	g
m	n	ŋ	l	r	j	w	h

Shaded phonemes have equivalents or near equivalents in Italian, and should therefore be perceived and articulated without great difficulty, although some confusions may still arise. Unshaded phonemes may cause problems. For detailed comments, see below.

1. Italian /t/, /d/, /n/ are pronounced with the tongue against the teeth rather than the gum-ridge.
2. /θ/ and /ð/ are often pronounced as /t/ and /d/: *tin* for *thin*, and *udder* for *other*, etc. Over-emphasising these sounds can lead to excessive effort on the learner's part, which can be more problematic than the original error.
3. There are various problems related to voicing, particularly with the contrast between /s/ and /z/, which are positional variants in Italian. This gives rise to errors such as '*zmoke*' for *smoke;* and the devoicing of plural and third-person -s, in cases where English requires voicing.

    Students sometimes have difficulty in accurately perceiving initial voiced consonants (in words like *big, dog*) as voiced, because of the late onset of voicing in English.
4. There is no equivalent in Italian for the phoneme /ʒ/, and words like *pleasure* or *occasion* tend to be pronounced with /zj/ under the influence of the spelling.

Italian speakers

5. /ŋ/ in Italian is a variant of /n/. English *ng* (as in *singer*) is often pronounced /ŋg/ by learners: /sɒŋg/ for /sɒŋ/.
6. There is no equivalent of /h/ in Italian, and students will either fail to pronounce it or over-compensate: 'Hi 'ope 'e is'.
7. In Italian final consonants are rare, and are usually found only in foreign loan words, e.g. *bar, sport*, etc. So final consonants in English may be given a following vowel, usually schwa: *I wentə to schoolə onə the busə*.
8. Learners from some regions may voice final unvoiced consonants: /aɪ wend om on də bæz/ for *I went home on the bus*.
9. Initial *w* can cause problems: for example *would* may be perceived or pronounced as /uːd/ or /huːd/.

Consonant clusters

Although Italian has many of the permissible consonant clusters of English (and some more besides), the language is less consonant-heavy than English. Words with more than one cluster (like *understandable*) prove particularly difficult. Final clusters often cause problems, especially those containing /θ/ or /ð/, e.g. *sixths, clothes*.

Influence of spelling on pronunciation

Learners may give Italian values to each letter and, because of the close relationship between spelling and pronunciation in Italian, expect each letter to be pronounced (e.g. /kniː/ for *knee*). Note particularly:
1. The letter *r* is always pronounced in Italian, and this is carried over into English, leading to mistakes in words like *farmer*.
2. Double consonants are pronounced as such in Italian; this can affect learners' pronunciation of words such as *summer, accurate, sitting, opposite*.
3. The letters *c* and *g* vary as to their pronunciation in Italian according to what follows: *c* is pronounced /tʃ/ before *i* or *e*, but as /k/ before other vowels; *g* is pronounced /dʒ/ before *i* or *e*, but as /g/ elsewhere; *sc* is pronounced /ʃ/ before *e* or *i*, but as /sk/ elsewhere. Typical errors resulting from this are:
   'achent' for *accent*
   'sinjer' for *singer*
   'sheen' for *scene*
   Italian *ch* is pronounced /k/, leading to occasional errors like 'kip' for *chip*.
4. A *w* in loan words from English or other languages is often

76

pronounced as /v/: *vat* for *watt*. Students tend to carry this over to all English words with a *w*.

5. Learners sometimes pronounce initial silent letters, as in *pneumonia* and *psychology*, where such initial letters are pronounced in Italian.

Rhythm and stress

Italian learners often claim that English people 'eat their words'. The stress-timed patterns of English cause great difficulty to Italian learners, particularly in terms of perception and comprehension. The characteristics of stress-timing need to be pointed out. Special attention needs to be paid to the presentation and production of weak forms, since learners will expect full value to be given to all syllables.

Some factors of assimilation and the change of meaning with word stress have equivalents in Italian, e.g. un poco (pron. /umpoko/); and the pairs an'cora *(still, yet)* and 'ancora *(anchor)*; or capi'tano *(captain)* and 'capitano *(they happen)*. The same is true of stress changes between parts of speech, which parallel English, e.g. *politics, political*, etc. However, few students are aware of what happens in their own language, and most consider such phenomena in English to be bizarre.

Finally it should be noted that the word for *stress* in Italian is accento, and this may be confused with *accent*.

Intonation

Some learners may be rather resistant to adopting English intonation patterns, hearing them as strange or even affected. Students may also have difficulty in recognising intonation patterns: differences in British English between *yes/no* questions (rising intonation) and *wh*-questions (falling intonation) cause particular problems. Contrasts in Italian are usually signalled by reordering the components of the sentence, so that the element under focus comes at the end, which coincides with the primary stress:

> Il treno arriva alle nove. (*The train arrives **at nine**.*)
> Alle nove il treno arriva. (*The train **arrives** at nine.*)

In English, of course, different emphases can be indicated by changes in the primary stress and the intonation pattern, without necessarily changing the order of the various elements. Italian learners need these distinctions to be pointed out.

Students also have problems in recognising the role of intonation in signalling affective meaning; speakers from some regions may sound arrogant or aggressive when making requests and asking questions.

Orthography and punctuation

Apart from errors resulting from the relationship between spelling and pronunciation, where learners' expectations often lead to phonetic spelling, other problems of accuracy come from the Italian spelling of cognates like psichiatra, psicologia, etc., giving rise to spelling errors such as *psicology.

Italian conventions in the use of upper and lower case differ slightly from English. Small letters are used initially in the names of the days and months, and in adjectives of nationality and the names of languages.

Style

Extended prose causes problems because of different conventions in the use of linguistic resources, and different ideas about what constitutes 'good style'. Students may use long, complex sentences, with more subordination than English would normally prefer, and elaborate periphrasis to avoid repeating the same word. Participle constructions may be overused, and abstract nouns may be used where a verbal construction would be more normal in English.

Grammar

General

The main difficulties for Italians learning English lie in the fact that English relies to a great extent on word order and phrase structure to indicate grammatical function, whereas Italian, although it has developed a long way from the free ordering of words of its Latin origins, relies nevertheless much more on morphological inflections. The variety of syntactic devices in English, and the relative lack of morphological signals, will often cause students to complain that English has no rules, has little grammar and is unpredictable.

Statements, questions and negatives; auxiliaries

The auxiliary *do* has no equivalent in Italian and causes conceptual difficulties. Interrogatives are formed by putting a heavy functional load on intonation:

> ** Where he work?*
> ** What you want?*

Negatives are formed by the use of the negative particle non.

> ** I not smoke.*
> ** I no speak English.*

There are also a set of negative particles, which are used with non to express *nothing, never, no-one*, etc. giving rise to the use of double negatives in English:

> ** I don't understand nothing.*

Confusion occurs with the negative of infinitives:

> ** It is useless to don't speak.*

Time, tense and aspect: forms

1. Italian has five tenses, in the sense that there are inflected forms for present, future, conditional, simple past and imperfect. Other tenses are formed by the use of auxiliaries.
2. The third person singular ending on the present tense is frequently omitted by Italian learners. (Italian words rarely end in -s, so students fail to pronounce the ending, and subvocalisation causes it to be left out in writing as well.) This error is particularly difficult to cure, although it rarely impedes communication.
   > ** he go   * she say*
3. Italian has a form similar to the English present perfect (constructed with the auxiliary verb *have* and past participles, which may be regular or irregular). But a group of verbs, mostly common intransitive verbs of motion and change of state, form this tense with *to be* (essere), and this gives rise to errors:
   > ** He is gone.*

   Italian reflexives also form the perfect with essere:
   > ** I am cut myself.*
4. 'Conditional', for Italians, indicates a morphologically signalled verb form rather than a sentence structure, so that references to 'first', 'second' and 'third' conditionals, and to 'conditional sentences' cause a certain amount of perplexity. Italians use the subjunctive in the *if*-clauses of what we would call second and third type conditionals, and may use *would* . . . as an equivalent in English:
   > ** If you would win a prize, you could share it with me.*
   > ** If I would have known . . .*

Time, tense and aspect: use

1. Progressive verbs exist in Italian, but their use is more limited than in English:
    What do you read? (for *What are you reading?*)
2. Italians use their present perfect as a reference to actions in the recent past. There is no firm line drawn to mark the limits of when an action may be considered to be sufficiently in the past to warrant the use of the simple or 'historic' past. Matters are further complicated by the fact that there are differences in usage between north and south Italy, and between spoken and written Italian. The distinction made in English of how the action is viewed with respect to the present has no real meaning for Italian speakers and is often difficult for them to grasp. Use of the present perfect for the simple past is frequent:
    I have seen her last week.
3. To talk about how long a state of affairs has been going on, Italians use the simple present tense (often misusing *since* for *for*, or using an *It is . . .* construction by analogy with Italian):
    I live there since ten years.
    I am a teacher since 1983.
    It is three years that I learn English.
4. A future tense can be used in the Italian equivalent of *if* clauses, and in other subordinate clauses where a present tense would be used in English:
    When the holidays will be over, I will . . .
5. In standard Italian there is no equivalent to the *going to* future, or to the use of the present progressive with future meaning; but the simple present does function with future time reference in Italian:
    What do you do this night? (for *What are you doing this evening?*)
    I go soon to home.

To be, to have *and* to do

The equivalent of *have* is used in Italian to talk about common physical states:
    I have cold.
    Have you hunger/hungry?
Auxiliary and full-verb forms of *have* are often confused:
    I hadn't breakfast this morning.
And the equivalent of *make/do* or *take* often corresponds to English full-verb *have*:

**I want to make/do a shower.*
**We did a party.*
**I did/took a coffee.*
The Italian equivalent of *to agree* is a structure with *be*:
**I am not agree at all.*

Auxiliaries and modals

Do, once learnt, tends to be overused by elementary learners:
**I usually do go out on Sunday.*
There are five modal auxiliaries in Italian, which have all the morphological and syntactic properties of other verbs, unlike their English equivalents. The special characteristics of English modals therefore cause problems:
**I can to go.*
**I would to go.*
**She musts come soon.*
**Do you can help me?*
I would is often treated as a translation of vorrei (= I *would like to*):
**I would very much go.*
The varied shades of meaning in the area of possibility, certainty, obligation, etc., expressed by the English modals, are difficult for Italian students to 'feel'. They tend, for instance, to overuse *must*, since in Italian different tense forms of dovere are used to shade meaning, rather than different modals:
**You must to know.* (for *You should/ought to know.*)
Other distinctions which may cause difficulty are those between *could* and *was able to*; *must* and *have to*; *mustn't, needn't* and *don't have to*; *didn't need to* and *needn't have.*
**You don't have to drive on the left in Italy.*
**Children under five mustn't pay.*
Comprehension problems may be caused by the fact that the weak spoken forms of modals like *can* and *must* may not be perceived by learners.

Non-finite forms

Although there is a 'gerund' in Italian, the form is not used in the same way or as frequently as in English. The infinitive tends to be used by learners after verbs instead of the gerund, and after adjectives instead of preposition + gerund:

Italian speakers

> *When he had finished to eat . . .
> *I am thinking to move to London.
> *It's not worth to buy that book.
> *I am tired to listen to your criticisms.

Many learners fail to realise that a gerund is needed after a preposition:

> *Before to go home, he . . .
> *I am looking forward to see you.

To may be dropped before an infinitive where there is no corresponding word in Italian:

> *I want go home.
> *I hope see you soon.

The 'object + infinitive' structure causes problems, since Italian tends to use a clause:

> *Does he want that I come, too?

The Italian infinitive of purpose structure uses per (= for):

> *She went out for to buy . . . / for buy . . . / for buying . . .

Clause structure: subjects and objects

Italian commonly expresses the idea of 'liking' with the equivalent of 'to please' (piacere). This means that the Italian subject corresponds to the English object, and vice versa, which can cause mistakes:

> *Your new car likes me.

A similar problem arises with the verb to miss: the Italian for I miss you is Tu mi manchi – literally You are lacking to me. This can cause Italians to use the English verb the wrong way round:

> *My home misses me.

In Italian, use of the subject pronoun is not obligatory in normal colloquial speech:

> *When a man finds a friend, finds also a treasure.
> *Is difficult to say.

The order of subject and predicate is freer than in English, and can be used to make distinctions of emphasis, style, etc.:

> *(It) would be necessary more time.
> *Is arriving Giovanni tomorrow.

Intrusive subject pronouns are common:

> *My family and I we have visited . . .

Object pronouns may be omitted:

> *Yes, I like.

The equivalents of explain, suggest and say can have two objects in Italian:

> *Please explain me your problem.
> *Can you suggest us a good restaurant?
> *Say me the truth.

Reported speech

Difficulty in grasping the English 'one-step' tense shift rules after introductory verbs in past or conditional tenses can often give rise to mistakes, especially since Italian can use conditionals in past reported speech clauses:

>*He said that he would have arrived at six o'clock. (for . . . that he would arrive . . . or . . . that he had arrived)

Word order in reporting *wh*-questions can be a problem:

>*Do you know where is my village?

Italian has one word only to cover the functions of *say* and *tell*:

>*He said me that he wanted . . .

Relatives

Students may have difficulty in understanding and producing clauses with zero relative pronouns like *That's the car I want*.

Redundant pronouns may be added:

>*That's the house that I told you about it.

The passive voice

Italian uses the passive voice much less than English, and students may have difficulty in forming English passives, particularly perfect and progressive forms.

>*Not enough houses have built in the last ten years.

>*Our new house is building now.

Some students seem to have been taught the passive in a rather mechanical way:

>(*)My bicycle has been stolen by somebody.

Italian cannot make an indirect object the subject of a passive verb, so clauses like *George was given a camera for his birthday* can seem peculiar to learners. And structures like *He was thought to be hiding* or *They are alleged to have demanded* do not come easily to Italian students.

Reflexive verbs

Reflexive verbs are more common in Italian than in English. The equivalents of *get up, wash, shave, dress, get ready, sit down*, for example, are all reflexive in Italian.

$^{(*)}$*I get myself up at 6.00 every morning.*
Italian reflexive pronouns are not different in form from personal pronouns:
Take care of you.
Italian reflexive pronouns can also be used as indirect objects, in cases where English would use possessives:
I broke myself the arm.
And they can express the idea of 'each other'.
We will meet us after dinner.
There is also an Italian impersonal reflexive construction; failure to find the correct English passive equivalent leads to errors such as:
In this region you/he/it produces many shoes.

Articles

Although misuse of articles rarely impedes communication, it is none the less one of the greatest problems for Italian learners. Italian has both definite and indefinite articles, which inflect for number and gender, but their use is different from English. The contrast between specific and generic causes problems, since in Italian nouns used in a generic sense take the definite article:
The dogs are useful pets.
I think the money is very important.
Italians do not use the indefinite article when identifying people's professions or status:
I am teacher.
When I was child . . .
Indefinite articles are often dropped after the equivalents of *as*, *with* and *without*:
I am speaking to you as friend.
You can eat it with spoon.
I studied English without teacher.
They are also not used in some common expressions referring to location:
She lives in mountains / in country.
However, articles can be used in Italian in a number of cases where they are dropped in English – for instance, when referring to countries, colours and eating meals:
I was travelling through the Italy.
My favourite colour is the red.
After the breakfast, we went to school.
Other difficulties include:

few / little vs *a few / a little*
in future vs *in the future*
last / next week vs *the last / the next week*
(the) church, school, prison, hospital, etc.

Quantifiers

Italians do not usually realise that *much* and *many* are rare in affirmative clauses:
   **She has much money.*
Most is often wrongly used with an article:
   **The most of my friends live in London.*
The use and position of *both* and *all* can cause problems:
   **We all are going to the cinema.*
Instead of *one . . . another*, Italians may use *a . . . another*:
   **He spent the morning running from a shop to another.*
Neither, either and *none* can all be nessuno in Italian:
   **None of the twins is at home.*

Possessive structures

Structures with possessive *'s* may be put the wrong way round:
   **my car's father*
And possessive *'s* may be used inappropriately:
   **the table's leg*
Italian possessive determiners inflect for number and gender. In the third person, there is no three-way distinction between *his, her*, and *its*: the choice of word in Italian depends on the gender (masculine or feminine) of what is possessed, not of the possessor:
   **Look – there's Maria and his boyfriend!*
   **He bought some flowers for her wife.*
Other common errors include the use of *your* for *her*; and mistakes like **the my book*, since Italian possessives frequently co-occur with articles.
   Confusion of possessive determiners and pronouns also occurs frequently, as they have the same form in Italian:
   **mine parents*
Forms like *a friend of mine* are difficult, and are avoided.

Number and countability

The countable/uncountable distinction is less clear-cut in Italian than in English, and some uncountable English words have countable equivalents in Italian. Examples are: *news, furniture, information, luggage, advice, weather, spaghetti* (and other pasta dishes), *bread*.

> **It's a terrible weather!*
> **I need two breads.*

Certain Italian phrases use a plural where English does not:

> **A second-hand car in good conditions.*

The Italian word for *people* (gente) is singular:

> **People is strange.*

Italian family names cannot be given a plural inflection:

> *the Smith (for *the Smiths*)

Pronouns

Who may be used without an antecedent in the sense of 'anyone who':

> **Who finds a purse in the street should take it to the police station.*

Italian use of the preposition di (= *of*) after the equivalents of *something, anything*, etc. gives rise to:

> **something of interesting*
> **nothing of important*

He or *she* are occasionally used instead of *it*, reflecting the gender of the equivalent Italian noun:

> **We started up the mountain, but she was too difficult to climb.*

Adjectives and adverbs

Adjectives in Italian usually follow the noun and inflect for number, which may lead beginners to make mistakes:

> *an idea stupid
> **the dears children*

More advanced learners may make mistakes with expressions like *the poor, the blind*, etc.:

> **We should give money to the poors.*

Italian does not have comparative or superlative inflections:

> **She is much more old than me.*

Some expressions in Italian use an adjective where English would use an adverb:

> *speak slow
> *walk quick

In Italian an adverb may separate a verb from its object or complement:
> *I like very much English.*
> *I live always in Rome.*

Prepositions

The precise meaning of some prepositions is a little elusive in both languages, and English often strikes Italian students as arbitrary. Typical errors caused by Italian transfer include:
> *to discuss about*
> *to read on the newspaper*
> *to go in England*
> *to listen something*

The Italian words for *before* and *after* are also commonly used as adverbs:
> *We went to the National Gallery; after, we went to the British Museum.*

Students have difficulty with 'preposition-stranding' in questions, relatives and passives. Some learners would find the following sentences hard to understand or produce:
> *Who did you buy it for?*
> *That's the woman I told you about.*
> *She's being operated on tomorrow.*

Vocabulary

Previous learning experience often leads students to rely on word for word translation, and there are the usual problems of false friends. Some of the more frequently encountered of these are:
> *in fact* used to mean *indeed*
> *actually* used to mean *now, at present*
> *sympathetic* used to mean *pleasant, friendly*
> *according to me* used to mean *in my opinion*
> *to know* used to mean *to meet (for the first time)*
> *library* used to mean *bookshop*
> *editor* used to mean *publisher*
> *lecture* used to mean *reading*
> *conference* used to mean *lecture*
> *morbid* used to mean *soft*
> *sensible* used to mean *sensitive*
> *eventual* used to mean *possible*
> *comprehensive* used to mean *understanding*

> *assist* used to mean *attend*
> *control* used to mean *check*

Other common areas of confusion, resulting from different or over-lapping coverage in the two languages include:

> *still, yet, again*
> *as, how, like* (all rendered in Italian by come)
> *which, what, who, that* (all rendered in Italian by che)
> *too, too much, too many* (all rendered in Italian by troppo)
> *very, a lot, many, much* (all rendered in Italian by molto)
> *why, because* (both rendered in Italian by perchè)
> *come, go*
> *bring, take*
> *dead, died* (both rendered in Italian by morto)
> *also, even* (both rendered in Italian by anche)
> *worse, worst*

Words may be borrowed from French:

> *stage for 'course', 'work experience'
> *depliant for 'brochure'

Suffixes are often wrongly constructed by analogy with other English or French words:

> *satisfated   *abandonated   *interpretated   *changement

And English loan-words may be re-exported with changed meanings, as in the use of gadget to mean 'freebie', 'promotional item'.

A sample of written Italian with a word-for-word translation

L'   altra notte ho   fatto un incubo   tremendo.   Mi
The other night [I] have made a   nightmare tremendous. Me

trovavo   nella   stazione di una cittadina a   me sconosciuta.
[I] found in the station of a   town   to me unknown.

Ero   appena scesa   dal   treno, quando fui
[I] was barely descended from the train, when [I] was

avvicinata   da due poliziotti   che mi chiesero i   documenti
approached by two policemen that me asked   the documents

con aria intimidatoria. Presa alla   sprovvista,   cominciai
with air   intimidating. Taken at-the unprepared, [I] began

a cercarli   prima nella borsa, poi   nelle   tasche   ed
to search them first   in the bag,   then in the pockets and

infine   nella valigia,   da   cui   estraevo ogni
finally in the suitcase, from which [I] extracted each

indumento ed   ogni oggetto, uno per uno, prima con   calma,
garment   and each object, one by one, first   with calm,

poi affanosamente anche perchè mi   stavo rendendo
then breathlessly   also   because to me [I] was rendering

conto   che quella non era mia valigia.   Cominciai
account [=realising] that that not was my suitcase. [I] began

allora a farmi   prendere dal   panico, a guardare in giro
then to make me to take by the panic, to look   in round

a destra e   a sinistra per cercare una via di scampo ma
to right and to left   for to search a   way of escape but

la stazione era   circondata da un filo   spinato ed a poco
the station was surrounded by a wire barbed and at little

a poco   mi   apparve non più   come una
at little [= little by little] to me [it] appeared not more as   a

stazione ma come un campo di concentramento. Ed   io non ero
station but as   a camp of concentration. And I not was

più   una viaggiatrice   qualsiasi   ma una deportata
more a   traveller [fem.] of whatever kind but a   deported [fem.]

e   quelli non erano poliziotti   ma soldati. Presa dall'
and those not were policemen but soldiers. Taken by the

angoscia e   dal   panico mi   svegliai di soprassalto
anxiety and by the panic me [I] awoke of start [= with a start]

e   il cuore mi   batteva   così forte che ci
and the heart to me was beating so   strong that there

vollero alcuni minuti   prima che mi   rendessi
wanted some minutes before   to me [I] render [subjunctive]

conto   che
account [= it took a few minutes until I realised] that

era   tutto un sogno.
[it] was all   a dream.

(by Anna Ortolani)

Speakers of Spanish and Catalan

Norman Coe[1]

Distribution

Spanish: SPAIN, including the Canaries; the whole of SOUTH AMERICA except Brazil and the Guianas; CENTRAL AMERICA; MEXICO; CUBA; PUERTO RICO and THE DOMINICAN REPUBLIC; Western Sahara; some urban centres in north Morocco; Equatorial Guinea; some parts of the USA.
Catalan: CATALONIA, ANDORRA, the BALEARIC ISLANDS, parts of Valencia and Alicante, France (eastern Pyrenees). Nowadays there are very few people who speak Catalan exclusively; most Catalan speakers also speak Spanish or French (depending on where they live).

Introduction

Spanish and Catalan are Romance languages, closely related to Italian and Portuguese; they belong to the Indo-European family. Variations in Spanish are noticeable within Spain itself, and also between metropolitan Spain and the varieties spoken in the Americas. However, these differences are largely confined to pronunciation and vocabulary, morphology and syntax being fairly standard everywhere. With a little experience, all varieties are mutually intelligible.

Despite its limited geographical spread, Catalan varies appreciably from one area to another, though the variations are largely within pronunciation and vocabulary. There is a large degree of mutual intelligibility, though the variety spoken in the Balearics is significantly different from mainland Catalan.

Phonology

General

While the Spanish and English consonant systems show many similarities, the vowel systems and sentence stress are very different, and these

---

[1] Additional information on Latin American usage supplied by John Shepherd and Richard Rossner.

can cause great difficulty for Spanish-speaking learners of English. European Spanish speakers, in particular, find English pronunciation harder than speakers of most other European languages. Speakers of Catalan, with its broader range of vowels and a stress system more similar to that of English, in general have less difficulty.

Some common features of the pronunciation typical of Spanish and Catalan speakers of English are:

- Difficulty in recognising and using English vowels.
- Strong devoicing of final voiced consonants.
- Even sentence rhythm, without the typical prominences of English, making understanding difficult for English listeners.
- Narrower range of pitch (in European speakers), producing a bored effect.

Vowels

Spanish has five pure vowels and five diphthongs; Catalan has eight pure vowels and eight 'falling' diphthongs. In neither language is length a distinctive feature. Consequently, learners find difficulty in differentiating between English vowels, especially where length is a part of the difference. Typically, at least two English vowels share the 'phonetic space' occupied by one Spanish/Catalan vowel, so one-to-one correspondences are practically impossible.

1. /iː/ and /ɪ/ correspond to Spanish/Catalan /i/, so *seat* and *sit*, *sheep* and *ship*, etc. are confused.
2. /ɑː/, /æ/ and /ʌ/ correspond to Spanish/Catalan /a/, so words such as *cart*, *cat* and *cut* are confused in perception, though *cart* as produced by a Spanish/Catalan speaker usually has an intruded flapped /r/, i.e. /kart/. (See also the section 'Influence of spelling on pronunciation' below.)
3. /ɔː/ and /ɒ/ correspond to Spanish/Catalan /o/, so *caught* and *cot*, etc. are confused.
4. /uː/ and /ʊ/ correspond to Spanish/Catalan /u/, so pairs like *pool* and *pull* are confused.
5. English /ɜː/ and /ə/ have no similarity to Spanish vowels. /ə/ is normally replaced by the strong pronunciation of the written vowel, so /abaut/ for *about*, etc. /ɜː/ is replaced by /i/ or /e/ plus flapped /r/, so /birt/ for *bird*; /bert/ for *Bert*, etc. Catalan, on the other hand, does have a neutral vowel, which appears in unstressed syllables containing the letters *a* or *e*; English /ə/ is therefore not such a problem for Catalan speakers.
6. As for diphthongs, there are four that are similar in English and

Spanish (except that the second element in Spanish tends to be stronger than in English): /aʊ/, /eɪ/, /aɪ/ and /ɔɪ/. These diphthongs are not difficult for Spanish-speaking learners. English /əʊ/, however, is often not distinguished from /ɔː/, so *coat* and *caught* (as well as *cot*) are confused, for example.

Catalan has a wider range of diphthong sounds than English; thus, though the exact values do not coincide, Catalan learners have little difficulty in producing acceptable variants.

Consonants

p	b	f	v	θ	ð	t	d
s	z	ʃ	ʒ	tʃ	dʒ	k	g
m	n	ŋ	l	r	j	w	h

Shaded phonemes have equivalents or near equivalents in Spanish and Catalan, and are perceived and articulated without serious difficulty, though even here there are some complications. Unshaded phonemes cause problems.

1. Initial voiceless plosives (/p/, /t/, /k/) are not aspirated as in English, so they often sound like /b/, /d/, /g/ to English ears.
2. Word-final voiced plosives are rare in Spanish and Catalan; learners tend to use /t/ for final /d/, /k/ for final /g/ and /p/ for final /b/.

   Other voiced word-final consonants also tend to be strongly devoiced, so '*rish*' or *rich* for *ridge*; /beiθ/ for *bathe*, etc.
3. Spanish and Catalan have the same three nasal phonemes as English, i.e. /m/, /n/ and /ŋ/, but their assimilation to the surrounding phonetic context differs from English, so for example /aiŋgoiŋ/ is common for *I'm going*.

   In Spanish, /n/ or /ŋ/ tends to replace /m/ in final position, so for example '*drean*' or '*dreang*' for *dream*. Final /n/ in Spanish is not always very distinct, and may be absorbed into a nasalised vowel and/or pronounced more like /ŋ/.

   In Spanish and Catalan, /k/ does not follow /ŋ/ at the end of a word, so *sing* is pronounced for both *sing* and *sink*, etc.
4. Spanish/Catalan speakers tend to give *b*, *d* and *g* their mother-tongue values, which vary according to context. These are quite similar to English initially, but between vowels they are softer continuous sounds, not stops: /b/ is more like /v/, /d/ like /ð/, and /g/

not exactly like any English sound. This can make learners' pronunciation of words like *robin, habit, ladder, reading, bigger* or *again* somewhat difficult for a native speaker to understand.

5. In Spanish, /z/ does not exist; learners use /s/ for /z/, so *pence* for both *pence* and *pens*, *lacy* for both *lacy* and *lazy*, etc. Moreover, the European Spanish pronunciation of /s/ often approaches /ʃ/, causing confusion between pairs like *see* and *she*.

   Catalan, on the other hand, has a /z/–/s/ distinction similar to that of English, so there is no general problem. However, Catalan /z/ does not appear word-finally, so Catalans will say *face* for both *face* and *phase*, etc.

6. Spanish, and most varieties of Catalan, only have one sound in the area of /b/ and /v/ (pronounced intervocalically as a bilabial fricative or continuant); hence confusion between pairs like *bowels* and *vowels*.

7. Of the English phonemes /ʃ/, /tʃ/, /ʒ/ and /dʒ/, European Spanish only has /tʃ/, with obvious consequences for learners. Confusion is common between words such as *sheep, cheap* and *jeep*; *pleasure* may be pronounced as '*pletcher*', '*plesher*' or '*plesser*', and so on. In Southern Latin America, /ʒ/ or /dʒ/ occur in words written with *ll*, e.g. llamar /dʒamar/.

   Catalan, on the other hand, has four phonemes similar to the English ones, though the voiced ones, /ʒ/ and /dʒ/, do not appear finally, causing problems with words like *bridge, beige*.

8. Spanish/Catalan /r/ is flapped and is normally pronounced in all positions; this carries over into English. (See also the section 'Influence of spelling on pronunciation' below.)

9. The nearest Spanish sound to English /h/ is a velar fricative like the *ch* in Scottish *loch* or German Bach (but written *j* or *g*). This often replaces English /h/. The sound is somewhat less harsh in American Spanish.

10. Spanish speakers often pronounce English /j/ (as in *yes*) rather like /dʒ/, leading, with devoicing, to confusion between *you, chew, Jew* and *year, cheer, jeer*, etc.

11. Spanish and Catalan speakers may pronounce /w/ rather like /b/ between vowels, e.g. /ariβalker/ for Harry Walker. Before a vowel, /w/ may be pronounced as /gw/ or /g/: /gwud/ or /gud/ for *would*.

Consonant clusters

Consonant clusters are in general less frequent in Spanish and Catalan than in English, so that learners have difficulty perceiving and producing English clusters. Typical simplifications:

> *'espres'* for *express*
> *'istan'* for *instant*
> *'brefas'* for *breakfast*
> *'tes'* for *test* and *text*
> *win* for *win* and *wind*
> *when* for both *when* and *went*
> *can* for both *can* and *can't*
> *cars* for *cars*, *carts* and *cards*, etc.
> *kick* for *kicked*; *grab* for *grabbed*

Some learners reduce final consonants still further producing, e.g., 'fre fru sala' for *fresh fruit salad*.

Note that /s/ plus another consonant, as in *Spain, sceptic, stop*, never occurs at the beginning of a word in Spanish or Catalan, so *'Espain'*, *'esceptic'*, *'estop'*, etc.

Influence of spelling on pronunciation

1. Spelling and pronunciation are very closely – and simply – related in Spanish, so beginning learners tend to pronounce English words letter by letter. In Catalan, the relationship between pronunciation and spelling is about as complicated as it is in English, so that English orthography seems less of a problem. However, with unknown words Catalan speakers also tend to pronounce letter by letter. Some examples are:
   > *asked* pronounced *'asket'*
   > *break*: *e* and *a* pronounced separately
   > *answer*: *w* and *r* pronounced
   > *friend*: *i* and *e* pronounced separately (but *d* dropped)
   > *chocolate*: second *o* and final *e* pronounced

2. Flapped /r/ is generally pronounced where written, so it intrudes before consonants (as in *learn, farm*) and for Spanish speakers also at the ends of words (as in *four, bar*).

   Furthermore, in Spanish and Catalan double *r* is rolled (and in Catalan initial *r* as well), and this habit carries over.

3. /ə/ does not exist in Spanish, so unstressed syllables are pronounced with the written vowel:
   > *teacher* /tit∫er/   *interested* /interestet/
   > *photograph* /fotograf/   *photography* /fotografi/

4. In European Spanish and Catalan double *l* is generally pronounced rather like the *-lli-* in 'million'; Latin American pronunciations include /j/, /ʒ/ and /dʒ/. Beginners may carry these pronunciations over into English.

5. In Spanish the letter *j* corresponds to a voiceless velar fricative. This

sometimes leads speakers to pronounce, e.g. *jam* in a way that sounds more like *ham* to English ears.

Rhythm and stress

Spanish is a syllable-timed language. In general, all syllables take about the same length of time to pronounce (though extra length may be used for emphasis); to an English ear, there is therefore not a great difference in prominence between stressed and unstressed syllables. In English, on the other hand, stressed syllables tend to carry pitch change and to be pronounced more distinctly, while unstressed syllables are reduced and often pronounced with a neutral vowel /ə/ or /ɪ/. Since content words (nouns, verbs, adjectives and adverbs) are stressed in English, they are therefore relatively prominent as compared with the unstressed grammatical words (articles, pronouns, prepositions, auxiliary verbs). So the stress and rhythm of an English sentence give a lot of acoustic clues to structure and meaning. When Spanish speakers pronounce an English sentence with even stress and rhythm, these clues are missing, and English listeners find it difficult to understand because they cannot so easily decode the structure. (For example, in *Ann is older than Joe, is* and *than* may be as prominent as *old*.)

Catalan shows a more marked difference between stressed and unstressed syllables, including a neutral vowel like /ə/ in unstressed positions. Catalan is also more stress-timed (with similar time-intervals elapsing between stress and stress, as in English, rather than between syllable and syllable), but these features are still not as marked as in English. Thus, while Catalan learners typically approximate more closely to English sentence rhythm, there is still a remaining margin of difference to be overcome.

Spanish and Catalan learners find variable stress intractable (see also the section 'Intonation' below), and they cannot usually either recognise or produce the difference in English expressions like:

the black bird   the blackbird
the green house   the greenhouse

Contrastive stress is also a problem. It is a problem for recognition, and in production one gets:

* *With sugar or without **sugar**?*
* *Mary didn't come but John, **yes**.*

i.e. the last word is more heavily stressed than the contrasting word.

Intonation

European Spanish and Catalan tend to use a narrower pitch range than English, and emphatic stress is expressed in extra length rather than in extra pitch variation. Thus some speakers may sound unenthusiastic or bored to English ears.

In English the intonation nucleus can fall on any stressed syllable in the sentence, depending on what is being emphasised. By contrast, in Spanish (and to a large extent in Catalan too) the nucleus falls on the last stressed syllable in the sentence. (If an element is to be stressed, the freer word order allows it to move to the end.) Thus learners can approximate to *John **painted the walls*** (as an answer to the question *What did John do?*). However, they find great difficulty in producing (and even recognising) the pattern ***John** painted the walls* (as an answer to the question *Who painted the walls?*).

Orthography and punctuation

Spelling

Spanish has high sound–spelling correspondence, so obviously the spelling of English does not come easily; in Catalan the correspondence is much more complicated, making the spelling of English less of a shock. For both groups it is common to reduce double letters to single ones:

*apear   *diferent   *necesary   *forgoten

The problem of spelling is exacerbated because learners do not distinguish English phoneme contrasts, and so they cannot exploit those sound–spelling regularities that do exist. For example:

hoping is confused with *hopping*
this is confused with *these*

Related to this is the difficulty in grasping basic regularities like the English tendency to write either two vowels plus one consonant or one vowel plus two consonants:

*breack   *crak   *shoutting

Contractions

Spanish and Catalan do not have contracted verb forms, and learners find them a problem. In listening to English, they find difficulty in picking up, for example, *will* or *would* in:

I'll come tomorrow.

They'd help us

and construe them as *I come, They help*, etc.

In speaking, early learners are reluctant to use contractions, preferring:

I will not come to *I won't come*, etc.

Subsequently, when they have grasped the idea, there is a tendency to overuse them, e.g.:

Are you Spanish? Yes, *I'm.

Punctuation

Spanish and Catalan punctuation conventions are similar to English, so there are relatively few problems. Commas are often used where English would prefer semi-colons, and semi-colons where English would prefer full stops. Beginners may carry over the Spanish use of an inverted question or exclamation mark at the beginning of a sentence:

*¿*When are you coming to see us?*

*¡*It was fantastic!*

Spanish and Catalan do not use inverted commas in reporting speech, but sometimes use –, thus:

– ¿Cómo te llamas? (What's your name?)

– Me llamo Sara. (My name's Sara.)

But sometimes there is no punctuation to indicate direct speech (see Spanish extract on page 111).

Spanish and Catalan both use a comma to separate decimals and a stop to separate thousands:

3.000 (three thousand)

3,25 (three point two five; typically pronounced, following the Spanish pattern, as **three point twenty-five*)

Capital letters

Spanish and Catalan do not use capital first letters for days of the week, months or national adjectives, so: *monday, *july, *spanish, etc.

Grammar

General

Grammatical similarities between Spanish, Catalan and English include: singular and plural forms of nouns; definite and indefinite articles;

97

regular and irregular verbs; past, present and future tenses; perfect and progressive verb forms; no declension of nouns, adjectives or pronouns. (Similarity of form does not, of course, guarantee similarity of use: see separate points below.)

However, compared with English, both Spanish and Catalan:

– have highly inflected verb systems;
– have freer word order;
– show gender and number in adjectives and nouns;
– have no modal auxiliaries;
– use the passive much less;
– have a subjunctive mood.

At the level of syntax (sentence structure), Spanish and Catalan show very little divergence, so the problems dealt with below are virtually always common to both. At the level of morphology, both Spanish and Catalan are highly inflected in the verb and have singular and plural forms of nouns and adjectives. Of these only the plural of the adjectives and articles has a noticeable effect on the learning of English; see section on 'Number' below. (Incidentally, it is striking that speakers of languages with scores of verb endings should find the -s of the third person singular of the English simple present tense so recalcitrant. Even advanced learners often make mistakes on this point.)

Word order

This is much freer in Spanish and Catalan than in English.
1. 'Subject–verb' and 'verb–subject' do not regularly correspond to statement and question respectively:
    The firemen arrived ten minutes later. (statement)
    * *Arrived the firemen ten minutes later.* (statement)
    (For questions, see next section.)
2. The freer word order allows words that are emphasised to be placed last:
    * *Yesterday played very well the children.*
    * *Played very well the children yesterday.*
    as well as:
    Yesterday the children played very well.
    The children played very well yesterday.
3. Frequency adverbs have several possible positions, but not the typical mid-position of English:
    * *Often she has helped.*
    * *She often has helped.*

4. Adjectives and nouns typically postmodify head nouns:
    * *They live in the house white.*
    * *Can you lend me a ball of tennis?*

This makes noun phrases like *Cambridge University Bridge Club* particularly difficult for Spanish and Catalan learners, because for them the elements of the phrase would more naturally be expressed in the reverse order:
    * *The Club of Bridge of the University of Cambridge.*

It is interesting that Spanish/Catalan speakers say, for instance, los Rolling for *the Rolling Stones* and un Christmas for *a Christmas card*, i.e. they construe the first word in the English noun phrase as the head noun.

5. In Spanish and Catalan, an indirect object must have a preposition (a), and the two objects can go in either order, so:
    * *They gave to Sam the book.*
    * *They gave the book to Sam.*

The English two-object structure *They gave Sam the book* is difficult for learners, and they try to avoid it.

6. Adverbials and object complements are regularly placed before a direct object:
    * *They took to the hospital her mother.*
    * *Mrs Smith speaks very well English.*
    * *Keep tidy Britain.*

Questions

1. There is no set word order for questions, and auxiliaries play no part in them:
    * *John has bought the books?*
    * *Has bought the books John?*
    * *Mary came?*
    * *When Mary came?*
    * *Came Mary?*
    * *Mary, when came?*

Naturally, subject and object questions cause difficulty both in recognition and production:
    * *Who did kill Oswald?*   *Who Oswald killed?*
    * *Who killed to Kennedy?*   *Who Kennedy killed?*

(For this use of *to* with a direct object, see the section 'Prepositions' below.)

2. Learners have difficulty with *do/does/did*:
    * *Did they went?*
    * *Do they went?*

Speakers of Spanish and Catalan

> *_Do she goes?_
> *_Does she goes?_
(See also 'Indirect speech' below.)

Question tags

In Spanish, the way to urge agreement to any positive statement, no matter what its form, is to add a rising no at the end. Given the complication (for Spaniards) of question tags in English, it is not surprising that this simple ploy carries over, e.g.:
> *_They're coming tomorrow, no?_
> *_You have a car, no?_
In Catalan the corresponding universal question tag is oi, but Catalans still tend to use _no_ in English.

Negatives

1. Auxiliaries play no part in forming negative sentences in Spanish or Catalan; the negative word goes before the verb phrase:
> *_Peter not found the key._
> *_Peter not has found the key._
The negative particle is no, and beginners may replace _not_ by _no_ accordingly:
> *_I no understand._
In short answers, the negative goes after the pronoun, adjective, adverb, etc.:
> *_Those no._   *_Green no._   *_Here no._
2. The double negative is standard:
> *_I not saw nobody._ or *_I didn't see nobody._
> *_Tom not helps her never._ or *_Tom doesn't help her never._
This makes it difficult for learners to appreciate the three English categories of:

assertive:	some	somebody	_always/once_, etc.
non-assertive:	_any_	_anybody_	_ever_, etc.
negative:	_no/none_	_nobody_	_never_, etc.

In particular, non-assertive forms are construed as negative:
> *_I waited but anybody came._
(See also 'Clause structure and complementation', point 4, below.)

Verbs

1. In Spanish and Catalan all verbs show the normal range of tenses (present, past, future, conditional) and composite forms (progressive, perfect). There is thus no separate category of modal auxiliaries as in English, and learners find the concept, the simplicity of their forms, and their uses difficult to grasp. Typical mistakes include:
   Maria cans cook.
   Do you can swim?
   May you come tomorrow?
   She could find the key. (meaning . . . *managed to* . . .)
   She had to win the match. (meaning . . . *should have won* . . .)
   They will can do it next week.
2. In many cases where in English there are two different words, or a word is used with two different structures, Spanish and Catalan have verbs with both transitive and intransitive possibilities:
   She went up the stairs.
   She went up the book. (meaning . . . *took the book up.*)
   They were waiting. *They were waiting the bus.*
   '*Mary laughed.*' *'What did she laugh?'*
3. There is a general problem with two- and three-part verbs, in many cases because the meaning of the English compound is not deducible from the meanings of the parts, and also because learners feel more comfortable with a synonym derived from Latin. (See 'Vocabulary', point 1, below.) In some cases, though, one Spanish/Catalan word expresses both the meaning of the English verb alone and also the meaning of a phrasal verb, e.g. tirar/llençar = *throw, throw away*, gastar = *wear, wear out.*
4. Particular problems of verbal structure include the fact that many English phrases consisting of '*be* + adjective' are expressed in Spanish and Catalan by '*have* + noun':
   have reason (= be right)
   have hunger
   have heat, etc.
   and in Spanish/Catalan *I like this* is expressed as *This pleases me*, leading to confusions such as:
   Football likes me.

Ellipsis

What can be dropped varies from one language to another. Where English uses *it*, *so*, *any*, etc. to stand for a complement that can be understood from the context, Spanish/Catalan often allows complete ellipsis:

> 'Do they want some money?' 'Yes, *they want.'
> 'Do you want to go?' 'No, *I don't want.'
> I like to get up early; *I'm used.
> 'Are they coming?' 'No, *I don't think.'

Time, tense and aspect

In form, Spanish and Catalan make a simple/progressive distinction:

> Maria visita. (= *Maria visits.*) / Maria está visitando. (= *Maria is visiting.*)

Spanish and Catalan also have a perfective aspect:

> Maria ha visitado. (= *Maria has visited.*)

However, although these forms correspond to English forms, they do not necessarily represent similar distinctions of meaning.

1. The simple present is often used for an action taking place now:
   > *Look! It rains!

2. The simple present is often used to refer to future time:
   > *Do I come tomorrow? (for . . . Shall I . . .?)
   > *I wait for you at home. (for I'll wait. . .)
   > *I see her this evening. (for I'm seeing her . . .)

3. The present tenses are used to refer to a period starting in past time and continuing up to the present (where English uses a perfect):
   > *How long are you working in your present job?
   > *It's a long time that I live here.

4. In Catalan and the Spanish of some areas of Spain, the present perfect can be used with time-when adverbials, and in some regions it is normal when referring to actions and events earlier on the same day:
   > *When has she received the letter?
   > *Today I've finished work early because I've started at seven o'clock this morning.

   In other areas of Spain and in Latin America, on the other hand, the simple past can be used (to emphasise that for the speaker there is no relation to present time) where British English requires the present perfect:
   > Ya lo leí = *I have already read it.*

5. Spanish and Catalan have more than one form corresponding to the past progressive in English, one of which means the same as *used to (do)*. This causes confusion:
   > *When we were young, we were playing a lot of tennis.

In general, this form is more frequent than in English, and is practically standard for the past of stative verbs (the equivalents of *have, know*, etc.):

* *When I was a teenager, I was having a motorbike.*
* *She wasn't knowing that he had died.*

6. The imperative often has an expressed subject:
    * *Come you tomorrow!*

7. In Spanish and Catalan, the subordinate clauses of most sentences referring to future time have the subjunctive, and learners are reluctant to use the present simple:
    * *When Mary will get here, tell her to come in.*

8. Spanish and Catalan have a frequentative verb (soler) which allows all tenses. Learners try to use a form of '*used to*' to express frequency in present time, e.g.:
    * *I use to do a lot of exercise.*

Passives

1. Spanish and Catalan have a passive form constructed in the same way as the English passive: with '*be* + past participle'; but in those cases where English uses the passive without an agent phrase, Spanish and Catalan tend to use a form reminiscent of the English reflexive:
    * *The house built itself before the war.*

2. Spanish and Catalan cannot form passives that parallel:
    They were given bikes for Christmas.
    Polly was owed a lot of money.

    These structures (where the indirect object has become the subject of a passive verb) are difficult for learners.

3. The Spanish/Catalan endings corresponding to *-ing* and *-ed* do not have a clear active and passive meaning respectively, with consequent confusion in English:
    * *The lecture was very bored.*
    * *I'm very interesting in Polish films.*

Infinitives

1. Spanish and Catalan often use the infinitive as an abstract noun (corresponding to the English *-ing* form):
    (*)*To smoke is bad for you.*

    As a consequence, learners may have difficulty in understanding sentences which have *-ing* forms as subjects.

2. Spanish and Catalan have an infinitive marker (a), but its distribution does not square fully with English *to*:
   It's difficult learn English.
   Let us to see.
   (See also the sections 'Clause structure and complementation' and 'Indirect speech' below.)

Articles

Here are some of the main differences in the use of the articles in Spanish and Catalan as compared with English:
1. The definite article goes with mass nouns and plural count nouns that are used with a general meaning:
   The food is more important than the art.
   Do you like the big dogs? (meaning . . . *big dogs in general*)
2. Spanish and Catalan use the definite article with possessive pronouns:
   That is the yours, and this is the mine.
3. Spanish and Catalan make no distinction between the indefinite article and the number *one*:
   We used to live in one flat; now we live in one house.
4. In some expressions where the distinction between one and many is considered irrelevant, singular count nouns need no article:
   Do you have car?
   Her sister is dentist.
5. The indefinite article has a plural form (corresponding roughly to *some*). This can cause beginners to make mistakes:
   I have ones nice American friends.

Gender

Spanish and Catalan have grammatical gender: all nouns, as well as related articles and adjectives, are masculine or feminine. Reference is made with the corresponding pronoun:
   *The table is dirty. *Clean her, please.*

Number

1. In Spanish and Catalan the form of the plural is similar to English, (-s ending), but the ending is used with articles, adjectives and possessives as well as nouns:
   *yellows flowers   *hers news shoes*

2. There are several words that can take plural forms in Spanish/ Catalan, where English has a mass noun, giving rise to, for example:
    *furnitures   *informations   *spaghettis   *thunders*
    I've got two news for you.
3. Those 'symmetrical' things that are plural in form in English (*trousers, pyjamas,* etc.) are usually singular in Spanish and Catalan:
    *a trouser   *a bathing trunk*
    There are no irregular plurals in Spanish or Catalan; learners are liable to construe *people* as singular, and to make mistakes like *a police,* *childs,* *childrens.*

Adjectives

1. Adjectives can stand without either a noun or proform *one:*
    They showed me two models, and I bought the small.
2. Comparatives and superlatives are expressed by using the equivalent of *more* and *most:*
    I am more old than my sister.
    In addition, there is only one word (más/més) for both *more* and *most:*
    Barcelona is the more large city of Catalonia.

Pronouns

1. Subject personal pronouns are largely unnecessary in Spanish/ Catalan because the verb ending indicates person and number:
    Rosa isn't French. *Is Spanish.*
    Have gone home because wanted to go to bed.
    Was raining.
    Over-correction may lead students to put in redundant personal pronouns:
    That's the man who he lives next door to us.
2. In Spanish and Catalan most personal pronouns have the same form for subject and object, so:
    *I saw she.   *They know we.*
3. Although Spanish/Catalan has equivalents to impersonal pronoun *it* and dummy *there,* their distribution does not totally correspond, and one finds:
    How much sugar/How many cakes is it in the cupboard?
4. There is no equivalent for the structure '*it is* + pronoun' as used to identify oneself:
    'Who is it?' *'Am I.'* (for '*It's me.*')

5. Reflexives sometimes do not correspond, in some cases a reflexive pronoun being used in Spanish/Catalan where English does not have one and vice versa, leading to:

   They enjoyed very much.
   She complained herself.

   Even where the verbs in both Spanish/Catalan and English are reflexive, there remains the problem that the reflexive pronoun in Spanish is the same as the personal pronoun:

   I showered me and went out.

6. Spanish/Catalan does not normally express a distinction corresponding to *They helped themselves* and *They helped each other.*

Possessives

1. Spanish and Catalan use the definite article, not a possessive, in sentences like:

   Mary washed the hair.

   If it is important to specify the person affected, this is achieved using a reflexive:

   Bill cut himself the finger.

2. Spanish and Catalan have the same word for *your* (formal), *his, her* and *their*, with consequent confusion in English:

   Sara and Joe had both got his shoes wet.

3. Catalan uses the definite article with possessives:

   The my cousin is in Portugal.

Possession

Possession and related concepts that in English are expressed by possessive cases of nouns (e.g. *Jim's bike, Mary's boss*) are expressed in Spanish and Catalan with an *of*-phrase:

   *the book of Rosa   *the gate of the garden*

Learners have problems in distinguishing between *a bottle of wine* and *a wine bottle*, etc. because una botella de vino / una ampolla de vi can express both meanings.

Noun phrases with two nouns to express a part–whole relationship, like *garage door, table leg*, will be expressed as:

   the door of the garage or *the garage's door*

Relative pronouns and clauses

1. Spanish does not distinguish between personal and non-personal relative pronouns:
   *the man which came   *the ball who is lost
2. The relative pronoun can never be deleted in Spanish or Catalan, and learners have difficulty in understanding English clauses with zero relative pronoun:
   The girls we saw looked quite happy.
   Did you like the woman we spoke to?
   (Examples like the last one, in which a relative clause finishes with a preposition whose object has been deleted, are particularly difficult for students.)

Clause structure and complementation

1. Purpose clauses are expressed with a preposition (para/per a) and the infinitive:
   They have gone for (to) buy a film.
2. Spanish and Catalan speakers tend to say, for example, *We are going to paint the house*, regardless of who is actually going to do the painting. So they find problems with such structures as:
   We are going to have the house painted.
   If necessary, Spanish/Catalan can express this, of course, but the structure, if transferred to English is:
   We are going to make (to) paint the house.
3. Although Spanish and Catalan have two non-finite forms (like our infinitive and *-ing* form), their distribution is different:
   They refused helping their neighbours.
   I'll never forget to see that accident.
4. In Spanish/Catalan some verbs express the 'person affected' immediately following the verb, where in English this is understood or requires a different structure:
   She explained (to) me the problem.
   They suggested Jim to take the job.

Indirect speech

Much of indirect speech in Spanish/Catalan corresponds to that of English: verb forms, pronouns, etc., change in order to adapt to the differences between the reporting situation and the original situation.
1. However, the structure of reported commands, requests, etc., is different. Spanish/Catalan achieve this with a subjunctive (and

therefore finite verb) in the reported clause, and learners try to use a similar structure in English:

> *I am asking that they go.*
> *They ordered (to) her that she should go/that she went.*

An extra complication arises when the reported clause is negative, which in English would of course be expressed by *not to do*, etc., so:

> *I want that you don't go/that you not go.*
> *The captain ordered the soldiers that they didn't retreat.*

2. Interestingly, indirect questions cause problems for intermediate and even advanced learners. When they have finally come to grips with English question word order, they construe reported questions as also needing this order:

> *I don't know where does Mary live.*
> *They asked me how much did I earn.*

Prepositions

1. Spanish has a 'personal preposition' (a), used in transitive sentences when the direct object is human:

> *They took to their mother to the hospital.*

2. In Spanish and Catalan, prepositions must always go with their noun phrase, and cannot go at the end of a clause:

> *For what have you come?*

Learners find difficulty in interpreting sentences like:

> I don't know who they're working for.
> Who does Fred sit next to?

3. In Spanish and Catalan, a preposition can be followed by an infinitive:

> *After to see the film, we went for a meal.*

4. While in many cases the 'central' meaning of a preposition in one language corresponds to that in another, there are always many exceptions to these simple correspondences. Areas of particular difficulty are:

   – *in/on/into*:
   > *in Monday   *on July   *lying in the beach
   > *They are into the room.

   – *to/at/in*:
   > *go at the beach   *arrive to the station
   > *We stopped in the crossroads.

   – *as/like*:
   > *She works like a waitress.
   > *They seem as their mother.

   – *for/by*:

*This park was designed for the Catalan architect Gaudí.
– *during/for*:
*They stayed there during three months.
But there are many other problem areas.

Vocabulary

1. Spanish and Catalan are developments of Latin; their vocabularies therefore correspond to the Latin-derived side of English: estructura = *structure*, derivar = *derive*, difícil = *difficult*, confusió(n) = *confusion*, and so on. While this fact offers the learners access to a large passive vocabulary, it also tends to make their language sound formal: they use *enter* rather than *go in*, *arrive at* for *get to*, *extinguish* for *put out*, etc. In particular, learners have difficulties with the forms and multiple meanings of two- and three-part verbs, such as *put on*, *put off*, *put out*, *look up*, *look for*, *look forward to*.

2. Spanish and Catalan refer to both the members of a male–female pair (or a family group) by using the plural of the male form:
   rey/rei = *king*, reina = *queen*, reyes/reis = *kings* or *sovereigns*
   hijo/fill = *son*, hija/filla = *daughter*, hijos/fills = *sons* or *children*
   So learners often use *fathers* for *parents*, *brothers* for *brothers and sisters*, *sons* for *children*, etc.

3. Numerals are a problem for several reasons:
   – The use of plurals does not correspond, so **five hundreds*
   – Spanish and Catalan largely avoid ordinals, so **the five of June*
   – punctuation of numbers (see the section 'Punctuation' above)
   – the number 0, which for Spaniards is cero/zero in virtually all contexts; hence problems with *nought*, *nil*, *love* and the 'o' of telephone numbers.

4. As in the case of all languages, there are many items of vocabulary which have a meaning relationship of one-to-many. For learners, the greater difficulty is typically when one item in the mother tongue is expressed in various ways in the target language. The problem with cero has just been mentioned. Other common examples are:
   casa = *house, home*; cómo/com = *how, as, like*; conocer/conèixer = *know, meet*; decir/dir = *say, tell*; dejar/deixar = *lend, let*; esperar = *wait for, hope*; hacer/fer = *do, make*; historia/història = *history, story*; mucho(s)/molt(s) = *many, much*; nervioso/nerviós = *excited, nervous*; romper/trencar = *break, tear*; llevar/portar = *carry, wear*; perder/perdre = *lose, miss*; pista = *track, (tennis) court, runway, ski slope*; porque, perquè = *because, why*; receta/recepta = *recipe, prescription*; tiempo/temps = *time, weather*; último/últim = *last, latest*.

5. Some common 'false friends':

Spanish/Catalan	English translation
actual	*current*
asistir/assistir	*attend*
beneficio/benefici	*profit*
caravana	*traffic jam*
conductor-a	*driver*
carrera	*race, degree course*
discutir	*argue*
(estar) constipado/constipat	*(have) a cold*
embarazada/embarassada	*pregnant*
éxito/èxit	*success*
en frente/davant (or enfront)	*opposite*
extranjero/estranger	*foreign(er)*
eventual	*possible*
(persona) formal	*reliable (person)*
lectura	*reading matter*
llbrería/lllbrerla	*bookshop*
pariente/parent	*relative*
pas(s)ar (un examen)	*take (an exam)*
pretender/pretendre	*intend*
(clas(s)e) particular	*private (class)*
profesor-a/professor-a	*teacher*
propaganda	*advertising*
probar/provar	*test, trial*
propio/propi	*own*
remarcar	*emphasise*
reunión/reunió	*meeting*
sensible	*sensitive*
simpático/simpàtic	*pleasant*
suburbio/suburbi	*slum*

A sample of written Spanish with a word-for-word translation

Sentado en el   suelo se   calzaba
Sat   on the floor himself he was shoeing [= putting on]

las ásperas botas de racionamiento   de suela clavateada
the rough   boots of rationing [= army boots] of sole   studded

y   puntera de metal: ellos se   las
and toecap of metal: they [for] themselves them [= the boots]

miraban   con   envidia.
they were looking [at] with envy.

¿Un regalito   de   la viuda Galán? dijo   Sarnita, y
A   present little of [= from] the widow Galan? he said Sarnita, and

Java se   levantó   y   le hizo   una seña . . .
Java himself he raised [= got up] and [to] him he made a   sign . . .

Ven, dijo, y Sarnita le   seguió: bastaba   la
Come, he said, and Sarnita him he followed: it was enough the

luz que se   filtraba   a través de la arpillera
light that itself it was filtering through   the sacking

para ver   el escenario de tables, desierto, la diminuta
for to see the stage   of boards, deserted, the tiny

concha del   apuntador, forrada con una tela   roja, las
shell   of the prompter, lined with a   cloth red, the

candilejas de cinc abollado, y   más allá,   la
footlights of zinc embossed, and more there [= beyond], the

oscura sala con los bancos de missa   en formación,
dark   hall with the benches of mass [= pews] in formation,

sin   pasillo central.
without aisle central.

(From *Si te dicen que caí* by Juan Marsé)

A sample of written Catalan with a word-for-word translation

Tenia   prop de divuit   anys quan vaig
I was having almost eighteen years, when I go [past auxiliary]

conèixer   en Raül, a l'estació   de
know [= when I met] the Raul, at the station of [= in]

Manresa. El   meu pare havia mort, inesperadament i   encara
Manresa. The my father had   died, unexpectedly   and still

jove,   un parell d'anys abans, i   d'aquells temps
young, a couple of years before, and of those times

conservo un record   de punyent soledat.   Les meves relacions
I keep   a memory of acute   loneliness. The my   relations

amb la   mare   no havien pas   millorat,   tot el contrari,
with the mother not had   at all improved, all the contrary,

potser   fins i tot empitjoraven   a mesura que
perhaps even   they were worsening at step   that [= in proportion as]

em   feia   gran.
myself I was making big [= I was growing up].

No existia,   no existí   mai   entre   nosaltres,
Not it was existing, not it existed never between us,

una comunitat   d'interessos, d'afeccions.
a   community of interests, of affections.

Cal   creure   que cercava . . .   una persona
It is necessary to believe that I was seeking . . . a   person

en qui   centrar   la   meva vida afectiva.
in whom to centre the my   life affective.

(From *Un amor fora ciutat* by Manuel de Pedrol)

Portuguese speakers

David Shepherd

Distribution

BRAZIL, PORTUGAL, ANGOLA, MOZAMBIQUE, GUINEA-BISSAU, CAPE VERDE ISLANDS, SAN TOME E PRINCIPE, Goa, Damão, Diu, East Timor, Macau.

Introduction

Portuguese is a Romance language closely related to Spanish. Educated speakers of European Portuguese (henceforth EP) have little trouble understanding each other; this variety also serves as the model for the *lingua franca* of Goa, Macau and the former African colonies. The prestige dialect in Portugal is that of the educated classes from the Coimbra-Lisbon region. Portuguese is also the native language of approximately 97% of Brazilians. Despite its size, Brazil shows few major variations in dialect in comparison with most European countries. The prestige variety of Brazilian Portuguese (henceforth BP) is that of Rio de Janeiro. The contrasts between European and Brazilian Portuguese are very much greater than those between British, American or Australian varieties of English. The pronunciation of the two varieties is very different; there are numerous divergences of vocabulary (for example, EP has more words of Arabic origin than BP, which has borrowed an increasingly large number of words from Indian languages and American English); and there are some grammatical differences. Despite these points of contrast, the two varieties are mutually comprehensible.

Phonology

General

The English and Portuguese vowel systems are quite different. While English has twelve pure vowels, BP has nine (EP eight plus one schwa /ə/), all of which can be nasalised.

113

Portuguese speakers

Among the features of Portuguese which give rise to a Portuguese accent in English are:

– Frequent nasal vowels.
– The insertion of intrusive vowels between consonants (especially in BP).
– For BP speakers especially, syllable-timed rather than stress-timed delivery, with over-emphatic pronunciation of most unstressed syllables.

Vowels

iː	ɪ	e	æ	eɪ	aɪ	ɔɪ
ɑː	ɒ	ɔː	ʊ	aʊ	əʊ	ɪə
uː	ʌ	ɜː	ə	eə	ʊə	aɪə / aʊə

Shaded phonemes have equivalents or near equivalents in Portuguese, and should therefore be perceived and articulated without great difficulty, although some confusions may still arise. Unshaded phonemes may cause problems. For detailed comments, see below.

1. /iː/ tends to be pronounced too short, and is confused with /ɪ/: *rich* for *reach*; *hit* for *heat*, etc.
2. /e/ is confused with /æ/: *head* and *had*.
3. /ɑː/ is shortened and confused with /æ/: *aunt* and *ant*; *can't* and *cant*.
4. /ɒ/ is confused with /ɔː/: *caught* for *cot*, or *spot* for *sport*; or even with /ʌ/: *hut* for *hot*.
5. /ʊ/ is confused with /uː/: *fool* for *full*.
6. /ʌ/ may be pronounced as /æ/: *lack* for *luck*, or even, because of orthographic interference, as /uː/: *mood* for *mud*.
7. Unstressed vowels are often given their full value, especially by BP speakers: *Ann* for *an*; *thee* for *the*. On the other hand, unstressed vowels at the ends of words may become whispered and almost inaudible: *sit* for *city*; *cough* for *coffee*; '*offs*' for *office*.

Diphthongs

There are fewer diphthongs in Portuguese than in English. The greatest problems arise with /ɪə/ and /eə/, which tend to be confused: *hear* and *hair.*

Consonants

p	b	f	v	θ	ð	t	d
s	z	ʃ	ʒ	tʃ	dʒ	k	g
m	n	ŋ	l	r	j	w	h

Shaded phonemes have equivalents or near equivalents in Portuguese, and should therefore be perceived and articulated without great difficulty, although some confusions may still arise. Unshaded phonemes may cause problems. For detailed comments, see below.

1. The 'dark' /l/ in final position or before a consonant is often pronounced as a vowel similar to /ʊ/: *'bottu'* for *bottle*, and *'heeoo'* for *heel*.
2. /p/, /k/ and /t/ are unaspirated initially in Portuguese, and may be confused with /b/, /g/ and /d/: *peg* and *beg*; *Kate* and *gate*; *tin* and *din*.
3. Initial and medial /t/ and /d/ are both pronounced quite forcefully and may be confused: *tale* and *dale*; *latter* and *ladder*. But when followed by /iː/, /ɪ/ or /e/, they are often pronounced as affricates, almost like /tʃ/ and /dʒ/: *'cheam'* for *team*; *Jean* for *dean*.
4. There is also confusion between /t/ (a short flap) and /r/ (a short trill): *better* and *bearer*; *heating* and *hearing*.
5. Vowels before final /m/, /n/ and /ŋ/ are nasalised, often to the point where the final consonant is inaudible.
6. An initial /r/ is an unvoiced trill or (BP) fricative; in BP learners it may sound similar to a strong initial *h*: *red* and *head*; *right* and *height*.
7. Final /z/ does not occur in Portuguese, and may be replaced by /s/ (*rice* for *rise*) or (with EP speakers) by /ʃ/ (*hash* for *has*).
8. /θ/ and /ð/ are realised either as /s/ and /z/, or as /t/ and /d/, leading to confusions such as *sinker* or *tinker* or *'dinker'* for *thinker*, and *breed* or *breeze* for *breathe*.

9. /tʃ/ and /dʒ/ are pronounced /ʃ/ and /ʒ/, leading to confusions between, for instance, *chair* and *share* or *pledger* and *pleasure*.
10. Initial /h/ has no equivalent in Portuguese and is either omitted (*ear* for *hear*, *as* for *has*), or inserted unnecessarily because of over-compensation: '*High ham is holdest friend*' for *I am his oldest friend*.
11. Few consonants can occur finally in Portuguese, and so a vowel is often added: '*parkie*' for *park*; '*cabbie*' for *cab*. Clusters between words may be simplified: '*widis*' for *with this*.

Consonant clusters

The range of consonant clusters is much wider in English than in Portuguese, often causing the insertion of extra vowels by Portuguese speakers to 'assist' pronunciation of English ('*closis*' for *clothes*). BP speakers tend to find particularly difficult initial clusters with *s* ('*estream*', '*estudy*'), while EP speakers tend to simplify final clusters.

Influence of spelling on pronunciation

Spelling and pronunciation are very closely related in Portuguese. Mistakes will be made at all levels of competence. A common error is to pronounce the letters *g* (before *i* or *e*) and *j* as /ʒ/ in words like *general* or *jury*, by analogy with Portuguese gelo, caju etc.

Rhythm and stress

EP is a heavily stress-timed language. Speakers of EP find it reasonably easy to perceive and produce stresses correctly in English, but their pronunciation of unstressed syllables may be excessively reduced. BP is syllable-timed, like Spanish, and this leads to difficulties of the following kind for BP speakers:
- inappropriate stress in long words and compounds, e.g. **poli'tical demonstra'tors*, **a telephone 'box*; **a tea 'cup*.
- inappropriate stress on auxiliary verbs, articles, conjunctions, prepositions, etc., suggesting an unintended emphasis:
    I saw **them yesterday.*
    They **were happy.*
    It was **his book, not **his** bag I wanted.*
- Perceiving unstressed words and syllables.

Intonation

Declarative sentences are given a marked low fall, often making the last word inaudible. All English question tags tend to be pronounced with a rising tune, irrespective of meaning.

Juncture

There is a tendency, where there are doubled consonants, to pronounce both and add an intrusive vowel, for example in *this stop, at that time.*

Orthography and punctuation

Portuguese speakers have considerable difficulty with English spelling. At all levels there is a tendency to represent English sounds (learned orally) with their standard Portuguese spelling forms. The following areas of error are typical:
1. All words ending in consonants (except *l, m, s, z* and *r*) tend to be given a final vowel sound. This vowel is often included when writing English.
    *She is a cookie.
2. Where the phonemes /ɪ/ or /iː/ occur:
    *'Inglish' for English
    *'clined' for cleaned
    *I have bin.
3. With the diphthong /aɪ/:
    *'traying' for trying
    *laying for lying
    *She is dating a 'nayce' gay.
4. With the phoneme /ʃ/:
    *'finiched' for finished
    *'choes' for shoes
5. Where words are similar in both languages, beginners will tend to use the Portuguese spelling; this often leads to words being written with a single instead of a double consonant (e.g. *dificult, *apropriate, *eficient).
6. Adjectives of nationality do not have capital letters in Portuguese:
    *portuguese   *english

Grammar

General

The Portuguese grammatical system has much in common with English and many other western European languages. There are similar 'parts of speech'; Portuguese adds an *s* to plural nouns, and has definite and indefinite articles, regular and irregular verbs, auxiliary and modal verbs, active and passive forms, and past, present and future tenses. There are perfect verb forms, although the present perfect has a more limited application in Portuguese, and informal BP does not have perfect progressive tenses. Portuguese is inflected in much the same way as French, Italian and Spanish, which means that the word order can be somewhat freer than in English.

Questions and negatives; auxiliaries

1. In Portuguese, question forms are marked by intonation, and not by the use of auxiliaries (there is no equivalent of auxiliary *do*) or (in *yes/no* questions) by changes of word order:
   You know John? He is married?
2. Overgeneralisation of *do* causes mistakes in indirect questions:
   *Please tell me what did he say.
   *She couldn't explain where he does work.
3. The negative form in Portuguese is marked by placing the word não before the main or auxiliary verb, independent of tense:
   *He no would like it.
4. The double negative is used in Portuguese:
   *He doesn't know nothing.
   *I haven't seen him nowhere.
5. Short answers to questions in Portuguese are formed by repeating the verb of the question:
   'Do you like dancing?' *'Yes, I like.' or *'Like.'
6. There is only one question tag in Portuguese, namely não é (verdade)? (literally *Is it not truth?*). The equivalent, *isn't it?*, is used indiscriminately in English.
   *They want to go at seven o'clock, isn't it?

There is

In BP the verbs haver and ter (the formal and colloquial equivalents of *to have*) are used to express *there is/are* etc. EP speakers use only haver, always in the singular.

There are/were a man from Scotland next door.
Had lots of people at yesterday's match.
Has wonderful beaches in Rio.
Exists a lot of problems.

Time, tense and aspect

A. Past time

Portuguese has simple past, present perfect, and past perfect tense forms.
1. Like English, Portuguese uses the present perfect for recent actions and events involving the present.
    The weather has been terrible (lately).
    I haven't seen him.
2. But where the equivalent of *already* can be added, a past tense is common:
    I already finished the exercise.
3. Where the equivalent of *ever* can be added, the simple past is used:
    Did you (ever) go to London? (for *Have you (ever) been to London?*)
4. To express the idea of duration, the simple present is used with há (= *it is*):
    It is years that I don't see him.
5. The presence of an adverbial referring to a finished or unfinished time-span has no relevance to tense choice in Portuguese:
    I have been to Rome last spring.
    I didn't visit my mother this week.
6. There is no present perfect progressive in spoken Portuguese. The simple present or present progressive are used in most equivalent situations:
    I am here since five o'clock.
    I am studying English for five years.
    She is living in Manchester since 1981.

B. Present time

1. BP has two commonly-used present tense forms: one roughly equivalent to the English simple present (e.g. Ele percebe – *He understands*), and the other equivalent to the English present progressive (e.g. Ele está trabalhando – *He is working*). Problems arise, however, with verbs (mainly stative verbs) which take the latter construction in Portuguese but not in English.
    She is not understanding.

2. EP forms its present progressive form with estar a + infinitive (literally 'to be at to do something').
    'What are you to do now?' 'I am to read the newspaper.'
Since this structure is used with both stative and active verbs, EP speakers, too, may confuse simple and progressive forms in English.
3. Portuguese can also use the equivalent of *go* as a present progressive auxiliary, leading students to misuse *going to*.
    *'What's your son doing now?' *'He's going to look for a job.'*
    (for *'He's looking for a job.'*)

C. Future time

Students may use future verb forms after conjunctions of time:
    I will be there when you will need me.
The future tense is used in Portuguese more often than in English to express guesses and suppositions.
    *There's the door. *Will it be Peter?*
    **How many hours will she work a day?* (for *How many hours do you suppose she works a day?*)

Modal verbs

Where English uses *can* to talk about skills, Portuguese uses only the main verb:
    **He swims.* (for *He can swim.*)
The English use of a special form (without *to*) of the infinitive after modals has no Portuguese equivalent:
    **He must to do it now.*
The complex distinctions between *must* and *should*, *must* and *have to*, *can* and *may* and so on are as difficult for Portuguese speakers as for other learners.

Conditionals

Because of developments in modern Portuguese grammar, especially in the spoken language, students may use parallel verb forms in the two halves of conditional sentences.
    **If I see him, I tell him.*
    **If I went to London, I visited the British Museum.*
    **If you had started on time you hadn't missed the train.*

120

Relatives

Portuguese has one word que corresponding to relative *who* and *which*.
> *I spoke to the man which seemed to be in charge.*
> *It's a ring who belonged to my grandmother.*

Learners have difficulty understanding and using English clauses with zero relative pronoun (like *The car he bought broke down in the first week.*).

The passive voice

In general the passive functions in a very similar way in Portuguese and English. Elementary students have the usual problems in constructing the forms correctly. More complex structures may cause difficulty:
> *Your application is considered.* (for . . . *being considered*)
> *The meeting has postponed.* (for . . . *has been postponed*)

Portuguese sometimes uses reflexive verbs where English uses passives:
> *English speaks itself here.*

In Portuguese the indirect object of an active verb cannot, as in English, function as the subject of a passive verb. Learners therefore have difficulty with sentences like *I was given a watch.*

Causative uses of *have* and *get* do not have Portuguese equivalents:
> *He told someone to paint his house.* (for *He had/got his house painted.*)

Non-finite forms

1. There is no equivalent in Portuguese for the substantival use of the *-ing* form (gerund). The infinitive is used instead:
   > *Do you mind to wait for a few minutes?*
   > *I'm tired to listen to her complaints.*
   > *She stopped to work at five o'clock after to finish her report.*
2. Portuguese infinitives are often preceded by a preposition such as de or a. In cases where a Portuguese infinitive has no preposition, students may drop *to* before the English equivalent.
   > *I tried telephone you.*
   > *She promised pay everything.*
3. The English 'object + infinitive' structure does not have a Portuguese equivalent:
   > *She wants that you phone her.* (for *She wants you to phone her.*)

Word order

1. Portuguese word order is generally freer than English, and it is common to move a non-subject topic element to the front of the sentence:
   (*) Cakes I like!

2. The verb follows the question word in indirect speech in Portuguese:
   *I wonder where is your office.
   *I asked who was her friend.

3. Adverbs and adverbial phrases can separate a verb from its object:
   *I like very much samba.
   *He wanted a lot to go to England.
   *I visited on Sunday afternoon her in her house.

4. Declarative word order is used in exclamations with como (= *how*):
   *How he is clever!

5. Personal pronouns may be placed before, after or between elements of the verb, depending somewhat on the variety of Portuguese:
   *He me explained the theory. (BP)
   *He explained me the theory. (EP)
   *I asked what to do to him. (for *I asked him what to do.*)

6. EP can use pseudo-cleft sentences introduced by Quem (= *Who*).
   *Who gave me the present was John.

7. Adjectives follow nouns in Portuguese:
   *It was a problem very difficult.

8. The difference in noun phrase word order can lead to misunderstandings: *administrative activities* may be understood as *administration of activities*; *few moving parts* can be understood as *little movement of the parts.*

9. Phrasal verbs do not occur in Portuguese; the word order with pronoun objects causes problems:
   The heating's still on. *Can you turn off it?

10. Prepositions cannot be detached from their objects in Portuguese. This may lead learners to use over-formal or unnatural question structures:
    With whom did she go?
    Relative and passive structures like the following are also found difficult:
    I hated the people I was working with.
    He can't be relied on.

Articles and countability

1. In Portuguese the definite article is used with the following:
   – nouns used in a general sense:
       *The bees produce the honey.
       *The life is difficult.
   – proper nouns:
       *The Paolo is a friend of the Maria's parents.
   – names of meals:
       *He didn't eat at the breakfast, the lunch or at the dinner.
   – the equivalents of *next* and *last*:
       *I hope to meet her the next Sunday.
       *I saw him the last weekend.
   – the names of streets
       *I bought it in the Oxford Street.
   – words for 'institutions' used in a general sense, where English prefers a possessive pronoun or no article:
       *to go to the church / the school / the bed   * in the hospital
2. Some typical mistakes reflecting Portuguese expressions without articles:
       *He arrived on tenth of May.
       *to have right to do something
       *to feel need to do something
       *to have strength to do something
       *You have reason. (meaning *You are right.*)
3. Some uncountable English nouns have countable equivalents in Portuguese:
       *I asked him for an advice and he gave me many informations about furnitures.
4. After the equivalents of *much, how much* and *so much*, Portuguese can use the singular form of a countable noun, as if it was uncountable.
       *We have much problem this year.
       *I had never seen so much tree.

Determiners

1. There are no equivalents for *any* or the *an* in *another*:
       *That does not make difference.
       *We visited him in other town.
2. In Portuguese, the equivalent of *all* can be used with singular countable nouns, and there is no equivalent for *each* or *every*, or for compounds such as *everything*:

Portuguese speakers

> *We went to see him all Tuesday. (for . . . *every Tuesday*)
> *He understands all.

3. Articles and other determiners are commonly used before possessives, especially in EP:
> *She wanted to borrow the my car.
> *One my uncle is a solicitor.
> *Do you know this my cousin?

Adjectives and adverbs

Attributive adjectives normally follow nouns in Portuguese, and add -*s* to agree with plural nouns:
> *That is a book very exciting.
> *What a city marvellous!
> *Those are the wrongs papers.

Nouns can be dropped after adjectives if their meaning is clear from the context.
> *The important is to help other people.

Pronouns

1. Subject pronouns are frequently dropped; object pronouns may also be left out if they can be understood from the context.
> *Don't like this music.
> *Is boring.
> *Visits her mother every weekend.
> *I've seen.

2. The impersonal subject *it* does not exist in Portuguese:
> *In Brazil, when is the summer, is sunny.
> *Is difficult to understand her.

3. Conversely, identification of é with *it is* can lead to the use of redundant pronouns:
> *The life it is difficult.

4. Some Portuguese verbs can be followed by a double-object construction while their English equivalents cannot:
> *Explain me your problem.
> *Repeat me the words of the song.

5. *One*, used as a pronoun, has no equivalent in Portuguese. It is normally expressed by a gente (literally *the people*).
> *The people have to admit . . . (for *One has to admit*. . .)

6. In Portuguese there is a single possessive determiner for *his* and *her*,

124

which agrees in gender with the thing possessed. When carried over into English, this can cause problems:

He phoned her sister and asked to borrow his apartment.

7. In formal and deferential styles in Portuguese, the second person possessives teu(s), tua(s) are replaced by the third-person forms seu(s), sua(s). This can cause students to confuse the English equivalents:

She likes your brother very much. (for She likes her brother very much.)

8. Reflexive pronouns are used with some Portuguese verbs whose English equivalents do not have them:

I always have coffee before I dress myself.

Prepositions and particles

There are a greater number of prepositions in English, which is therefore more precise in its definitions of time, location and movement. Problems occur when a Portuguese preposition has more than one English equivalent.

1. Até is used for both time (= *until*) and distance (= *as far as*):

He walked until the station.

2. Durante can mean *during, throughout* or *for*:

I lived in London during three years.

3. Para means *for, to* and *at*:

She bought a present to her sister.
He is travelling for Edinburgh next week.
They gave a lot of importance for their possessions.
He was looking for the pretty girl. (for . . . looking at . . .)

4. Para is also used with an infinitive meaning *in order to*:

John travelled for to spend his holidays at the coast.

5. Em means *in* (for time) and also *at* and *on*:

She always comes home in Christmas.
It's nice to go to the beach in a hot day.
He's in the beach.
I'll meet you in the cinema. (for . . . at the cinema)
They're sitting on the table. (for . . . at the table)

6. There is no separate equivalent for the preposition *into* with verbs such as *go, transform, change* etc.

Then the Prince changed in a frog.

7. Other common mistakes reflecting Portuguese prepositional usage:

surprised with   *to count with* (for *on*)   *interested with/for*
indignant with   *worried with*   *to resemble with*
to dream with/in   *to pay attention in*   *based in*
to talk in (for *about*) *to rely in*   *to think in* (for *about*)

satisfied in   *passionate for*   *to like of something*
to marry with somebody

Vocabulary

Because Portuguese is a Latin-based language, EP and BP speakers find reading academic or scientific prose much less difficult than understanding colloquial spoken English.

Some common problems

1. The equivalents of *come* and *go* have a slightly different semantic relationship in Portuguese. *Go* may be used to refer to a movement from speaker to listener:
   'Are you coming here or not?' *'Of course I'm going, right now.'*
   Similar errors are made with *bring, fetch, give* and *take*:
   Bring this book to John. He's next door.
2. The verb ficar is very widely used in Portuguese. It can mean *to stay*, but can also refer to a change of state of a person, e.g. *to become, to turn, to grow, to remain*:
   He stayed furious because he waited so long. (for *He became furious . . .*)
3. Portuguese has the same word for *why* and *because*:
   He didn't come why he felt tired.
4. Portuguese has the same word for *as* and *like*:
   He looks as a teacher.
5. *Be careful* and *take care* use the same verb stem and the equivalent of the preposition *with* or *of* in Portuguese:
   Take care of him or *Be careful with him.* (for *Beware of him.*)
6. The Portuguese word obrigado (= *thank you*, or *much obliged*) can be used to express polite refusal. When the words *thank you* in English are given the same stress and intonation pattern (i.e. the *you* is stressed, as the penultimate syllable is stressed in obrigado), it gives an impression of impoliteness and sarcasm.
7. There are no equivalents for *just* and *ever* when used as intensifiers, as in *Have you ever . . .?*; *He lives just nearby.*
8. Confusions arising because there is one Portuguese word for two or more words in English:
   rob – steal
   lend – borrow
   speak – talk
   amuse – enjoy

still – *yet*
as well – *too*
then – *therefore*
hear – *listen*
see – *look*
across – *through*
say – *tell*
after – *afterwards* – *then*

False friends

A very small selection:

abuse	(abusar = *use frequently*)
actual(ly)	(actual(mente) = *current, nowadays, at the moment*)
cigar	(cigarro = *cigarette*)
cobra	(cobra = *snake*)
constipation	(constipação = *a cold*)
discuss	(discutir = *to argue* or *debate*)
disgrace	(desgraça = *accident, misfortune*)
disgust	(desgaste = *worn-out*)
distracted	(distraído = *absent-minded*)
educated	(educado = *well-mannered*)
expect	(esperar = also *to hope* and *to wait*)
expert	(esperto = *intelligent, sly*)
facilities	(facilidades = *proficiency*)
familiar	(familiar = *decent, respectable*)
intend	(entender = *to understand*)
library	(livraria = *bookshop*)
licence	(licença = *leave of absence*)
local	(local = *place*)
lunch	(lanche = *snack*)
ordinary	(ordinário = *vulgar*)
parents	(parentes = *relatives*)
presently	(presentemente = *at the moment*)
pretend	(pretender = *to intend, to plan*)
primarily	(primeiramente = *first*)
private	(BP privada = *toilet, privy*)
push	(puxe = *pull*)
rat	(rato = *mouse*)
real	(real = *royal; sure; that exists*)
use	(usar = *to wear*)
vulgar	(vulgar = *ordinary*)

Paralinguistic elements

Portuguese tends to be spoken at a lower pitch than British English, but at a higher volume. The strong syllable stress and lack of markers for question forms (polite requests are made in the imperative) often create the (erroneous) impression that the speaker is rude, irritated or angry.

Normally accepted non-emotional eye contact is lengthier among Brazilians than with most Europeans. People stand closer together when they talk, and physical touching is more widely acceptable. These conventions can be misinterpreted.

A sample of written Portuguese with a word-for-word translation

Ao acordar　　disse　para a　　mulher:　　　　Escuta, minha filha:
On to wake up he said to　　the woman [wife]: Listen, my　　girl:

hoje　é dia de pagar a　　prestação　de televisão, vem　aí　o
today is day of to pay the instalment of television, comes here the

sujeito　com　a　　conta, na certa.　　Mas acontece que　ontem　　eu não
subject with the bill,　　on certain. But happens　that yesterday I　no

trouxe　dinheiro da　　　cidade, estou a　nenhum.　　　– Explique isso
brought money　from the city,　　am　　on none [slang]. – Explain this

ao　　homem – repondeu a　　mulher. – Não gosto dessas　coisas.
to the man　　– answered the woman. – No like　of these things.

Dá　　um ar　de vigarice,　　gosto de cumprir rigorosamente as
Gives an　air of swindling, I like of to fulfil rigorously　　the

minhas　　obrigações.
my [plural] obligations.

(O Homem Nu by Fernando Sabino)

Acknowledgement

The author would like to thank Tanya Shepherd who helped at all stages of the preparation of this chapter, and Barbara Skolimowski and Chester Graham who provided suggestions for the European Portuguese examples.

Greek speakers

Sophia C. Papaefthymiou-Lytra

Distribution

GREECE, CYPRUS.

Introduction

Greek is an Indo-European language, but is not very closely related to any other language in this family. Greek and English phonology, syntax and vocabulary are very different in nature, and English is therefore not an easy language for Greek speakers.

Phonology

General

The Greek and English phonological systems are broadly dissimilar. Greek speakers have serious difficulty in perceiving and/or pronouncing correctly many English sounds. The English vowel system, which makes far more distinctions than the Greek system, causes problems. Stress and intonation patterns are also very different.

Among the features of Greek which give rise to a 'Greek accent' in English are :

- Less energetic articulation than English, with lax vowels, less lip-rounding and less spreading.
- Lack of contrast between weak and strong forms in natural speech as compared with English.
- Lack of elisions and assimilations; this makes the English of Greek speakers sound slow, drawling and rather formal.
- Tendency to speak at a higher volume and on a more uniform pitch level than most English people do.
- Different stress and intonation patterns.

Vowels

iː	ɪ	e	æ	eɪ	aɪ	ɔɪ
ɑː	ɒ	ɔː	ʊ	aʊ	əʊ	ɪə
uː	ʌ	ɜː	ə	eə	ʊə	aɪə / aʊə

Shaded phonemes have equivalents or near equivalents in Greek and should therefore be perceived without serious difficulty. Greek-speaking learners do, however, have difficulty in articulating these sounds correctly. Diphthongs tend to be articulated as two separate vowels pronounced in two syllables.

Unshaded vowels may cause more problems.

1. /ɪ/ is usually replaced by /iː/, causing pairs like *sit* and *seat* to sound similar.
2. /æ/ is usually replaced by /e/ or the Greek sound /a/. So for example *bad* may be pronounced /bad/ instead of /bæd/.
3. /ʌ/ is usually replaced by the Greek sound /a/. So for example *but* may be pronounced /bat/. And pairs like *bat* and *but*, *lack* and *luck* may be confused.
4. /ɜː/ and /ə/ are usually replaced by /e/. So for example *bird* may be pronounced /berd/ instead of /bɜːd/.
5. Long vowels /ɑː/, /ɔː/ and /uː/ are usually shortened and replaced by their nearest Greek equivalents /a/, /o/ and /u/ respectively.
6. /ɒ/ and /əʊ/, like /ɔː/, are usually replaced by the Greek vowel /o/. So for example *off* is pronounced /of/ instead of /ɒf/, *home* is pronounced /hom/ instead of /həʊm/. There is serious confusion between English words which are distinguished by these vowels, such as *nought/not/note*, *cord/cod/code*, *walk/woke*, *hop/hope*, *want/won't*.
7. /ə/ in diphthongs such as /eə/, /ɪə/, /ʊə/ is usually replaced by the nearest Greek sound /a/. So, for example, *hear* is pronounced /hɪa/ instead of /hɪə/.

Consonants

p	b	f	v	θ	ð	t	d
s	z	ʃ	ʒ	tʃ	dʒ	k	g
m	n	ŋ	l	r	j	w	h

Most of the shaded phonemes approximate only roughly to English sounds; although learners will perceive them easily, accurate articulation may prove difficult.

Unshaded phonemes, as well as some shaded phonemes in certain environments, may cause problems.

1. /ʃ/ is often pronounced as /s/. So, for example, *shirt* may be pronounced '*cert*'.
2. /ʒ/ is often replaced by /z/. *Garage*, for example, may be pronounced '*garaz*'.
3. /s/ before /m/ becomes /z/. *Small*, for example, may be pronounced '*zmall*'.
4. In Greek, /b/ is usually preceded by /m/, and /d/ by /n/. So *able* may be pronounced /eɪmbl/, and *idle* /aɪndl/.
5. /ŋ/ is usually pronounced as /ŋg/. For instance, *sing* is pronounced /sɪŋg/ instead of /sɪŋ/.
6. /h/ is non-existent in Greek. It is often replaced by the rougher Greek sound /x/ (like *ch* in *loch*). For instance, *him* may be pronounced /xɪm/.
7. The letter *r* is pronounced wherever it is written, leading to mistakes in British English where *r* precedes a consonant or comes at the end of a word (as in *card, hair*).
8. /tʃ/ and /dʒ/ may be pronounced like /ʃ/ and /ʒ/ respectively, leading to confusion, for instance, between *choose* and *shoes*, or *ledger* and *leisure*.

Influence of spelling on pronunciation

Greek spelling is phonetic: there is almost a one-to-one correspondence between sound and graphic symbol, with few ambiguities. As a result Greek learners, especially beginners, have a tendency to pronounce all the letters that are written, often giving them their Greek values:

Greek speakers

/kʊld/ for *could*
/me/ for *me*
/water/ for *water*
/eleven/ for *eleven*
/eɪgt/ for *eight*
/sekretari/ for *secretary*

Stress

There are some similarities in patterns of word and sentence stress in Greek and English. Note, however, that Greek tends to have one stressed syllable in each word, unlike English words, which may also have syllables with secondary stress. As a result, Greek learners tend to pronounce one primary stress in English words and give all other syllables weak stress:

/sʌbstɪˈtjuːʃən/ for /ˌsʌbstɪˈtjuːʃən/

Rhythm

1. Greek has syllable-timed rhythm. Each syllable has approximately the same duration, regardless of the number or position of stresses in an utterance. In English, however, the stressed syllables in an utterance are evenly spaced regardless of the number of unstressed syllables that intervene. Greek learners tend to transfer their syllable-timed rhythm into English.
2. Beginners may also have difficulty in perceiving and articulating secondary and weak stresses in sentence patterns. Very often they unnecessarily stress 'weak forms' such as *but, were, than*, etc., pronouncing them as they are spelt. And they may find it difficult to hear such words when they are pronounced at natural speed.

Intonation

Intonation patterns differ in Greek and English. Some features of Greek intonation carried over into English (such as the use of a high fall where English would use a low rise) may make speakers sound abrupt and impolite. Special practice is needed in the intonation of polite requests, suggestions, commands, offers, question tags and interruptions, and in the use of stereotyped responses such as *Mm, Yes, I see, That's right* with appropriate intonation patterns.

Orthography and punctuation

Spelling

1. Most Greek alphabetic symbols are different from the English letters, and beginners need practice in handwriting.
2. Beginners may tend to use one letter consistently for each sound, as in Greek, leading to mistakes like:
     *sistem *Inglish *kut *taim (for *time*) *trein (for *train*)
3. Students may leave out silent letters:
     *bot (for *bought*) *tok (for *talk*)

Punctuation

Punctuation conventions in Greek are generally similar to those in English but there are a few radical differences which may cause problems. The main differences are that semicolons, question marks and quotation marks are written differently in Greek, which can cause problems for beginners:
     Greek semicolon: ·
     Greek question mark: ;
     Greek quotation marks: « »

Grammar

General

The Greek and English grammatical systems are similar in many ways. There are the same 'part of speech' categories, and Greek has, for instance, singular and plural noun forms, definite and indefinite articles, regular and irregular verbs, active and passive verb forms and past, present and future tenses. There are perfect verb forms but the present perfect, for instance, is not used in Greek in the same way as in English. Greek has no equivalent of the English present progressive or present perfect progressive forms (though the meanings expressed by these forms can be expressed in Greek in other ways). There is, however, a rough equivalent of the past progressive form.

Greek is a highly inflected language – articles, adjectives, nouns and pronouns have four cases, for example. Word order is consequently freer in Greek than in English, where the grammatical function of a word is mostly indicated by its position in the sentence. Greek learners have difficulty with word order in English.

Greek speakers

Greek has grammatical gender – nouns and pronouns are masculine, feminine or neuter – but there is no systematic relationship between gender and meaning. Adjectives always conform to the gender of the noun to which they refer. The lack of any systematic inflectional system in English leads Greek learners to feel that English has 'no grammar'. However, word order and the choice and structure of verb forms present them with serious problems.

Questions and negatives

The auxiliary *do* has no equivalent in Greek and inversion is not used to make questions; spoken *yes/no* questions differ from affirmatives by intonation only:

> *You come back from school early every day?*
> **What she is doing?*
> **How many brothers she has?*

Negatives are formed by putting δεν (= *not*) before the main verb, omitting the auxiliary:

> **They not come to see us.*
> **What he not do yesterday?*
> **He not agree with me.*

Time, tense and aspect

A. Past time

1. Greek has past perfect and present perfect tenses (formed with εχω, the equivalent of *have*, + aorist infinitive) as well as past and imperfective tenses. There are no progressive forms, though in many cases the imperfective tense functions like the past progressive in English.
2. The present and past perfect are not much used in Greek; the past tense is commonly used instead:
   > **He did not yet return the money he borrowed.*
   > *I am sorry I am late. *Did you wait long?*
   > **I just finished reading that book when he telephoned me.*
3. To say how long a present state has been going on, Greek may use a present tense:
   > **I know them since I was a kid.*
   > **He works at the office for many years.*
4. Overgeneralisation of the English present perfect may lead to mistakes like:
   > **She has married long ago.*

5. Greek accepts either the past or the present tense after a reporting verb. Learners, however, tend to use the present tense where English uses a past tense after a past reporting verb:
    He did not say if she is at home.
6. Learners often use the imperfective instead of *used to*, as in:
    He was going out a lot, but now he is married and stays at home.

B. Present time

1. The third person singular ending is often omitted:
    He go to school every day.
2. The lack of a Greek present progressive causes mistakes:
    'Where's Tom?' *'He waters the flowers.'*
    Look! Those two boys fight!
    I am eating breakfast after I am getting dressed.
3. In the present progressive the verb *to be* is often omitted:
    They running fast.
    She playing tennis.
    On the other hand, it is sometimes unnecessarily added in the simple present:
    We are walk to school every day.
    She is speaks English.

C. Future time

1. Greek and English future tenses are constructed quite differently, and Greek has no equivalent of the *going to* future:
    I will to see them tomorrow.
    They will fighting each other soon.
2. Greek learners may use a simple present tense instead of a future tense:
    I go to school tomorrow.
3. On the other hand, problems are caused by the English use of the present tenses in subordinate clauses referring to the future:
    I shall meet him before the train will go.

Conditionals and 'unreal' forms

1. Greek conditional sentences may have the same verbal structure in both clauses. This is transferred into beginners' English:
    If my car will be ready I will meet you at the station.
    If she would have money she would buy you a present.

2. Past conditionals are difficult:
   *If you had fixed the car we had went for a ride.
3. Learners have difficulty with structures after *I wish* and *if only*:
   *Mary is gone. I wish / If only she is here.

The passive voice

1. The use of the passive is roughly equivalent in Greek and English. A common mistake is to omit *-ed* from the past participle or to drop the auxiliary:
   *The sky is cover with clouds.
   *The girl punished.
2. Learners may have difficulty with complex passives and make mistakes like:
   *The house is building for a long time.

Modal verbs

The English modals and semi-modals *can, may, must, have to, ought to*, etc. do not have one-to-one equivalents in Greek. Inevitably there are differences which lead to mistakes. Some common problems:
1. Beginners tend to use *to* + infinitive after modals:
   *I cannot to come to see you.
2. Past modal structures cause problems. Instead of making the modal verb past, students may use a present modal with a past main verb:
   *I can saw it.
   *We must made it.
3. The differences between *can* and *may*, *must* and *have to*, etc. take time to master.

Complementation

1. English *-ing* forms often correspond to Greek infinitives – for example, after prepositions:
   *Before to reach home she ate all the sweets.
2. Infinitives are often used instead of *-ing* forms as complements of verbs and adjectives:
   *I must stop to smoke. It's bad for my health.
   *Please excuse me to be so late.
   *She is busy to write a book.

3. Greek learners often use *to* + infinitive in cases where English uses the infinitive without *to* – for example after the verbs *see, hear, watch, feel, make, let, help*:
    * *She saw them to come down the stairs.*
    * *I made her to eat the food.*

Infinitive of purpose

1. In English, a negative infinitive of purpose is generally introduced by *in order* or *so as*. This may be dropped:
    * *He crossed the road not to see me.*
2. Learners may replace the infinitive after *to* by a past tense form (an overgeneralisation or transfer from Greek):
    * *I called George to told him the good news.*
3. An infinitive of purpose may be replaced by a main clause:
    * *I want the book I read it.*
4. An infinitive of purpose may be preceded by *for*, as in:
    * *George went to London for study English.*

The causative structure

This does not exist in Greek. Learners tend to replace it with the equivalent Greek form which, in English, results in confusion about who does what for whom:
    * *She had cut her hair at the hairdresser's.*

Word order

Word order is free in Greek, which causes learners to make frequent mistakes.
1. A sentence may begin with the direct or the indirect object or complement:
    * *The book to Mary I gave on Saturday.*
    * *Wonderful is the house you bought.*
2. An adverb may separate a verb inappropriately from its subject, object or complement:
    * *I last night did my homework.*
    * *The teacher speaks always English in class.*
    * *The girls will be tomorrow very happy.*
3. Adverbs of place may precede adverbs of time in cases where English would use the reverse order:

> **They will be tomorrow here.*
4. The equivalent of *ago* may precede an expression of time:
> **I sent the letter ago three days.*

Articles

1. In Greek, the definite article may accompany nouns which are used in a general sense. This leads students to make mistakes with uncountable and plural nouns in English:
   > **The gold is very expensive.*
   > **The honesty is a great virtue.*
   > ** We must buy the bread for two days.*
   > **The dogs are faithful animals.*
2. Definite articles are used with proper names in Greek:
   > **She speaks the French very well.*
   > **The Peter is my friend.*
3. In Greek, the indefinite article is not used before a subject complement:
   > **She is doctor.*
   > **Alex is good footballer.*
   > **His new car is Porsche.*

Gender

Nouns in Greek are masculine, feminine or neuter. Pronouns are used accordingly. Beginners often write or say such things as:
> **My bag is in my room. Can you bring her here?*
> **The river is long. He runs all the way to the sea.*

Number

1. Some uncountable English nouns have countable Greek equivalents:
   > **Can you give any informations?*
   > **I left all my luggages at the station.*
   > **I have many works to do.*
2. Irregular plurals are also a problem:
   > **There are a lot of sheeps in the meadow.*

Adjectives and adverbs

1. In Greek, adjectives are inflected. They conform to the number (as well as the gender and case) of the noun to which they refer. This is a potential source of mistakes for beginners:
   *There are four greens chairs in the room.
2. In Greek, adverbs of manner often resemble adjective forms:
   *All cars must move slow on this part of the road.
3. Very often, adjectives such as *friendly, lovely* are treated as adverbs:
   *She looked at him friendly.

Pronouns and determiners

1. Personal pronouns are often omitted:
   *Is very hot today.
   *When he saw his father, sat down.
   *We saw him play football and we liked.
   *I want to tell me the truth.
2. On the other hand, noun subjects or fronted objects may be picked up by redundant pronouns:
   *My brother he came to see me.
   *Mary who sits next to me she is sixteen years old.
   *The car I bought it yesterday.
   After infinitive complements, object pronouns may be inserted unnecessarily:
   *That is not fit to drink it.
   Unnecessary pronouns may also be inserted in relative clauses: see the section below.
3. *It* may be used instead of *there* to introduce indefinite subjects:
   *It is a chair in the next room.
4. Other pronouns and determiners easily confused by learners are:
   some – any
   anything – nothing
   my – mine
   this – that
   other – another
   much – many
   little – few
   few – a few

Greek speakers

Reflexive pronouns

1. There is often confusion between object pronouns and reflexive/emphatic pronouns, as in:
   I often talk to me.
   John did not do it him.
2. Reflexives are sometimes used after verbs like *wash* or *shave*, which in Greek require medio-passive.
   Bob shaved himself before he left for work.

Relative clauses

1. Greek learners tend to use *who* in relative clauses which modify nouns that are masculine or feminine in Greek, and *which* in relative clauses which modify nouns that are neuter in Greek, regardless of meaning.
   The river who runs across the valley is shallow.
2. Learners may have difficulty in understanding and producing relative clauses with zero relative pronouns like:
   The people we went to see weren't at home.
3. Additional subject and object pronouns may be inserted unnecessarily.
   The man who he is upstairs is Peter.
   That is the man whom I saw him.
   John, look what I make it.

Conjunctions

That tends to replace *what* in indirect questions:
   I do not remember that you said to me.

Comparisons

1. Beginners often transfer Greek forms of comparison into English:
   Mary is taller from Jane.
   Mary is more tall than Jane.
2. The same Greek word may correspond to both *as* and *like* in certain contexts. This is a potential source of confusion:
   She looks as her mother.
   I, like ecologist, want to protect the environment.

140

Prepositions

1. Greek learners have considerable difficulty with English prepositions. Most Greek prepositions have rough English equivalents, but
problems arise in cases (too many to list) where an English expression does not require the 'same' preposition as is used in Greek:
    * *She was dressed with a white suit.*
    * *He walked in the bridge.*
    * *Dinner was prepared from my mother.*
2. Problems also occur when a preposition in Greek has more than one
English equivalent, depending on the context. Some examples are:
    – μέχρι = *to* or *till*
        * *We walked till the river and back.*
        * *They shall stay with us to next month.*
    – σε = *in* or *into*:
        * *He was into the room all day.*
        * *She came in the room and took a book.*
    – σε = *on*, *at* or *in* to refer to time:
        * *We have a meeting at Saturday.*
        * *I usually get up on five o'clock.*
    – από = *from, of, in* or *since*:
        * *She has been here from Sunday.*
        * *He is deprived from his fortune.*
3. Prepositions may be incorrectly omitted after certain verbs under the
influence of Greek:
    * *He came and asked my pencil.*
    * *He explained me the matter.*
    * *They knocked the door and then left.*
4. In other cases, inappropriate prepositions are added after verbs,
again under the influence of Greek:
    * *They left to England last Friday.* (for *They left for England . . .*)
    * *He entered in the room noiselessly.*
5. Learners have difficulty with 'preposition-stranding' structures
where a preposition is placed at the end of a clause. A common error
is to omit the preposition:
    * *Who did you buy it?*
    * *That's the woman I was talking.*
6. Learners often replace *for* with *since* and *since* with *from*:
    * *Mary has lived here since two years.*
    * *I have been teaching from 1994.*

Phrasal verbs

1. In Greek there are no lexical items equivalent to English phrasal verbs. Greek learners have difficulty with them and tend to avoid using them, preferring to use one-word verbs, which can give a rather formal and bookish impression:

    He returned on Sunday. (for *He came back on Sunday.*)
    I telephoned him. (for *I rang him up.*)
    They visited us last weekend. (for *They called on us last weekend.*)
    We had no petrol. (for *We ran out of petrol.*)

2. With two-part phrasal verbs the object pronoun is often placed after the particle instead of before.

    **I rang up him yesterday.*

Vocabulary

1. Some English words are loans from Greek (e.g. *telephone, television, crisis, phenomenon, catastrophe*). Others have been borrowed into Greek (e.g. *jeans, pullover, goal, picnic*). This facilitates learning in certain cases, but there are also some 'false friends' which may lead to confusion. For example, Greeks may misuse:

    agenda to mean *notebook*
    agnostic to mean *foreign, stranger*
    barracks to mean *small shop*
    cabaret to mean *bar*
    ephemera to mean *newspaper*
    fortune to mean *storm*
    graphical to mean *picturesque*
    idiotic to mean *private*
    pneumatic to mean *witty, intellectual*
    sympathise to mean *like*
    trapeze to mean *table*

2. Learners may have difficulties in cases where one Greek word has several English equivalents, or where a related pair of English words does not have an exact counterpart in Greek. Examples:

    miss/lose
    beat/hit/strike/knock
    woman/wife
    house/home
    finger/toe
    office/desk/study
    made of / made from

know/learn/study
interesting/interested
remember/remind
make/do
room/space
Excuse me / Sorry
very/much
too/very
say/tell
annoy/bother
3. Phonetically motivated confusions are also a possible source of mistakes:
   man/men
   woman/women
   prize/price

A sample of written Greek with a transliteration and a word-for-word translation

Ήτανε τόσο δυνατό το χτύπημα, που δεν βρήκε   το κουράγιο να
Itane toso dinato to htipima, pou den vrike   to kourajio na
Was   so   hard   the blow,   that not found he the courage to

διαμαρτυρηθεί. Τι   νόημα   θα είχε μια οποιαδήποτε διαμαρτυρία;
diamartirithi. Ti   noima   tha ihe mia opiadipote diamartiria?
protest.   What meaning will had a   whatever   protest?

Ο   άλλος   τη δουλειά του: έκοβε συνέχεια   το κρέας.
O   allos,   ti doulia tou: ekove sinehia   to kreas.
The other, [continued] the work his: cut he continuously the meat.

Και το μαχαίρι, αυτό το κατακαίνουριο, το αστραφτερό μαχαίρι,
Ke to maheri, afto to katakenourjio, to astraftero maheri,
And the knife,   that the all new,   the shiny   knife,

είχε γίνει   αγνώριστο.   Παγωμένο λίπος είχε κολλήσει στην
ihe jini agnoristo.   Pagomeno lipos ihe kolisi   stin
had become unrecognisable. Cold   fat   had stuck on the

λεπίδα του και στην λαβή,   μικρά κομμάτια κρέας.
lepida tou ke stin lavi,   mikra komatia kreas.
blade its and on the handle, small pieces [of] meat [genitive].

Δεν μπορούσε να δει καλά, το φως   λιγοστό, η   καρδιά
Den boruse   na di kala, to fos   ligosto, i   kardia
Not could he to see well, the light [was] little, the heart

143

του	αναστατωμένη.	Πώς	να	το	πιάσει	στα χέρια	του	το
tou	anastatomeni.	Pos	na	to	pjiasi	sta herjia	tou	to
his	[was] upset.	How	to	it	take	he in hands	his	the

εξαθλιωμένο	μαχαίρι,	πώς	να	το	καρφώσει	στο στήθος	της . . .
exathliomeno	maheri,	pos	na	to	karfosi	sto stithos	tis . . .
miserable	knife,	how	to	it	nail-he	in the breast	her . . .

(From *The Passport* by A Samarakis)

An example of the written English of an elementary Greek learner

Dear Jim,

I have to see you for two years, so I sent you this letter, with a photogaphy of my party. But the most important think which make me sent you this letter, is that I'll go to stay to Hollywood, with my grandmother! After my grandfather's died she is alone, so she want me to stay with her! At first I had arguments with my father, but at the end he said o.k.!

I'm happy about going to Hollywood. I'll see top stars and I'll go to famous places! Of course, I'm a little unhappy, because I'll see my friends and my family after a long time. But I'm so happy, that I think I'll fly!

> With love,
> Fotini

Russian speakers

Bruce Monk and Alexander Burak

Distribution

THE RUSSIAN FEDERATION, Armenia, Azerbaijan, Belarus, Estonia, Georgia, Kazakhstan, Kyrgyzstan, Latvia, Lithuania, Moldova, Tajikistan, Turkmenistan, Ukraine, Uzbekistan.

Introduction

Russian belongs to the Slavonic branch of the Indo-European family of languages. It is very closely related to Belarussian and Ukrainian; the other Slavonic languages are Polish, Czech, Slovak, Slovene, Serbian, Croatian, Bulgarian and Macedonian. At the present time the majority of the 148 million people in Russia speak Russian as their native language. An estimated 80 million people in the former republics of the Soviet Union also have Russian as their first language with another 40 million people in these newly independent countries using Russian as a second language or *lingua franca*.

Phonology

General

The two major features which distinguish the Russian sound system from English are the absence of the short–long vowel differentiation and the absence of diphthongs. English rhythm and stress patterns are also hard for Russian speakers to master.

Vowels

iː	ɪ	e	æ	eɪ	aɪ	ɔɪ
ɑː	ɒ	ɔː	ʊ	aʊ	əʊ	ɪə
uː	ʌ	ɜː	ə	eə	ʊə	aɪə / aʊə

Shaded phonemes have equivalents or near equivalents in Russian, in the form either of individual sounds or of combinations of sounds, and are perceived and articulated without serious difficulty, although some confusions may still arise. Unshaded phonemes may cause problems. For detailed comments, see below.

1. The sound /ɜː/, which is not found in Russian, causes Russian learners of English the greatest difficulty. They often substitute the Russian sounds /э/ or /o/. (The Russian sound /э/ is similar to the nucleus of the English diphthong in *bare* or the English vowel in *bell*.) Particularly troublesome are words beginning with *w*, such as *work, worm, worth, worse*.
2. /ɑː/ tends to be replaced by the more frontal Russian /a/.
3. /æ/ tends to be replaced by a more close sound resembling /e/, leading to confusion between pairs such as *sat* and *set*.
4. The second parts of diphthongs, and the second and third parts of triphthongs, tend to be 'overpronounced'.
5. The sound /ɔː/ is often replaced by the more frontal Russian /o/ or diphthongised into /oʊ/. A confusion often arises between words like *cot, caught* and *coat* or *bought* and *boat* or *not, nought* and *note*.
6. In general, long vowels are pronounced insufficiently 'tense', which makes them sound similar to short vowels. *Field* may be pronounced like *filled*, for example, or *seat* like *sit*.
7. The difference in length of long vowels depending on the final consonant (compare *pea, peal* and *peat*) is also difficult to master.
8. Diphthongs apart, Russian speakers tend to pronounce most English vowels as glides, e.g. /ɒ/ is often pronounced almost like /wɒ/, /ɔː/ as /əʊ/, /ɜː/ as /eə/, etc. This seems to be due to the difficulty Russians have with differentiating in their pronunciation between long (tense) and short (lax) English sounds. The beginnings of tense (long) sounds tend to be pronounced in a relaxed way with tenseness starting to appear towards the middle of the articulation; short sounds tend to be diphthongised due to their slight lengthening.

Consonants

p	b	f	v	θ	ð	t	d
s	z	ʃ	ʒ	tʃ	dʒ	k	g
m	n	ŋ	l	r	j	w	h

Shaded phonemes have equivalents or near equivalents in Russian, and are perceived and articulated without serious difficulty, although some confusions may still arise. Unshaded phonemes may cause problems. For detailed comments, see below.

Of the 24 English consonants, the sounds /θ/, /ð/, /ŋ/ and /w/, which are not found in Russian, prove very difficult.

1. /θ/ and /ð/ present major difficulties and are often replaced by /s/ and /z/. Typical mistakes: *sin* for *thin*; *useful* for *youthful*; *zen* for *then*.
2. /ŋ/ is usually replaced by the Russian /g/ or dental /n/. So for example *wing* might be pronounced *wig* or *win*.
3. The difference between /w/ and /v/ is often not clearly felt, leading to confusion between, for instance, *while* and *vile*, or *west* and *vest*.
4. The sounds /t/, /d/, /l/, /n/ are often made with the tongue touching the top teeth, which gives them a foreign sound.
5. Final voiced consonants such as /b/, /d/, /g/ are devoiced in Russian, causing learners to pronounce such words as *lab*, *said* and *pig*, for instance, as *lap*, *set* and *pick*.
6. The sounds /p/, /k/ and /t/ are not aspirated in Russian, which causes learners to mispronounce them at the beginnings of words in English. So for example *pit* may sound rather like *bit*, *come* like *gum*, or *tart* like *dart*.
7. Learners may replace /h/ by a rougher sound (like *ch* in Scottish *loch*) due to more fricative noise produced in the course of its articulation.
8. Russian learners tend to 'soften' (palatalise) most English consonants before front vowels such as /iː/, /ɪ/, /e/, /eɪ/, /ɪə/, in words like *tea* (where the sound /t/ begins to resemble /ts/), *deed* (where the sound /d/ begins to resemble /dz/), *key* (where a faint suggestion of the sound /j/ appears after /k/ due to palatalisation), etc.
9. 'Dark' /l/ (as in *full* or *hill*) often replaces 'clear' /l/ (as in *light* or *fly*).
10. The sound /ʃ/ is always hard or 'dark' in Russian, so Russian

learners of English tend to make /ʃ/ before vowels and at the end of words harder ('darker') than the correct English sound, which is slightly palatalised.

11. The sound /tʃ/ is always slightly soft ('palatalised') in Russian, so learners tend to replace the hard ('dark', unpalatalised) English sound /tʃ/, as in *chase*, with its palatalised Russian version.

12. Russian has no sound /dʒ/ although it does have separate sounds /d/ and /ʒ/. The sound /dʒ/ only occurs in Russian in borrowed words from English, e.g. *jeans, Jack*, etc., and some other languages. As a result Russian learners of English tend to pronounce the English sound /dʒ/ as two separate sounds without sufficient fusion of its components.

13. The Russian counterpart of the English sound /j/ is pronounced with a lot more fricative noise.

14. The letter *r* in words like *doctor* is sometimes pronounced as /r/ by Russians when first learning English, inappropriately if they are aiming at a standard British pronunciation.

Consonant clusters

1. The combinations /θ/ + /s/, /ð/ + /z/ or /s/ + /ð/ (as in *months, clothes, sixth*) are generally a major challenge even for quite good learners, who often tend to substitute /ts/ and /z/.

2. Link-up problems arise in pronouncing /t/, /d/, /s/, /z/ followed by /j/, as in *situation, education, Did you see the film?, issue, casual*, etc., where Russian learners of English ignore the phonetic phenomenon of accommodation/assimilation of adjacent sounds.

3. In combinations of two plosive consonants (such as /p/, /b/, /t/, /d/, /k/, /g/), the first plosive is usually exploded in Russian. This is carried over into the pronunciation of such words as *asked, hugged, lobbed*, etc.

4. Russians tend to insert the neutral sound /ə/ in the combinations /tl/, /dl/, /tn/, /dn/, leading to pronunciations such as *little* /lɪtəl/, *button* /bʌtən/, *modern* /mɒdən/.

5. The initial clusters /tw/, /tr/, /pr/, /dr/, /br/ are also difficult, leading to problems with words like *twice, tree, price, dry, bright*. Russian learners of English tend to pronounce the component letters in these clusters separately, sometimes inserting a neutral vowel between the two sounds, instead of fusing them together to produce undividable sounds like /tr/ in *tree*, where the initial English cluster sounds similar to the initial sound in *chair*, or /dr/ in *dry*, where the initial English cluster sounds a shade like /dʒ/, etc.

Rhythm and stress

Russian stress patterns are as variable as English ones. However, Russian speakers tend to lose secondary stresses in long English words:

competition /kəmpɪˈtɪʃn/
intelligibility /ɪntələdʒəˈbɪlɪtɪ/
compatibility /kəmpətəˈbɪlɪtɪ/
imperturbability /ɪmpətəbəˈbɪlɪtɪ/

Sentence rhythm presents problems. For instance, learners often pronounce the slower 'strong' forms of words like *as*, *than*, *can*, *must* or *have*, instead of the faster 'weak' forms.

Intonation

The Russian low fall is not deep enough and the low rise does not begin low enough and tends to 'shoot' upwards abruptly. Other problems:

1. Russians tend to finish their *yes/no* questions with a fall, which can make them sound impolite:
   Did you tell her?
2. Tag questions may also cause confusion:
   It's a nice day, isn't it?
3. Alternative questions are often ended with a rise:
   Do you want coffee or tea?

Influence of spelling on pronunciation

Great difficulties often arise for Russians, as for other learners, from the lack of correspondence between what is written and the way that it is pronounced. Typical mistakes:

knife /knaɪf/
comb /kɒmb/
break /briːk/
risen /raɪzn/
singing /sɪŋgɪŋg/
mind /mɪnd/
through /θraʊ/ or /θroʊg/, etc.

Writing and punctuation

Writing

Although Russians use the Cyrillic alphabet, many English letters are similar in form to Russian letters: *a, o, e, n, m, p, c, k, g, x, y, M, T, H* (certain of them are pronounced differently). Russians may experience difficulties in writing *s, r, i, h, l, f, b, t, j, I, G, Q, N,* which do not occur in Cyrillic.

Punctuation

Russian punctuation marks and the rules for their use are basically similar to English. The main difference is in the use of commas to mark off nearly all subordinate clauses in Russian. This leads by transference to the following typical mistakes:

*I think, that you're right.
*I don't know, which book to choose.

Inverted commas are usually written like this: „ "

Grammar

General

The grammatical systems of Russian and English are fundamentally different. English is an analytic language, in which grammatical meaning is largely expressed through the use of additional words and by changes in word order. Russian, on the other hand, is a synthetic language, in which the majority of grammatical forms are created through changes in the structure of words, by means of a developed system of prefixes, suffixes and inflectional endings which indicate declension, conjugation, person, number, gender and tense. Russian therefore has fairly complicated systems of noun and adjective declension and verb conjugation, but the Russian sentence has no real fixed word order.

The Russian and English verb systems express rather different kinds of meaning. Russian has only three tenses: past, present and future. The verb system is mainly built on the notion of aspect. This is the contrast between actions which are uncompleted (imperfective aspect) and those which are completed (perfective aspect). These contrasts are indicated through affixation. Perfect and progressive forms of verbs, as understood in English, do not exist. Strictly speaking, there are no auxiliary verbs like *do, have* or *will* in Russian, although the verb bit' (*to be*), for example,[1] used to build future tense forms or some passive voice forms, could be construed as a kind of auxiliary verb, e.g. V dva chasa ya **budu rabotat'** doma (*I'll be working* at home at two o'clock) or Rabota **bila**

---

[1] In transcription from Cyrillic, an apostrophe after a letter (as in bit') indicates that the sound is palatalised.

zdelana v srok (*The work **was done** in/on time*). By the same token the Russian verbal particle pust (similar in meaning to the English *let*), used to build some imperative mood forms, could also be conceived as a kind of auxiliary, e.g. **Pust** on **pridyot** zavtra (*Let him **come** tomorrow*).

'Phrasal' verbs do not exist in Russian, and the use of prepositions is far more limited than in English.

Nouns have grammatical gender.

There are no articles in Russian.

With such basic differences between the grammatical systems of the two languages it is inevitable that there will be certain major difficulties for a Russian learning English.

Questions and negatives; auxiliaries

1. The auxiliaries *do, have, will* and *be* have no equivalent in Russian. Typical mistakes in statements, questions and responses are:
    *I no like it.
    * When you went there?
    * How you like it?
    'Do you like football?' *'Yes, I like.'
2. *Do* is often confused with *does*, and vice versa:
    *She don't go there now.
3. Negative question forms may be wrongly used:
    *Don't you know when he's coming? (for Do you know. . .?)
4. Not having auxiliary verbs, Russian lacks question tags. Russians have great difficulty in forming these and often make mistakes when using them. They also tend to employ them far less frequently than native speakers:
    *You like her, doesn't it?
    *Is many people in room, isn't it?
    *Did you see him, didn't you?
    *You didn't do it, didn't you?
5. Russian learners find the use of short answers and reply questions difficult:
    'Can he play tennis?' (*) 'Yes.' (for 'Yes, he can.')
    'Are you tired?' *'No, not tired.' (for 'No, I'm not.')
    'Don't forget to write.' (*)'No.' (for 'I won't.')
    'It was a very pleasant evening.' (*)'Yes.' (for 'Yes, it was.'/'Yes, wasn't it?')
    'I don't understand.' *'No? I explain again.' (for 'Don't you? I'll explain it again.')
6. Russians have difficulty with the use of *Let* in imperatives:

Russian speakers

> *Let they to do it.*
> *Let's no do it.*

Time, tense and aspect

A. Past time

Russian has no perfect or past progressive tenses. One simple past form is used to refer to actions and events denoted by perfect and progressive tenses in English. Typical mistakes are:

> *I read when he came.*
> *He said he already finished work.*
> *I still didn't read the book.*

B. Present time

1. In Russian there are no present perfect or present progressive forms. There is only one simple present tense. This leads to mistakes like:

> *Where you go now?*
> *Your article is typed now. Please wait.*
> *How long you be/are here?* (for . . . *have you been here?*)

2. In reported speech Russian speakers often do not observe the sequence of tenses rule:

> *He said he live here long.*
> *I knew she (is) in town.*

3. In the third person singular Russians often omit the suffix -(e)s:

> *He very like her.* (for *He likes her very much.*)

C. Future time

1. A simple present tense may be used to refer to the future:

> *I promise I come tomorrow.*

2. There are no future perfect or future progressive tenses:

> *She will work here ten years by Thursday.*
> *This time tomorrow I will lie on the beach.*

3. In subordinate clauses of time the future tense is used in Russian where a present tense would be used in English:

> *When she will ring you, tell her I called.*

4. Mistakes are made with sequence of tenses:

> *She said she go tomorrow.*
> *They said they no come.*
> *He said he will come.*
> *They said they will do the work by five.*

To summarise, mistakes in using English tenses generally occur because the Russian verb system has only two aspects (perfective and imperfective) expressed mostly through affixation, whereas the English verb is viewed from three perspectives which can be combined, i.e. as expressing 'simple', continuous and perfect actions or events. Russian basically has three active verb categories, whereas English has 16 if one counts future-in-the-past forms. Hence the difficulty learners experience in sorting them out.

The passive voice

Russian learners do not usually find the basic forms of the passive too problematic. The complex forms in the continuous and perfective aspects cause the most difficulty:
>*The house is (was) building.
>*The book has finished.

Conditionals

1. In subordinate clauses of condition the future tense is used in Russian where the present tense would be used in English:
   >*If she will come, I will tell her.
2. More problems inevitably arise in complex conditional forms:
   >*If he would (to) helped me I had did it.

Modal verbs

1. The system of modal verbs in Russian is simpler than in English, and interference may therefore cause mistakes such as the following. The constructions *to be able to* and *to have to* need particular care:
   >*I can to do it.
   >*You must to work hard.
   >*Yesterday he must go home early.
   >*I shall must phone him.
   >*She will can do it.
2. Answers to questions with *may* and *must* cause difficulty:
   >'May I come in?' *'No, you may not/can't.' (meaning 'Please don't.')
   >'Must I do it now?' *'No, you must not.' (meaning 'No, you needn't.')

To be

1. The link verb *to be* is not used as a rule in the present tense in Russian:
   *He good boy.
   *They no nice.
2. In all tenses Russians experience difficulties in the use of the *there is* construction:
   *Is table in room?
   *Many tables are in room, yes?
3. When the *there is* construction has been learnt, Russians may still confuse it with the use of *it* as a dummy subject:
   *There is hot here, is it?
   *It is very good stereo in room.

To have

1. Russian learners can experience difficulty in making the association between the English verb *to have* and its Russian equivalent, the 'u menya est' construction (literally 'at me is').
2. At beginner level mistakes are sometimes made in the use of *has/have*.
   *He have book.

Non-finite forms

1. The more complex *-ing* forms and infinitives (progressive, perfect and passive) cause difficulty:
   *I heard of his appointing headmaster. (for I heard that he had been appointed headmaster.)
   *I like inviting by my friends. (for I like being invited by my friends.)
   *She is said to live here long.
   *She is believed to write a new book.
2. The 'infinitive of purpose' is difficult to master:
   *I came for to help you.
   *I came that to help you.

Verbal complements

1. 'Object + infinitive' structures cause problems for Russian learners.
   *I could see that he goes across the street.

*I could see him to go across the street.
*They made me to do it.
2. Causative structures are also difficult:
   *I've just made it. (for I've just had it made.)
   *I must go to cut my hair. (for I've got to have my hair cut.)

Word order

1. Since Russian expresses basic grammatical relations through inflections, word order in the Russian sentence is rather more free than in English. Moreover, it is common for Russian sentences to begin with adverbial phrases of time and place. This leads to certain typical mistakes:
   *Yesterday on table lied my book.
2. Clause-final prepositions cause problems of style:
   *At what are you looking?
   *With whom were you talking when I saw you?

Articles

Russian has no articles. The mistakes Russian learners of English make in the use of the English articles are too numerous to list here. There is a general confusion in the understanding of the basic differences between *the, a/an* and the zero article.
1. One of the initial problems for Russian learners is learning how to use the articles in general:
   *New house is building near cinema that is near us.
   *Have you mother?
2. Then there is the problem of choice between the definite and indefinite articles:
   *Have you the mother?
   *Is she a woman you told us about?

Quantifiers

Ways of talking about quantities and amounts usually cause considerable difficulty. The commonly misused and confused quantifiers are *few (of), a few (of), little (of), a little (of), much (of), many (of), none (of)* and some others:
   *I have many money.

> **I have few days before I go.* (In the sense: *I have a few days left before I go.*)

Russians tend to use *many, much* and *little* inappropriately in affirmative sentences:

> *(*)I have many friends.* (for *I have a lot of friends.*)
> *(*)I have much time.* (for *I have a lot of time.*)
> *(*)I have little time.* (for *I don't have much time.*)

Gender

Nouns in Russian are masculine, feminine or neuter. This leads learners to make mistakes with personal pronouns:

> '*Where's book?*' **'She is on the table.*'
> '*Where's my umbrella?*' **'He is here.*'

Number

1. The category of number exists in Russian. However, the countable/ uncountable distinction causes problems, since some English uncountable nouns have countable Russian equivalents:

   > **Her hairs are nice.*
   > **I have one news.*
   > **I'll give you a good advice.*
   > **'Where are money?' 'They on table.'*

2. Special care is also needed with *this/these, that/those*:

   > **I don't like this songs.*

Noun compounds

Noun compounds of the type *the boy's book, John's book* are a problem at beginner level. Learners try to use *of*-phrases (e.g. **the book of the boy*) where animate/proper noun possessives are the norm.

Numerals

The plural ending *-s* is often added to *hundred, thousand, million* and *billion* due to the influence of the Russian language:

> **two hundreds roubles*
> **twenty millions*

Adjectives and adverbs

1. The greatest difficulties arise for Russians in the formation of the degrees of comparison of the adjectives *bad*, *good* and *far*:
    * *He is more bad than I think.*
    * *They are badder.*
    * *It is farer.*
2. Adjectives can also be confused with adverbs, for instance, *bad/ badly*, *good/well*:
    * *He speaks English very good.*
    * *She plays piano bad.*

Relative pronouns

1. Usually *who* is confused with *which* because the same Russian word can be used for both:
    * *The people which came I no like.*
2. *That* is confused with *what*:
    * *I know what he work here.*

Interrogative pronouns

Mistakes occur in the use of *who*, *which* and *whose*:
    * *Who of you know/s English?*
    * *Who book is this?*

Indefinite pronouns

Everybody and *everyone* are often associated with the plural number because the corresponding pronoun is plural in Russian:
    * *Everybody/Everyone were there.*

Negative pronouns

Nobody/no-one are often used instead of the quantifier *none* in sentences like:
    * *Nobody/no-one of them were there.*

Prepositions and adverb particles

1. The use or omission of prepositions results in errors:
   *I listen music very much.
   *I want to explain you this.
   *It'll be dark for three o'clock. (for... *by three o'clock.*)
   *He work on factory.
   *Can you comment this?
   *What are you laughing?
2. Russian has no equivalent of English adverb particles; nor does post-position exist. Phrasal verbs therefore cause difficulties, especially when the particle follows the object, as in *I'll look it up.*

Vocabulary

False friends

There are quite a few words that sound similar in English and Russian, but that have different meanings or shades of meaning. Examples are:
aktual'niy (= *current*, not *actual*)
simpatichniy (= *nice, friendly*, not *sympathetic*)
biskvit (= *sponge cake*, not *biscuit*)
manifestatsiya (= *demonstration*, not *manifestation*)
salyut (= *firework display*, not *salute*)
perspektiva (= *prospect*, not *perspective*)
perspektivniy (= *promising, future, long-range*, not *perspective*)
dekada (= *ten days*, not *decade*)
miting (= *a rally*, not *a meeting*)
kharakteristika (= *a (character) reference, a letter of recommendation*, not *a characteristic*)
pretendovat' (= *to lay claim to, to have pretensions to*, not *to pretend*)
operativniy (= *effective, quick, practical, current, timely*, not *operative*)
moment (= *point, element, aspect* as in a presentation, not *moment*)
ekonomniy (= *thrifty, frugal, practical*, not *economic*)

A more complete list of Russian-English false friends is to be found in the dictionary by V. V. Akulenko, Anglo-Russkiy i Russko-Angliskiy Slovar' 'Lozhnykh Druzey Perevodchika'. (English-Russian and Russian-English Dictionary of 'a Translator's False Friends'.) Moscow: Soviet Encyclopaedia Publishing House, 1969.

Other confusions

A number of widely-used words have different rules of usage from their closest Russian equivalents.

1. *yet/already*:
   > **Have you see her already?* (meaning *Have you seen her yet?*)

   Russians would find it difficult at beginner level to differentiate between *Have you seen her yet?* where *yet* signals a legitimate question, and *Have you seen her already?* in the sense *What? So fast?* or *How did you manage to do that?*

2. *so/such*:
   > **He is so clever man.*
   > **It is such difficult.*

3. *say/tell*:
   > **He said me that you are ill.*
   > **The story says about the war.*

4. *Please*:
   > *'Here's a book for you.' 'Thank you.' *'Please.'*

   or:
   > *'Give me the book, please.' *'Please.'* (instead of *Here you are.*)

5. Rather overused are *to my mind, you see, you know, well*:
   > *'What time does the film start?' *'To my mind, at seven.'*
   > **Well, you see, I often go to the Crimea, you know.*

6. Failure to use 'conversational fillers' in other situations may make Russians sound impolite when, in fact, they do not mean to be so:
   > *'Would you like to go there?' *'No, I wouldn't.'* (for *'Well, I'm afraid I can't because . . .'*)
   > **Tell me please how to go to the station.* (for *Excuse me, could you tell me the way to the station, please?*)

7. The expression *of course* tends to be inadvertently misused:
   > *'Can you speak French?' *'Yes, of course.'* (for *'Yes, I can.'*)

Attitudes to language learning

All children in Russian secondary schools learn a foreign language. The majority of pupils learn English (British English being taken as the norm with American English slowly gaining ground), although French, German, Spanish and a number of other languages are also taught. Communicative methods are widely used, with an emphasis on oral skill. Russian citizens are therefore reasonably experienced language learners, and they are generally enthusiastic about language lessons, no doubt because they live in a multicultural and multilingual society in a period of sweeping socio-economic changes that allow and encourage unrestricted contacts with the English-speaking world.

Samples of written Russian with transliterations and word-for-word idiomatic translations

Знаете ли   вы, что . . . взяв   обыкновенный русский
Znayete li   vi, shto . . . vzyav obiknovenniy russkiy
Know [interrogative] you, that . . . taking ordinary   Russian

алфавит и   расположив буквы определённым образом,
alfavit i   raspolozhiv bukvi opredelyonnim obrazom,
alphabet and disposing   letters definite   way,

можно получить не только кандидатскую, но и   докторскую
mozhno poluchit' ne tol'ko kandidatskuyu, no i   doktorskuyu
can   receive not only candidate,   but and doctor

диссертацию?
dissertatsiyu?
dissertation?

Did you know that by using the ordinary Russian alphabet and placing the letters in a certain way you can obtain not only an MA thesis but even a doctoral one?

(From *Literaturnaya Gazeta*, 7 November 1984)

После десятимесячного   отсутствия вернулся к жене и
Posle desyatimesyachnovo* otsutstviya vernulsa k zhene i
After ten month   absence   returned to wife and

детям   участник прошлогодних соревнований по
detyam uchastnik proshlogodnikh sorevnovaniy po
children participant last year   competitions on

спортивному ориентированию Ф. Уклоняев.   Сразу же
sportivnomu orientirovaniyu F. Uklonyaev. Srazu zhe
sport   orienteering   F. Uklonyayev. At once

после возвращения   спортсмен начал усиленную
posle vozvrashcheniya sportsmen nachal usilennuyu
after return   sportsman began strengthened

подготовку к   новым весенним стартам.
podgotovku k   novim vesennim startam.
preparation for new   spring   starts.

* this ending is written -ogo but pronounced -ovo.

Mr F. Uklonyayev (= the Dodger), who participated in last year's sports orienteering championship, has returned to his wife and children after a ten-month absence. Immediately upon his return the athlete started intensive training to take part in the forthcoming spring events.

(From *Literaturnaya Gazeta*, 12 June 1985)

Polish speakers

Grzegorz Śpiewak (phonology) and
Lucyna Gołębiowska

Distribution

POLAND; Polish communities in the USA, Germany, Brazil, Canada and elsewhere.

Introduction

Polish is an Indo-European language, a member of the (West) Slavonic branch. As such, it is most closely related to Czech and Slovak, and more distantly to Russian, Byelorussian, Ukrainian, Bulgarian, Macedonian, Serbo-Croat and Slovene.

Since the change of political system in 1989, when Poland began to tighten its links with the West, the role of English, always a popular language, has dramatically increased. English is now considered an essential part of a good education, and is widely taught in and out of schools. Many employers organise in-service EFL courses.

Because English, like Polish, is an Indo-European language, and because it is ever-present in mass culture and enjoys high prestige, Polish speakers, especially the young, do not find it particularly difficult.

Phonology

General

Polish learners of English often despair of the apparent lack of consistency between spelling and pronunciation. Learners at elementary levels expect each letter to be pronounced, and give Polish values to each letter. The multitude of stress patterns in English is also an unpleasant surprise to Poles, given the regular penultimate-syllable stress of their mother tongue. Their initial impression of English pronunciation is that 'everything sounds together' or that the English 'eat their words'.

Features of the Polish pronunciation of English that contribute to a Polish accent in English include: the use of full instead of reduced vowels in unstressed syllables, giving the impression of 'pronouncing

too much'; certain intonation contours; a prominent rolled /r/ –
especially word-finally; final devoicing (especially /s/ in place of /z/); and
mispronunciation of *th*, /ŋ/ and sibilants. For details, see below.

Rhythm and stress

Polish speakers have major problems mastering the stress-timed rhythm
of English. They often cannot recognise weak forms and attempt to
pronounce all the words with nearly equal prominence, which affects
their rhythm and speed. In particular:
1. Full vowels are pronounced in place of /ə/ in words like *banana* or
   photographer.
2. Grammatical items such as *and, that, as, a, the* are given their
   'strong' pronunciation in all contexts.
3. A number of words are mis-stressed due to the influence of the native
   penultimate-syllable stress. Polish learners need a lot of help with the
   pronunciation of word families with stress-shifts (e.g. *'politics,
   po'litical, poli'tician*), and also with words like *vegetable, reachable,
   comfortable*, where the *a* is wrongly pronounced as /eɪ/ and stressed
   (possibly by analogy with *table* and *able*), making such words
   difficult to understand.
4. Polish learners often fail to perceive and produce secondary stress in
   longer words, e.g. *ˌinfor'mation, ˌmulti'plicity*.

Juncture

1. Polish has no linking /j/ or /w/, so sequences like *my uncle, do it* are
   pronounced separately.
2. Likewise, Polish learners do not link consonants to vowels in
   sequences like: *have an apple, come for a meal*.
3. When two plosives follow each other (as in *used to, like Carol, and
   diving*), Poles typically pronounce both separately, typically devoicing the first one if it is voiced.
4. Sequences of /d/, /t/, /s/, /z/ followed by /j/ in phrases like *would you,
   as you know, did you, miss you* are pronounced as separate sounds
   without assimilation (e.g. /wʊdjuː/ instead of /wʊdʒə/).

Vowels

Vowels represent an area of great difficulty and potential confusion. The reason for this is that Polish has 8 vowels in total (6 oral and 2 nasal), compared to the 22 vowels of English. Polish has no length distinction and no diphthongs or triphthongs. As a result, English vowels cause major problems to Poles, both as regards perception and articulation. The table below illustrates some of these problems:

	English	Polish
close vowels	iː ɪ ʊ uː	i ɨ u
mid vowels	e ə ɜː ɔː	ɛ o
open vowels	æ ʌ ɑː ɒ	a

As the symbols indicate, none of the English vowels has an exact equivalent in Polish. What is more, Polish has only one open vowel compared to as many as four in English. Consequently, open vowels are the single most difficult area for Polish speakers, both as regards hearing the differences between them and producing accurate vowel sounds. In addition, the following points are worth noting.

1. There are no weak vowels in Polish: schwa and /ɪ/ are regularly replaced by full vowels.
2. Both /e/ and /æ/ are typically pronounced as /ɛ/; hence the notorious problems with pairs like *man – men, bad – bed, pat – pet*.
3. /ɪ/ is pronounced as /i/ rather than the more similar but centralised Polish /ɨ/, leading to confusions between pairs such as *feet – fit, sheep – ship*.
4. /ɑː/ may be confused with /æ/, leading to mispronunciation of words like *father*, and inconsistency in the choice between British and American variants of words like *pass, after*.
5. /ow/, the Polish approximation of the diphthong /əʊ/, is often pronounced in place of /ɔː/. As a result pairs like the following are often confused: *saw – sew, bought – boat, law – low*.
6. Even though /ɜː/ is a relatively easy vowel to learn, Poles regularly replace it with /o/ when they see it written as such (as in *work, word, world*).
7. The second elements of the closing diphthongs /eɪ/, /aɪ/, /ɔɪ/, /əʊ/, /aʊ/ are pronounced as /j/ and /w/ respectively (importing Polish sequences like: /a/ + /j/, /u/ + /w/, which are not diphthongs).
8. The variation in length of long vowels according to what follows (as in *pea, peas, peace*) is difficult to master.

Consonants

p	b	f	v	θ	ð	t	d
s	z	ʃ	ʒ	tʃ	dʒ	k	g
m	n	ŋ	l	r	j	w	h

English consonants do not cause major comprehension problems for Polish learners. The main difficulties lie in their accurate production and in predicting their value from spelling. Shaded phonemes have equivalents or near equivalents in Polish, and are articulated without serious difficulty, although some confusions may still arise. Unshaded phonemes may cause considerable production problems. For detailed comments, see below.

1. /θ/ and /ð/ are regularly replaced by any of the following: /f/, /v/, /s/, /z/, /t/, /d/ or even /ts/, /dz/. Interdentals are a nightmare for elementary learners, and need a lot of practice.
2. By contrast, even advanced learners often mispronounce /ʃ/, /ʒ/, /tʃ/ and /dʒ/, replacing them with the harsher non-palatal Polish /š/, /ž/, /tš/, /dž/ respectively.
3. The Polish equivalent of English /h/ is not a voiceless vowel, but a fricative, similar to the final sound in *loch*, and most learners pronounce English /h/ in this way. Moreover, Polish learners expect *h* to be pronounced wherever they see it written, and do not omit it in sequences like *give him the book, take her out.*
4. The sound /r/ has a distinct rolled quality in Polish, often imported into English especially at elementary levels (together with the postalveolar place of articulation). Learners of British English also need to be taught *not* to pronounce /r/ in word-final position and before consonants, as in *first, work, her, water, far, there.* (American English is easier for Poles in this respect.)
5. Polish devoices most final voiced consonants, which leads to confusion between pairs like: *bed – bet, his – hiss, dog – dock.* The problem is particularly acute with weak forms of words like: *is, his, was,* which are all pronounced with a very audible final /s/. One way to deal with this problem is to offer a lot of practice in linking final consonants to following initial vowels, as in *his uncle, is a man, was at home.*
6. On the other hand, /l/ and /r/ after unvoiced consonants, in words

like *please, try, cream, prison*, are incorrectly pronounced with full voicing.

7. There is no dark /l/ in standard Polish, which causes difficulty with words like *table, able, little, role.*
8. Polish learners typically mispronounce *ng* as /ŋg/ (before a vowel) or /ŋk/ (in final position). *Singing* may be pronounced /sɪŋgɪŋk/ and *ring him* /rɪŋk hɪm/; *sting* sounds like *stink*; *wing* is pronounced like *wink.*
9. Polish lacks aspiration of /p/, /t/, /k/, which affects the sound of both the consonants and the following vowels in words like *part, top, cat.*
10. Nasal consonants are pronounced very softly (with palatalisation) before front vowels, e.g. in: *knee, meat, need.*
11. Very few learners are aware that the place of articulation of /t/, /d/, and /n/ is dental in Polish but alveolar (on the gum ridge) in English.

Intonation

To the majority of Polish speakers English intonation sounds exaggerated, affected, or overdone, which causes considerable resistance to imitating English contours for fear of sounding funny. Poles typically mispronounce *wh*-questions, producing a fall-rise instead of a falling tone. On the other hand, they do not mark falling tones sufficiently in statements, giving the impression of sounding flat.

Influence of spelling on pronunciation

Apart from the confusion arising from the inconsistency between spelling and pronunciation, Polish speakers have difficulty with words that are written with silent letters or syllables: e.g. *psychology, salmon, whistle, know, knife, camera, secretary, comfortable.*

Orthography and punctuation

Spelling

Initially, Polish learners experience some difficulty with English spelling. This results from the fact that Polish spelling is largely phonetic. With time, however, they adapt to the new system.

Note that days of the week and months are not capitalised in Polish, and there is a rule about not capitalising adjectives. This leads to mistakes like:

*english books   *tuesday

On the other hand, in letters, as a sign of respect, all Polish equivalents of *you* and *your* are capitalised; hence mistakes like:

*I'm writing to You . . .

Punctuation

Punctuation conventions are roughly the same in Polish and English. The main difference is that commas are used to mark off subordinate clauses:

*I think, that it's OK.
*I'll call you, when/if she comes.

Inverted commas are written differently: „ "

Grammar

General

Polish, unlike English, is a highly inflected language, and therefore has a much freer word order. Nouns, for example, have grammatical number, gender (masculine, feminine, neuter) and seven cases, shown by changes in form. Adjectives conform to the gender, number and case of the noun to which they refer. Each verb (with or without a preposition) governs a particular case. The grammatical function of a word is indicated by these means, rather than by its position in the sentence as in English.

Verbs are usually either imperfective or perfective; the imperfectives form three tenses (present, past and future), the perfectives two (past and future). Time and tense are generally perceived as one, in fact both terms have the same Polish equivalent: czas.

Polish uses the passive much less than English, has no phrasal verbs, no primary or modal auxiliaries (as understood in English), no perfect or progressive verb forms.

There are no articles in Polish.

Naturally, all those differences confuse Polish learners of English.

Questions and negatives

Polish interrogatives are primarily made by adding an initial question word, or simply by using question intonation. Negatives are made by preceding the verb with nie (= *no*). The whole idea of auxiliaries is therefore novel and creates considerable problems. Typical mistakes (especially at beginners' level) include:

> *She no(t) do(es) it.*
> *Do/Does she it?*
> *I very not like school.*
> *Where they live?*
> *(Why) You are standing?*
> *He is working now, yes?*

Note also:

> *Did you finished?*
> *He do(es)n't knows.*

Overgeneralisation, on the other hand, often leads to errors such as:

> *Do you can swim?*

Polish *yes/no* questions require a question word (czy). As a result, learners frequently panic because they think they cannot remember its English equivalent, and either say nothing at all, or produce, for example:

> *If does she work here?* (for *Does she work here?*)

On numerous occasions Polish requires multiple negation, which results in mistakes like:

> *Nobody doesn't understand.*
> *She never doesn't know nothing.*

Note also:

> *She doesn't know something.* (for *She doesn't know anything.*)

Question tags, short answers and reply questions

Polish short answers are a simple *Yes/No*. Reply questions and question tags are equivalent to *Yes?*, *Really?* and a few others. They are not tense related. This results in over-abrupt responses and errors such as:

> 'Can he play chess?' (*) 'No.' (for *No, he can't.*)
> 'Do you live here?' (*) 'Yes.' (for *Yes, I do.*)
> *They have (not) finished, yes /isn't it?*

It is worth noting that question tags, short answers and reply questions are not as frequent in Polish as they are in English, so Poles tend to avoid them altogether. This may make speakers sound impolite when, in fact, they do not mean to be so.

Note also:

> 'He never comes on time.' *'Yes.' (for 'No.')

It *and* there *as subjects*

1. Where an English sentence has impersonal *it* as subject, Polish often has no subject pronoun. This leads to mistakes like:
   *Today is cold.
   *Here is quiet.
   *Already is making dark. (for *It's already getting dark.*)
   *Is three o'clock.
   Note also:
   Rain/Snow was falling. (in preference to *It was raining/snowing.*)
   *There is cold/warm. (for *It is cold/warm.*)
2. *There* as a grammatical subject introducing an indefinite noun phrase appears to be especially difficult for Polish learners:
   *In my room is a/the table. (for *There is a table in my room.*)
   *Is a table in your room?
   *There is my/the book on a/the table.
   *There is my school. (for *My school is there.*)

Time, tense and aspect

There is considerable confusion in the use of all English tenses, most of all perfect and progressive, as they have no Polish equivalents.

A. Past time

1. Polish uses a past tense in situations where English requires a present perfect:
   *She still didn't come.
   *Were you ever in China? (for *Have you ever been to China?*)
   *I saw that film. (for *I've seen that film.*)
   *Sorry I'm late. Did you wait long?
   *She cried. (for *She's been crying.*)
   On the other hand, Polish learners will say:
   *I have done it last week.
   *When have you seen Tom?
2. Lack of progressive tenses in Polish leads to mistakes like:
   *I watched TV when you telephoned.
3. Conversely, the past progressive is sometimes overused:
   *Mozart was living in the 18th century.
   *We were dancing often when we were going to school.
   *He was believing this.
4. The past perfect is sometimes used for a sequence of past events, as in:

> *I had eaten breakfast and I went to school.

and for past events that are perceived as distant:

> *They had emigrated before the war.

B. Present time

1. A single Polish present tense expresses ideas which in English require various present or perfect tenses. This results in:
   > *They work now.
   > *We watch TV since two hours.
   > *I live here all my life.
   > *How long do you learn/are you learning English? (for How long have you been learning . . .)
2. The simple present third person singular ending is often omitted:
   > *She live here.
3. Other typical mistakes include:
   > *I'm living here all my life.
   > *Are you hearing the noise? (for Can you hear . . .?)

C. Future time

1. The choice between *going to* and *will* is usually made at random:
   > *The film is going to end after ten minutes. (for . . . will end in ten minutes.)
2. The simple present rather than the progressive may be used to refer to the future in sentences like:
   > *Where do you go?
3. Even though the future tense of some Polish verbs resembles the progressive aspect, Polish learners seem to overlook this:
   > *I will learn English all Sunday.
4. All perfect tenses are a problem, most of all the future perfect:
   > *He will come back by Monday. (for He will have come back by Monday.)
5. For future time reference Polish uses the future tense in subordinate clauses of time:
   > *When I will return, I will telephone you.
   > *It will finish by the time we will get there.

Sequence of tenses

In reported speech, after a past reporting verb, Polish uses the tenses of the original speech, hence:

> *He said me that you are busy.

And also:
> *I realised that she doesn't know about it.*
> *He thought that he can go.*
> *I didn't know he will come.*

Overgeneralisation leads to mistakes like:
> *I don't know if/when he comes. (for I don't know if/when he will come.)*

The passive voice

Compared with English, Polish uses the passive much less, though in most cases there are exact equivalents. Learners tend not to use it, and when they do, they usually find the progressive passive especially difficult:
> *It is done/doing now. (for It is being done now.)*

Typical mistakes include:
> *She born in March.*
> *Bread finished.*

Note also:
> *I am interesting in music.*

Conditionals

For future time reference Polish uses the future tense in subordinate clauses of condition:
> *If I will pass, I will celebrate. (for If I pass, I will celebrate.)*

The subordinate clauses in the 'second' and 'third' conditionals are identical in Polish. This, together with the limited number of Polish tenses, leads to great confusion, and virtually any combination of English tenses is possible. Most typically:
> *If you would go, I would go too. (for If you went, I would go too.)*
> *If she knew, she will/would tell. or *If she had knew, she would had told. or *If she would have known, she had told. (all for If she had known, she would have told us.)*

Modal auxiliaries

Most English modal auxiliaries have rough Polish equivalents. The Polish verbs, however, do not follow any special rules for questions, negatives or tenses. Furthermore, Polish has only one type of infinitive, so the choice between an infinitive with or without *to* already creates problems, not to mention perfect and progressive infinitive forms. All this results in a great deal of confusion.

1. Overgeneralisation of rules concerning the formation of negatives and interrogatives leads to:

   *Do you must/can, etc. (to) work?

   Note also:

   *He mustn't come. (for He needn't come.)

2. The use of tenses creates problems:

   *I will must (to) go.

   *They must read it yesterday.

3. The difference between *You must* and *You have to* is often lost, as is that between *You can . . .* and *You may . . .*

4. Short answers are often used incorrectly:

   'May I sit down?' *'Yes, you may.' (for *Please do.*)

5. *Shall I . . .?* in offers of assistance is generally avoided, giving way to *Can/May I . . .?, Do you want me to . . .?* or **Do you want that I . . .?*

6. *Can* rather than *may* is used to talk about current possibility:

   *She can know the answer.

7. Perfect and progressive infinitives tend not to be used at all:

   *She could see it. (for *She could have seen it.*)

   *He must work now. (for *He must be working now.*)

In sentences like the above, most learners will say *Maybe . . .* or *I'm sure that . . .* and avoid using modals altogether.

Infinitives and *-ing* forms

1. English *-ing* forms usually correspond to Polish infinitives:

   *I enjoy to dance.

   *You must stop to smoke.

2. Polish uses a subordinate clause where English uses an 'object + infinitive' structure, hence:

   *He wants that I come. (for *He wants me to come.*)

   *Would you like that I open the window?

3. Polish also uses a subordinate clause where English uses an 'object + present participle' structure:

   *I saw how she came / was coming. (for *I saw her coming.*)

Reflexive verbs

Reflexive verbs are more common in Polish than in English. Most typically learners say:

> *I woke myself, then I washed myself, I shaved myself and I dressed myself.*
> *They kissed themselves. (for They kissed.)*
> *They looked at themselves. (for They looked at each other.)*

Word order

Word order is relatively free in Polish, though this does not cause as many problems as one might expect.

1. One area of difficulty is the position of adverbs:
   > *I don't well speak English.*
   > *I don't speak well English.*
   > *I very like apples.*
   > *I like very much apples.*
   > *I eat every day/often bread.*
   > *Often I go to cinema.*

2. Final prepositions sound very odd to Polish learners, so they are likely to say:
   > *At what are you looking?*
   > *From where is Tom?*
   > *What do you listen?*
   > *Tell me about what it is.*

3. The verb often immediately follows the relative pronoun in Polish, hence:
   > *This is (the/a) house where live my friends.*
   > *(The/A) Question which asked (the) teacher was easy.*

4. Word order in Polish indirect questions is the same as in direct questions (there is no inversion); *yes/no* questions require a question word whether or not they are direct. Learners who have mastered English direct questions may therefore say:
   > *Tell me where are they.*
   > *Tell me are they at home.*
   > *She wants to know what do you want.*

   Note also:
   > *He asked how will you do it. (see 'Sequence of tenses')*
   > *I don't know if to do it.*

Polish speakers

Articles

There are no articles in Polish. As a result, some learners tend not to use them at all, many use them at random, still others overuse them. Even the most basic distinction between 'definite' and 'indefinite' causes great confusion:

> *I have (the) dog.
> *He is (the) doctor.
> *I like the/a chocolate.
> *(A) Film I saw yesterday was fantastic. (for The film I saw yesterday was fantastic.)

Possessive determiners and pronouns, personal pronouns

1. Possessive determiners and pronouns are the same in Polish, hence:
   > *This book is my.
2. Possessive determiners are often dropped in Polish when it is clear from the context who the possessor is:
   > *I must do homework.
   > *Eat breakfast. (for Eat your breakfast.)
3. In general, there are considerable problems with subject and object personal pronouns, as well as possessive determiners and pronouns:
   > *I can't see his. (for I can't see him.)

Other determiners

Polish learners have a problem discriminating between *many/much*, *a few/a little*, etc., hence:

> *How many juice do you want?
> *I need a little apples.

The use of *some* and *any* (irrespective of their role) also causes confusion:

> *I haven't (some) oranges. (for I haven't got any oranges.)

Relative pronouns

Because the same relative pronoun który (= *which*) is used for humans, animals and inanimate objects, the following type of mistake is possible:

> *(The/A) Student which asked (the) teacher didn't know (the) answer.

Note also:

> *This is all what I want.

Countability, number and concord

1. The nouns *news, money, advice, information* and *furniture* are countable in Polish:
    **I have one advice for you.*
2. The Polish word for door (drzwi) exists only in the plural; life (życie) exists only in the singular:
    **The door(s) are open.* (for *The door is open.*)
    **People's life . . .*
3. Most Polish collective nouns are either unambiguously singular or plural (pronouns and verbs must be used accordingly). Therefore, sentences like *The government are . . .* sound odd to Polish learners, and they are much more likely to say *The government is . . .* Typical mistakes include:
    **(The) Police is looking for the criminal.*
    Note also that wszyscy (= everybody/everyone) requires a plural verb:
    **Everybody are here.*
4. The Polish equivalents of *how many, many, a few* require a singular verb. So do the equivalents of *a lot* and *half*, even when they refer to plural countable nouns:
    **How many is present?*
    **Half of them is absent.*

Gender

Polish singular nouns are masculine, feminine or neuter. Pronouns are used accordingly, hence mistakes like:
    *Look at the cow/mouse. *She is so big.*
    *'Where is my coat?' *'He is there.'*

Adjectives and adverbs

1. Adverbs are sometimes used in Polish where English requires adjectives, hence:
    **It looks/sounds beautifully.*
    **I feel terribly.*
2. A Polish attributive adjective can be used independently of the noun (or the pronoun *one* which has no Polish equivalent):
    **Give me (a/the) red.* (for *Give me the red one.*)
    **The most important is to finish.*

Prepositions

1. Polish learners have considerable difficulty with English prepositions, although most have rough Polish equivalents. There are, however, differences in usage, hence:
     in work/school (for *at work/school*)
     on university
     on the party
     on Christmas
     on the bottom/top
     near the table (for *at the table*)
     in TV/radio
     since ten days
     after ten days (for *in ten days*)
     typical for him
     better/bigger etc. *from*
     angry on
     marry with her
     arrive to
     before the museum (for *in front of the museum*)
     exam from mathematics
     good/bad from mathematics
     made from (for *made of* and *made with*)
     between the students (for *among the students*)
2. Problems also arise when Polish does not require a preposition:
     listen me/music
     explain me this / why you . . .
     repeat me this / why you . . .
3. Prepositions are often incorrectly added under the influence of Polish:
     go to home
     be in home
     discuss about this
     believe in this (for *believe this*)
     ride on a bicycle
     climb on a tree
     leave from
     in next/last week

Phrasal verbs

There are no phrasal verbs in Polish, so a Polish learner is more likely to say *return* than *give back*, *write* than *write down*, *cut* than *cut up*, *invent* than *make up*, *finish* than *use up*, *check* than *look up*, etc.

Vocabulary

1. There are a considerable number of words that are identical in Polish and English (*radio* – radio) or very similar (*alphabet* – alfabet). Most of these are either of Greek or Latin origin. There are also numerous loans from English (*sweater* – sweter). Naturally, this facilitates learning. It also results in mistakes, such as in the case of **parking* (Polish parking = *a car park*), **camping* (camping, kemping = *a camping site*) and **sleeping* (sleeping, sliping = *a sleeper*).
   For a list of some 'false friends', see the *Cambridge International Dictionary of English*.
2. Learners readily accept the fact that two or more Polish words have one English equivalent. A glass, for example, is either szklanka, used mainly for drinking tea, or kieliszek, for alcohol. (Since there is a considerable difference in size between the two, a doctor's recommendation to drink one or two glasses of red wine daily can be understood to mean double the prescribed amount.)
3. It is the opposite situation that causes most confusion, however. The following pairs of words are usually associated with one Polish equivalent: *clock/watch, house/home, finger/toe, politics/policy, job/work, this/that, these/those, so/such, yet/still, yet/already, say/tell, speak/talk, remember/remind, lend/borrow, learn/teach, look/watch, hear/listen, make/do, enjoy oneself/play, take/pass* (an exam), *Excuse me/Sorry*.
4. The English word *please* is often understood to be the exact equivalent of the Polish proszę. In fact proszę has a much wider range of usage: it is also used as an answer to *Thank you* (roughly *Not at all*), and can mean *Here you are, Pardon, Come in, please* or *Follow me, please*.
   *May I please you? (for *Come in/Follow me.*)
5. The expression *of course* tends to be misused:
   'Do you live here?' **'Yes, of course.'*
6. The Polish equivalent of *have* is used to talk about ages:
   *He has two years. (for *He is two years old.*)

Forms of address

Polish demands a certain degree of formality, therefore even adult learners find it difficult to address their teacher by his or her first name

Polish speakers

– even _you_ seems difficult for some. In Poland, unless people are well acquainted, they address one another using pan (_Mr_), pani (_Mrs_) and, sometimes, panna (_Miss_). This leads to a number of mistakes:

　*_Mr Adam, can I ask you something?_
　*_Please mister/Mrs. (for Excuse me.)_
Note also:
　*_A mister/Mrs is waiting for you._

A sample of written Polish with a word-for-word translation

Nie ma pisarza, który   by   nie myślał
No has writer, which [conditional particle] no thought [masculine]

o   sławie. Może   tylko w średniowieczu spotyka
about fame. Maybe only in middle ages   meet [impersonal]

się   bezimienne książki, których   autorzy, ukrywając
[reflexive particle] unnamed   books, (for) which authors, hiding

swoje   nazwisko, zwracają się   przy
my/your/his/her/our/their surname, turn   [reflexive particle] near

końcu dzieła z   modlitwą do Boga albo z   prośbą do czytelnika, by
end   work with prayer   to God or   with request to reader,   to

o   nich pamiętał   w kościele.
about them remembered [masculine] in church.

An idiomatic translation

There is no writer who would not think about fame. It is only in the Middle Ages, perhaps, that one comes across unnamed books, whose authors hide their names, and only near the end of their work, do they turn to God with a prayer or (turn) to the reader with a plea to remember them in church.

(from _Alchemia słowa_ by Jan Parandowski)

178

Farsi speakers

Lili and Martin Wilson

Distribution

IRAN, Afghanistan, Pakistan, Southern Russia, India.

Introduction

Farsi is an Indo-European language, which has been greatly influenced by Arabic. The alphabet of modern Farsi consists of 32 characters written in Arabic script, from right to left. This was adopted after the Arab conquest in the seventh century, at which time a great deal of Arabic vocabulary was also introduced, making Farsi an unusual blend of two very different origins and influences. Farsi speakers have difficulty in learning English, especially during the early stages, largely because of the unfamiliar Latin script.

Phonology

General

The Farsi and English phonological systems differ in their range of sounds, as well as in their stress and intonation patterns. Farsi has only eleven vowels and diphthongs to 32 consonants, while English has 22 vowels and diphthongs to 24 consonants. Farsi speakers, therefore, have great difficulty in perceiving and articulating the full range of English vowels and diphthongs. In addition, there are five English consonant phonemes that do not have near equivalents in Farsi.

Farsi speakers

Vowels

iː	ɪ	e	æ	eɪ	aɪ	ɔɪ
ɑː	ɒ	ɔː	ʊ	aʊ	əʊ	ɪə
uː	ʌ	ɜː	ə	eə	ʊə	aɪə / aʊə

Shaded phonemes have equivalents or near equivalents in Farsi, and should therefore be perceived and articulated without great difficulty, although some confusions may still arise. Unshaded phonemes may cause problems. For detailed comments, see below.

The most common pure vowel errors are likely to be:
1. /ɪ/ is often pronounced as /iː/: *sheep* for *ship*.
2. /ʌ/ is often pronounced as /ɑː/: *cart* for *cut*.
3. /æ/ is often pronounced as /e/: *bed* for *bad*.
4. /ʊ/ is often pronounced as /uː/: *fool* for *full*.
5. /ə/ is often pronounced as a stressed vowel related to its orthographic form.
6. /ɔː/ is often pronounced rather like /ɒ/: *cot* for *caught*.
7. /ɜː/ often becomes /e/ + /r/.

With diphthongs the problems are accentuated and in particular the following are likely to cause special difficulty:
8. /aʊ/ is often pronounced as a sound approaching /ɑː/.
9. /eə/ is often pronounced as /e/ + /r/.
10. /əʊ/ is often pronounced closer to /ɒ/.
11. /ʊə/ is often pronounced as /uː/.

Consonants

p	b	f	v	θ	ð	t	d
s	z	ʃ	ʒ	tʃ	dʒ	k	g
m	n	ŋ	l	r	j	w	h

Shaded phonemes have equivalents or near equivalents in Farsi, and should therefore be perceived and articulated without great difficulty, although some confusions may still arise. Unshaded phonemes may cause problems. For detailed comments, see below.

1. /ð/ and /θ/ tend to be confused or pronounced as /t/: *ten* for *then*; *tinker* for *thinker*.
2. /ŋ/ may be pronounced as two separate phonemes, /n/ and /g/, because of its orthographic form.
3. /w/ and /v/: although /v/ has a near equivalent in Farsi, the two phonemes tend to be confused.
4. /r/ is a weak roll or tap in Farsi and many learners have great difficulty in producing the English /r/.
5. /l/ exists in Farsi as the 'clear' /l/ (as in *leaf*), but there is no equivalent of the 'dark' /l/ (as in *feel*), and learners are likely to have problems with this.

Consonant clusters

Consonant clusters do not occur within single syllables in Farsi, and Farsi speakers therefore tend to add a short vowel, either before or in the middle of the various English clusters. Examples of initial two-segment clusters that cause difficulty are *bl, fl, pr, pl, gr, gl, thr, thw, sp, st*.

> 'perice' for *price*
> 'pelace' for *place*
> 'geround' for *ground*
> 'gelue' for *glue*

The intrusive vowel in initial position usually approximates to the phoneme /e/, so *start* becomes 'estart'.

With initial three-segment clusters the problem becomes greater. The intrusive /e/ is particularly common before clusters beginning with /s/. Clusters such as *spl, spr, str, skr* in initial position produce pronunciations such as:

> 'esperay' for *spray*
> 'esteraight' for *straight*
> 'esceream' for *scream*

Final consonant clusters are also likely to cause problems, with learners again inserting an /e/:

> 'promptes' for *prompts*
> 'warmeth' for *warmth*

Farsi speakers

Influence of spelling on pronunciation

As there are no direct links between Farsi and English spelling (apart from a few transliterations, such as *stainless steel*), the Farsi speaker has no previously known orthographic patterns which are likely to interfere with his or her pronunciation. However, spelling in Farsi is more or less phonetic, except for the omission of short vowels, and, as a result, Farsi speakers tend to associate particular letters with particular sounds. This can cause problems with reading aloud and when words are initially encountered only in their written form. In particular Farsi speakers are likely to have difficulty with phonemes which have a wide variety of orthographic representations. For example, the phoneme /iː/, which has a single orthographic form in Farsi, can have any of the following forms in English: *ee, e, ea, ie, ei, ey, i* or *ay* (as in *quay*).

It is particularly hard for Farsi speakers to recognise that the post-vocalic *r* is not a consonant in standard British English, but usually indicates a lengthening of the vowel sound.

Stress

In Farsi stress is highly predictable, and generally falls on the final syllable of a word. Thus learners have great difficulty in mastering the unpredictable stress patterns of English. Particular problems occur when stress alters meaning, as in *'content* and *con'tent*. Weak forms also cause considerable problems. There is no equivalent of a weak form in Farsi, and vowels in unstressed syllables lose neither quantity nor quality. So learners are likely to retain the full value of, say, the *a* in *can*, even in an unstressed position. It follows that they will also have problems in perceiving weak forms in speech.

Intonation

Farsi sentences are divided into a series of tone groups, with each tone group containing one prominent stressed syllable, which makes a change of tone direction. Intonation groups can be divided into 'suspensive' (with more to follow), and 'final'. The basic final patterns are similar to those used in English, with a fall typical for a completed statement, a rise for a *yes/no* question, and a fall when an interrogative word is used. For the suspensive tone groups there is a rise to high tone on the stressed syllable, which is maintained to the end of the tone group. When carried over into English, some of these intonation patterns can produce an unusual high-pitched 'whining' effect, which is disconcerting.

In general, Farsi-speaking students do not have major difficulties with the main intonation patterns, although some of the more unusual patterns which imply distinctive attitudes and meanings present difficulties. Some students will tend to adopt a chanting tone when reading aloud, with a lack of clearly indicated stress, and little or no tonal variation.

Juncture

Farsi speakers often have similar problems with English juncture to those they have with consonant clusters. Therefore, with a word boundary such as in *next street*, they will often insert an extra /e/ in several places, and produce something like *'neksetestreet'*.

In Farsi, words are spoken without assimilation (phonetic change) in juncture, so whenever this occurs in English, as in *Would you* /wʊdʒə/, it is likely to cause difficulties.

Orthography and punctuation

As stated above, Farsi is written in Arabic script, and this is completely different from the Latin script of English. It is written from right to left with the letters joining each other according to very definite rules. Farsi students of English usually have to learn a completely new alphabet and new way of writing. Some short vowels are left out in normal Farsi orthography and this can lead to mistakes in English. There are no capital letters in Farsi and their use in English is difficult for learners to master. Beginners are also likely to have problems in the following areas:
1. Letters with mirror images, e.g. *b* and *d*, *p* and *q*.
2. Combinations of letters that could be confused if read from right to left, e.g. *tow* and *two*; *pot* and *top*; *form* and *from*.

Spelling is invariably phonetic in Farsi, and students' written English tends to be the same.

Farsi numbers, although Arabic, are different from those used in English. They are, however, written from left to right, and normally cause relatively few problems.

Punctuation

Until the late nineteenth century punctuation was little used in Farsi, but during the last hundred years, a system similar to that used in

Farsi speakers

English has been adopted. There is, however, a greater degree of freedom in the use of commas and question marks. The question mark is reversed, ؟, and the comma is inverted, ،. Full stops are used approximately as in English, but quotation marks are rarely used, and then not in a set way.

Generally there is less punctuation in Farsi, and Farsi writers have a tendency to join sentences together more with conjunctions such as *and* and *but*.

Paragraphing is a recent introduction, and indentation or separation usually only occurs in newspapers.

Grammar

General

As Farsi is an Indo-European language, it is similar in many ways to English. There are, however, some areas that are very different from English, and these can cause considerable interference for the Farsi speaker learning English.

Word order in Farsi is fundamentally different from English and will cause difficulties in the early stages. Adjectives always follow their nouns; verbs are usually placed at the end of a sentence.

Yesterday girl beautiful (I) saw.

Questions

The auxiliary *do* has no equivalent in Farsi. *Yes/no* questions in formal Farsi are signalled by a special question word, aya, or by use of a rising tone. Farsi speakers, therefore, tend to overuse questions marked only by intonation and, more seriously, omit the auxiliary when it is obligatory:

When you came to England?

Negatives

In Farsi both regular and irregular verbs are conjugated in such a way that the first/second/third person verb endings become part of the verb. Therefore it is possible to make a statement negative merely by prefixing the verb (both past and present tenses) with na. *Not* may well be treated in the same way:

She not eat supper. (for *She doesn't eat supper* or *She didn't eat supper.*)

184

Auxiliaries

In Farsi the equivalent of the auxiliary *to be* is sometimes added to nouns as a suffix instead of being used in its full form. Therefore Farsi speakers will sometimes omit it in English:

She (a) teacher. (for *She is a teacher.*)

Although *to have* exists as an auxiliary verb in Farsi, it is used only in a structure equivalent to the English progressive. Its use with the English present and past perfect tenses in statements, questions, and negatives may cause some difficulties. *I have bought my ticket*, translated literally into Farsi, means *I am buying my ticket.*

Special confusion – Chera (= Why not?)

Farsi has a special positive response to a negative question. This can loosely be translated as *Why not?* When this is used in English, as it often is by Farsi speakers, it sounds unintentionally aggressive:

'*Aren't you going out tonight?*' *'*Why not?*'

It is essential to explain that this is not an acceptable reply in English.

Question tags

Farsi does not possess a wide range of question tags. Na (= *No*) has to serve in nearly all situations. Students, therefore, find all question tags extremely complex:

He said he was coming, no? (for *He said he was coming, didn't he?*)

You said you would pay me back, no? (for *You said you would pay me back, didn't you?*)

Time, tense, and aspect

A. Past time

1. *Simple past and present perfect*

In Farsi the simple past tense is equivalent to both present perfect and simple past tenses in English. Therefore a Farsi speaker may sometimes use the wrong tense:

I bought my ticket. (for *I have bought my ticket.*)

I saw 'Star Wars'. (for *I have seen 'Star Wars'.*)

I lost my purse. Did you see it?

2. *Past progressive*
The past progressive tense in Farsi is formed with the equivalent of *to have*, and this leads Farsi speakers to produce:
>*When I arrived, he had eating his dinner. (for When I arrived, he was eating his dinner.)*

B. Reported speech

In Farsi, speech is usually reported directly in the form in which it was spoken. The complex rules of reported speech governing tenses in English can therefore cause confusion. This may lead the Farsi speaker to produce:
>*He said I am feeling ill. (for He said he was feeling ill.)*

Questions and requests are also reported directly and so the Farsi speaker might produce:
>*He asked are you going home. (for He asked if I was going home.)*

As quotation marks are very rarely used in Farsi, when reporting direct speech in English, the Farsi learner might produce:
>*He said I am ill. (for He said: 'I am ill.')*

C. Present and future tenses

The present tense in Farsi is used for a variety of functions:
1. It is used in the same way as the English present progressive for an action taking place in the present. This might lead the Farsi speaker to produce:
>*He reads book. (for He is reading a book.)*
2. It is used for an action beginning in the past and still continuing, which might lead the Farsi speaker to produce:
>*I live here for two years. (for I have lived here for two years.)*
3. It is used for the future, which may cause a confusion of the future and simple present in English and lead to the Farsi speaker producing:
>*He comes next week. (for He will come next week.)*

The various functions of the present tense in Farsi thus lead students writing in English to confuse the uses of the present progressive, present perfect, and to some extent future tenses.

There is also a present progressive tense, formed with the equivalent of *to have*, which has a meaning similar to the English present progressive; this might lead the Farsi speaker to produce:
>*He has walk. (for He is walking.)*

There is a general present which is similar to the English simple present, used to describe general truths; this is therefore not likely to lead to confusion.

There is also a future tense in Farsi, formed with an auxiliary equivalent to *to want*. This is very formal – it is never used in speech, and only rarely in modern writing – but it may lead the Farsi learner to produce:

> *I want go tomorrow. (for *I shall go tomorrow.*)

Modal verbs

Modal verbs do not work in the same way in Farsi as in English. In Farsi both the equivalent of *can* and the associated main verb are inflected, and this may be carried over into English.

> *I could went.

Although the equivalent of *must* in Farsi is not inflected, one word is used both for present and past tenses. This may lead the Farsi speaker writing in English to produce:

> *Yesterday I must went to the bank. (for *Yesterday I had to go to the bank.*)

It is however in the use of modals that the real difficulty arises. Farsi does not have the range of meanings expressed through modals in English, and most of them will cause problems. For example, the range of different meanings expressed by *must, have to, ought to, need to*, and *should* in English is expressed by one modal verb in Farsi, with the differences in the meaning being conveyed by additional phrases or other verbs. So Farsi speakers may have problems with the differences between the English modals, particularly between *should* and *must*.

Non-finite forms

There is no gerund form in Farsi, and the infinitive form is normally used in its place. Where distinctions are required in English, Farsi speakers find difficulties:

> *Instead to fight, they danced.

Word order

In Farsi word order in sentences usually follows the pattern: subject, object, verb. This may lead to confusion. Moreover, adjectives normally follow the noun they modify, which may lead Farsi speakers to produce:

> *I girl young saw. (for *I saw a young girl.*)

Furthermore, in Farsi adverbs of time are usually placed between subject and object, which could lead to confusion when writing in English:

>   *I yesterday visited him.* (for *Yesterday I visited him.*)

The active and passive voices

In Farsi there are passive forms for all tenses, but they are not used as widely as they are in English. Passive voice in Farsi is mainly formed by either omitting the personal pronoun in the third person plural (as in Farsi verb inflection indicates the agent) or by adding the Farsi equivalent of *to become* to the past participle of the passive verb. Thus Farsi speakers may produce:

>   *It becomes built.* (for *It is built.*)

Articles

The definite and indefinite articles have no equivalent in Farsi. Suffixes are added to nouns to indicate whether they are definite or indefinite. The system is quite different from English and Farsi speakers have considerable difficulty with all areas of article use. On the one hand Farsi speakers tend to omit articles before nouns when it is necessary to put one:

>   *His father is postman.*
>   *He plays piano.*
>   *Tiger is dangerous.*
>   *English people always talk about weather.*
>   *Irish are very friendly.*
>   *Shall we to cinema?*
>   *I listen to radio.*
>   *He is best.* (for *He is the best.*)

On the other hand Farsi speakers may add articles to nouns when they should be omitted:

>   *I go to the school every day.* (for *I go to school every day.*)
>   *Most of the people think . . .* (for *Most people think . . .*)
>   *The rocket flew into the space.*
>   *Criminals are a danger to the society.*
>   *In spring the nature is beautiful.*

Adjectives and adverbs

Adjectives and adverbs are usually used in similar ways in Farsi and there is no set pattern for forming adverbs from adjectives. In many cases the same word is used both as an adjective and an adverb. When a word can only be used as an adjective, (like the Farsi word for *dangerous*) then it is necessary to use a phrase (*'in a dangerous way'*) as its adverbial equivalent. Therefore Farsi speakers are likely to confuse adjectives and adverbs in both form and meaning, and to use rather awkward adverbial phrases.

Comparatives and superlatives

Comparatives and superlatives are always formed by the addition of a suffix, so the two different methods used in English are very confusing to the Farsi speaker. Thus Farsi learners when writing English may produce:
> *He is more better. (for He is better.)
> *This road is dangerouser than that one.

The preposition used with comparatives in Farsi is the equivalent of *from*, thus Farsi speakers may produce:
> *His feet are smaller from mine. (for His feet are smaller than mine.)

The definite article before the superlative may also be omitted, leading Farsi speakers to produce:
> *One of best musicians . . . (for One of the best musicians . . .)

Gender and number

In Farsi there is no *he/she* gender distinction, a single pronoun being used for both. This is likely to lead to regular errors, even at quite advanced levels:
> *My mother is a dentist. He works in London.

Plurals in general do not cause Farsi speakers major difficulties. However, nouns in Farsi do not take plural forms when used with numbers and this is likely to carry over into English:
> *I saw two man.
> *Ten ship sailed by.

Prepositions

In Farsi, prepositions are frequently used after verbs, but often they are different from the ones used in English. Farsi speakers tend to translate these prepositions directly into English:
> *He climbed from the hill. (for He climbed up the hill.)

189

> *She threw it out from the window.
> *I travelled there with car.

Phrasal verbs

Phrasal verbs do not exist in Farsi, and learners find them very confusing. Two difficulties arise:
1. The difficulty of accepting that the addition of a particle can totally change the meaning of a verb, as in *to **run up** a skirt* (i.e. to make one quickly).
2. The fact that the verb can be separated from the particle by its object. One error that frequently results is the omission of the particle:
   > *He cannot do his buttons.
   > *I put my coat.

Subordinate clauses

A. Relative

There is only one relative pronoun in Farsi and this is used for humans, animals, and inanimate objects. It is also used when the pronoun is the subject or the object of the verb, or when a possessive is required. The selection of the correct relative pronoun in English, therefore, causes serious problems.
> *The man which was here . . .

The object pronoun in a relative clause, which is omitted in English, is included in Farsi:
> *The man, which I saw him . . .
> *The book, which I gave it to you . . .

In Farsi the indefinite suffix is used with the noun that comes before the relative pronoun, which might lead Farsi speakers to produce:
> *A man who I saw . . . (for *The man who I saw . . .*)

In Farsi prepositions always appear at the beginning of the relative clause, thus making structures like *Who did you buy it for?* difficult for students, who even in informal situations tend to produce the more formal structure: *For whom did you buy it?*

B. Conditional

Conditional sentences referring to the present and future are formed essentially in the same way in Farsi and English. The expression of the past (or Type 3) conditional is different. In Farsi the past tense is used in the main clause, giving rise to:

> *If I had finished my work, I was going to the party.* (for *If I had finished my work, I would have gone to the party.*)

C. Concession

In Farsi, the equivalents of *although* and *but* can be used in the same sentence. This use is frequently carried over into English:

> *Although he had no money, but he travelled to America.*

D. Conjunctions

Conjunctions are used much more frequently in Farsi than in English, particularly at the beginning of sentences. As the most commonly used conjunction in Farsi is *and*, speakers have a tendency to join many clauses together, usually with a string of *ands*.

Vocabulary

Although Farsi is an Indo-European language, there are few similarities between English and Farsi vocabulary, with only a few high-frequency words such as the equivalents of *mother* and *brother* showing their common Indo-European origins. On the other hand, Farsi contains many vocabulary items with Arabic roots. The rest nearly all have old Persian or Pahlavi roots.

The advent of modern technology has brought in a number of scientific and technical words of European origin, such as *radio*, *television* and *helicopter*, many of which are used internationally; but their pronunciation has been adapted to Farsi patterns, and they produce their own kind of interference problems, e.g. *radio* pronounced '*rahdioo*'. In the 1970s there was an attempt by the government to 'Persianise' all foreign technical words, but this met with only limited success. After the Islamic revolution, however, a more successful attempt was made to translate all the Western terms into Farsi.

Acquiring English vocabulary is, therefore, much more difficult for a Farsi speaker than, for example, a European student, and teachers must not expect the same rate of progress. It cannot be assumed either that a large amount of vocabulary will be absorbed naturally through reading or everyday conversation. In particular, Farsi students tend to learn large quantities of vocabulary by heart through lists of synonyms, but find it very hard to understand or use more than a fraction of this language accurately.

Compound nouns in Farsi are frequently translated directly into English, giving rise to strange errors:
a work house (kar khane – lit. *house of work*) = *a factory*
a book house (ketab khane – lit. *house of books*) = *a library*

False friends

As there are few similarities between Farsi and English vocabulary, there are relatively few false friends. Most problems arise from words which have been borrowed by Farsi and now have different meanings. When such words are encountered in English, they are assumed to have the same meaning as in Farsi:
lastik = *tyre*, not *elastic*
machin = *car*, not *machine*
nylon = *plastic bag*, not *nylon*
chips = *crisps* (as in US English), not *chips*
estanless = *stainless steel*

Culture

Almost all Farsi-speaking learners of English will be Iranian. The Iranian education system is extremely formal, and lays great emphasis on the value of formal literary language and rote learning. As a result, it is often difficult to persuade Iranian students to accept the importance of mastering colloquial spoken forms, and of writing in a simple, clear style.

Most Iranians expect the teacher to be an authoritarian figure, and they expect to be tested or 'quizzed' regularly. Examinations are taken very seriously, and the grades and marked scripts are scrutinised with great care. Iranians, however, are natural communicators, as Iranian society places great importance on the art of conversation. Introduced with care, communicative methodology will lead to a rapid development of oral/aural skills, particularly with young learners. Nevertheless, it is prudent to take advantage of Iranian students' willingness to accept formal methods, such as choral drilling, rote learning, and regular testing, rather than to insist on a totally communicative approach. An exclusively communicative methodology may cause students to feel that a course is not really 'serious'.

Study in Britain may involve a cultural as well as an educational shock. Iranians brought up in post-Islamic revolutionary Iran may well find the changes very difficult to accept. They may well come with an anti-Western attitude, often with a strong vein of Islamic fundamentalism.

Those reacting against Western mores may show a degree of hostility to many EFL materials, with their emphasis on boy/girl relationships, fashion, and the consumption of alcoholic beverages. Hostility to women teachers, however, is unlikely.

A sample of written Farsi

صدها سال است که مردم فارسی‌زبان همواره دیوان حافظ را می‌خوانند و از آن لذت می‌برند و این یادگار گرانبهای لسان‌الغیب را عزیز و گرامی می‌شمارند.

«حافظ» دارای این خصلت دوگانه است که در عین قالب بودن برای محققین و نویسندگان و ادبا و دانشمندان، سخت مورد علاقه و دلبستگی همگان هم است.

A direct transliteration

Sadhaa saal ast ke mardome Farsizabaan hamvare divane Haafez raa mikhaanand va az aan lezzat mibarand va in iaadegaare geraanbaghaaie lesanalgheib raa aziz va geraami mishemaarand.

'Haafez' daaraaie in kheslate dogaaneh ast ke dar eine gdaaleb boudan baraaie mohagheghin va nevisandegaan va odabaa va daaneshmandaan, sakht morede alaagheh va delbastegie hamegaan ham hast.

A word-for-word translation

Hundreds year is that people Farsi language always anthology Hafez read and from that enjoy and this heritage precious fortune teller love and respect . . .

'Hafez' has this virtue dual is that at the same time interesting being for students of literature and writers and literary critics and scientists, hard liked and loved general public also.

Farsi speakers

An idiomatic translation

For hundreds of years Farsi speakers have enjoyed reading Hafez's anthology, respecting and loving the precious heritage of this 'fortune teller' . . .

Hafez has the dual virtue that at the same time as he is interesting to students of literature, writers, literary critics and scientists, he is popular with and loved by the general public.

(From *Hafez's Anthology* edited by A. Bagheri)

Handwriting difficulties: a sample written by a Farsi-speaking student

The English language is the most important language in the world. and everyone who want to find a better job must learning English.
I want to learning English because I want to stady in English language University. Now I can't speak and understand English but when I wand to go to university I must know the meaning of the English word That I must use in university

Arabic speakers

Bernard Smith

Distribution

ALGERIA, BAHRAIN, EGYPT, IRAQ, JORDAN, KUWAIT, LEBANON, LIBYA, MOROCCO, OMAN, PALESTINE, QATAR, SAUDI ARABIA, SUDAN, SYRIA, TUNISIA, UNITED ARAB EMIRATES, YEMEN REPUBLIC.

Arabic is a second major language in Chad, Israel, Mauritania, Djibouti, Bangladesh; also in Azerbaijan, Uzbekistan, Turkmenistan, Tajikistan, Kazakhstan, Kyrgyzstan and Chechnya.

In addition, Arabic being the language of the Koran, the holy word of Islam, all Muslims of whatever nationality are to some extent familiar with Arabic, can recite extensively in it, and are therefore influenced by it in their ideas of how language works. Islam has a significant following in Senegal, Mali, Niger, Nigeria, Guinea, Somali Republic, Kenya, Iran, Afghanistan, Pakistan, Malaysia, Indonesia, Brunei, the Philippines, northern China, Mongolia and Turkey, approximately 400,000,000 people in all, and increasing.

Introduction

Arabic is a Semitic language, having a grammatical system similar to Assyrian, Aramaic, Hebrew and Ethiopian. There is a universal 'pan-Arabic' language, which is taught in schools, used by the mass media in all Arab countries, and for all communications of an official nature. Within each country, often in quite small areas, a wide variety of colloquial dialects have developed, differing one from another not only in pronunciation, but also in common lexical items and, to some extent, in structure. The differences from country to country are more marked than, say, differences between UK, US and Australian English.

Phonology

General

The Arabic and English phonological systems are very different, not only in the range of sounds used, but in the emphasis placed on vowels and consonants in expressing meaning. While English has 22 vowels and diphthongs to 24 consonants, Arabic has only eight vowels and diphthongs (three short, three long and two diphthongs) to 32 consonants.

The three short vowels in Arabic have very little significance: they are almost allophonic. They are not even written in the script. It is the consonants and long vowels and diphthongs which give meaning. Arabic speakers tend, therefore, to gloss over and confuse English short vowel sounds, while unduly emphasising consonants, avoiding elisions and shortened forms.

Among the features of Arabic which give rise to an 'Arabic accent' in English are:
– More energetic articulation than English, with more stressed syllables, but fewer clearly articulated vowels, giving a dull, staccato 'jabber' effect.
– The use of glottal stops before initial vowels, a common feature of Arabic, thus breaking up the natural catenations of English.
– A general reluctance to omit consonants, once the written form is known, e.g. /klaɪmbed/ for *climbed*.

Vowels

iː	ɪ	e	æ	eɪ	aɪ	ɔɪ
ɑː	ɒ	ɔː	ʊ	aʊ	əʊ	ɪə
uː	ʌ	ɜː	ə	eə	ʊə	aɪə / aʊə

Shaded phonemes have equivalents or near equivalents in Arabic and should therefore be perceived and articulated without great difficulty, although some confusions may still arise. Unshaded phonemes may cause problems. For detailed comments, see below.

While virtually all vowels may cause problems, the following are the most common confusions:
1. /ɪ/ and /e/ are often confused: *bit* for *bet*.
2. /ɒ/ and /ɔː/ are often confused: *cot* for *caught*.
3. Diphthongs /eɪ/ and /əʊ/ are usually pronounced rather short, and are confused with /e/ and /ɒ/: *red* for *raid*; *hop* for *hope*.

196

Consonants

p	b	f	v	θ	ð	t	d
s	z	ʃ	ʒ	tʃ	dʒ	k	g
m	n	ŋ	l	r	j	w	h

Shaded phonemes have equivalents or near equivalents in Arabic and should therefore be perceived and articulated without great difficulty, although some confusions may still arise. Unshaded phonemes may cause problems. For detailed comments, see below.

1. Arabic has only one letter in the /g/–/dʒ/ area, which is pronounced as /g/ in some regions, notably Egypt, and as /dʒ/ in others. Arabic speakers tend, therefore, to pronounce an English *g*, and sometimes even a *j*, in all positions according to their local dialects.
2. /tʃ/ as a phoneme is found only in a few dialects, but the sound occurs naturally in all dialects in junctures of /t/ and /ʃ/.
3. There are two approximations to the English /h/ in Arabic. The commoner of them is an unvoiced, harsh aspiration; Arabic speakers tend therefore to pronounce an English /h/ rather harshly.
4. /r/ is a voiced flap, very unlike the RP /r/. Arabic speakers commonly overpronounce the post-vocalic *r*, as in *car park*.
5. /p/ and /b/ are allophonic and tend to be used rather randomly:
   I baid ten bence for a bicture of Pig Pen.
6. /v/ and /f/ are allophonic, and are usually both pronounced as /f/.
   It is a fery nice fillage.
7. /g/ and /k/ are often confused, especially by those Arabs whose dialects do not include the phoneme /g/. Pairs like *goat/coat* and *bag/back* cause difficulty.
8. Although /θ/ and /ð/ occur in literary Arabic, most dialects pronounce them as /t/ and /d/ respectively. The same tends to happen in students' English.
   I tink dat dey are brudders.
9. The phoneme /ŋ/ is usually pronounced as /n/ or /ng/, or even /nk/.

Consonant clusters

The range of consonant clusters occurring in English is much wider than in Arabic. Initial two-segment clusters not occurring in Arabic include:

pr, pl, gr, gl, thr, thw, sp. Initial three-segment clusters do not occur in Arabic at all, e.g.: *spr, skr, str, spl.* In all of the above cases there is a tendency among Arabic speakers to insert short vowels to 'assist' pronunciation:

> *'perice'* or *'pirice'* for *price*
> *'ispring'* or *'sipring'* for *spring*

The range of final clusters is also much smaller in Arabic. Of the 78 three-segment clusters and fourteen four-segment clusters occurring finally in English, *none* occurs in Arabic. Arabic speakers tend again to insert short vowels.

> *'arrangid'* for *arranged*
> *'monthiz'* for *months*
> *'neckist'* for *next*

Teachers will meet innumerable examples of such pronunciations, which also carry over into the spelling of such words in Arab students' written English.

Note: For a detailed comparative analysis of English and Arabic consonant clusters (and much other useful information) see *The Teaching of English to Arab Students* by Raja T. Nasr (Longman, 1963).

Influence of English spelling on pronunciation

While there are no similarities between the Arabic and English writing systems, Arabic spelling within its own system is simple and virtually phonetic. Arabic speakers tend, therefore, to attempt to pronounce English words phonetically. Add to this the reverence for consonants, and you get severe pronunciation problems caused by the influence of the written form:

> *'istobbid'* for *stopped*
> *'forigen'* for *foreign*

Rhythm and stress

Arabic is a stress-timed language, and word stress in particular is predictable and regular. Arabic speakers, therefore, have problems grasping the unpredictable nature of English word stress. The idea that stress can alter meaning, as in *a toy 'factory* and *a 'toy factory*, or *con'vict* (verb) and *'convict* (noun) is completely strange.

Phrase and sentence rhythms are similar in the two languages, and should cause few problems. Primary stresses occur more frequently in Arabic, and unstressed syllables are pronounced more clearly, with neutral vowels, but not 'swallowed' as in English. Arabs reading English aloud will often avoid contracted forms and elisions, and read with a rather heavy staccato rhythm.

Intonation

Intonation patterns in Arabic are similar to those of English in contour and meaning. Questions, suggestions and offers are marked much more frequently by a rising tune than by any structural markers, and this is carried over into English.

When reading aloud, however, as opposed to conversing, the Arabic speaker tends to intone or chant, reducing intonation to a low fall at the ends of phrases and sentences.

Juncture

As the glottal stop is a common phoneme in Arabic, and few words begin with a vowel, there is resistance in speaking English to linking a final consonant with a following initial vowel.

Junctures producing consonant clusters will cause problems, as described under the section 'Consonant clusters'. A juncture such as *next spring* produces a number of extra vowels.

The many instances of phonetic change in English through the juncture of certain phonemes, e.g. /t/ + /j/ as in *what you need* /wɒtʃuː niːd/, or /d/ and /j/ as in *Did you see him?* /dɪdʒuː siː hɪm/ are resisted strongly by Arabic speakers, who see any loss of or change in consonant pronunciation as a serious threat to communication.

Orthography and punctuation

Arabic orthography is a cursive system, running from right to left. Only consonants and long vowels are written. There is no upper and lower case distinction, nor can the isolated forms of letters normally be juxtaposed to form words.

Arabic speakers must, therefore, learn an entirely new alphabet for English, including a capital letter system; and then master its rather unconventional spelling patterns. All aspects of writing in English cause major problems for Arabic speakers, and they should not be expected to cope with reading or writing at the same level or pace as European students who are at a similar level of proficiency in oral English.

Typical problems are:
– Misreading letters with 'mirror' shapes, e.g. *p* and *q*; *d* and *b*.

– Misreading letters within words by right to left eye movements, e.g. *form* for *from*; *'twon'* for *town*. These errors occur in the writing of Arab students, too, of course.
– Malformation of individual letters, owing to insufficient early training, or the development of an idiosyncratic writing system. This is most usually seen with capital letters (often omitted), with the letters *o, a, t, d, g,* and the cursive linking of almost any letters. Many adult Arabs continue to print in English rather than attempt cursive script.

The numerals used in Arab countries are different from the 'Arabic' numerals used in Europe, though they are written from left to right. Reading and pronouncing numbers is a major problem.

Punctuation

Arabic punctuation is now similar to western style punctuation, though some of the symbols are inverted or reversed, e.g. ؟ for ?, and ، for ,.

The use of full stops and commas is much freer than in English, and it is common to begin each new sentence with the equivalent of *And* or *So*. Connected writing in English tends therefore to contain long, loose sentences, linked by commas and *and*s.

Grammar

General

As Arabic is a Semitic language, its grammatical structure is very different from that of Indo-European languages. There are, therefore, far fewer areas of facilitation, and far greater areas of interference. This must be borne in mind when Arabic speakers are mixed with, say, European students.

The basis of the Arabic language is the three-consonant root. A notion such as *writing, cooking,* or *eating* is represented by three consonants in a particular order. All verb forms, nouns, adjectives, participles, etc. are then formed by putting these three root consonants into fixed patterns, modified sometimes by simple prefixes and suffixes.

Root	/k/ /t/ /b/	(= *writing*)
A person who does this for a living	kattaab	(= *a writer*)
Passive participle	maktoob	(= *written* or *a letter*)
Present tense	yaktubuh	(= *he writes it*)

Root	/dʒ/ /r/ /h/	(= *wounding* or *cutting*)
A person who does this for a living	djarraah	(= *a surgeon*)
Passive participle	majrooh	(= *wounded* or *a battle casualty*)
Present tense	yajruhuh	(= *he wounds/cuts him*)

There are over 50 patterns, and by no means all forms are found for each root, but this is the structural basis of the language.

It follows that Arabic speakers have great difficulty in grasping the confusing range of patterns for all words in English: that nouns, verbs, and adjectives follow no regular patterns to distinguish one from another, and may, indeed, have the same orthographic form. Such regularities of morphology as English has, particularly in the area of affixes, will be readily grasped by Arabic speakers, e.g. *-ing, -able, un-*, etc.

Word order

In principle the Arabic sentence places the verb first, followed by the subject. This convention is followed more in writing than in speech, especially the better style of writing, and may carry over into English writing:

*Decided the minister yesterday to visit the school.

Questions and negatives; auxiliaries

The auxiliary *do* has no equivalent in Arabic. Where no specific question word is used, a question is marked only by its rising intonation:

*When you went to London?
You like coffee?

Note that the Arabic for *where?* is wayn?, which is inevitably confused with *when?*. Negatives are formed by putting a particle (laa or maa) before the verb:

*He not play football.

To be

There is no verb *to be* in Arabic in the present tense. The copula (*am, is, are*) is not expressed. It is, therefore, commonly omitted in English by Arabic speakers, particularly in the present progressive verb forms:

Arabic speakers

> * *He teacher.*
> * *The boy tall.*
> * *He going to school.*

Pronouns

Arabic verb forms incorporate the personal pronouns, subject and object, as prefixes and suffixes. It is common to have them repeated in English as part of the verb:

> * *John he works there.*

Time, tense, and aspect

A. Past time

1. Arabic has a past, or perfect tense, which signifies an action completed at the time of speaking. There is, therefore, in colloquial Arabic, no distinction drawn between what in English would be a simple past or a present perfect verb:

   > * *I lost my camera. Did you see it?*

2. There is a past perfect tense, used approximately as in English, formed by the past tense of the verb *to be*, followed by the past tense verb (*he was he ate = he had eaten*):

   > * *He was ate his dinner when I came.* (for *He had eaten his dinner when I came.*)

3. There is a past progressive tense formed by the past tense of the verb *to be* followed by the present tense verb (*he was he eats = he was eating*).

   > * *He was eat his dinner when I came.* (for *He was eating his dinner when I came.*)

4. In reported speech Arabic tends to use the tense of the original speech, not the past tense conventions of English.

   > * *He said he (is) going to London.*

   The use of direct speech is more common, giving rise to such errors as:

   > * *He told me I am* (for *he was*) *going to London.*
   > * *He said me she will meet me tomorrow.*

B. Present time

1. Arabic has a simple present tense form, which signifies an action unfinished at the time of speaking. It covers the areas of the English

simple and progressive present tenses, including their use to refer to future time. The lack of a present tense of the verb *to be*, coupled with this single present tense, causes a wide range of error in present tenses in English:

He go with me now / every day.
He going with me now / every day.
He is go with me now / every day.
What you do?
When you come / coming back?

2. This present tense also refers to duration of time up to the time of speaking, expressed in English by the present perfect:

I learn / I learning English two years now.

3. This present tense is also used as a subjunctive after *that* for subordinate clauses, a very common pattern in Arabic, which only occasionally overlaps with English usage:

He wants that he go with me.
It was necessary that he goes to the office.
(*)*It is impossible that he stay here.*

4. With a few verbs of movement, a present participle pattern (literally *going, walking*, etc.) is used (without a copula) to express movement happening at the time of speaking or in the near future. This approximates in a limited way to a present progressive tense, and Arabic speakers use it easily, though omitting the copula.

Where you going tomorrow?
I going to London.

C. Future time

1. There is no future tense form in Arabic. As often happens in English, a present tense form is used to refer to the future.

2. Various future-indicating particles are used in colloquial and pan-Arabic to indicate a reference to the future. They are placed before the present tense verb and, thus, approximate to the English use of *will* and *shall*.

Modal verbs

There are no modal verbs in Arabic. Their function is performed by normal verbs, often impersonal, or prepositions followed by a subjunctive (present) tense:

I can go: *I can that I go.*
           From the possible that I go.
I must go: *From the necessary that I go.*

> **On me that I go.*
> *I may go: *From the possible that I go.*

Arabic speakers, therefore, have problems in grasping and using the form and function of modal verbs, and will add regular verb endings to them and use auxiliaries with them.

> **Does he can do that? Yes, he cans do that.*

There is also a strong tendency to overuse *that* clauses both with modals and other verbs taking an object + infinitive construction in English. (See 'Non-finite forms' below.)

> **It (is) possible that I come with you?*
> **I can that I help you.*
> **He wants that he helps you.*

Non-finite forms

The gerund does not exist in Arabic. Its functions are performed by verbal nouns of separate patterns, or by regular verb forms.

In *Smoking is bad for you*, the Arabic equivalent of the verbal noun *smoking* is of a quite separate pattern from any tenses of the verb *to smoke*.

The Arabic equivalent of *I enjoy smoking* would be **I enjoy I smoke*.

In *I prefer working to playing*, the Arabic equivalent construction would be **I prefer (that) I work to (that) I play*.

Similarly, there is no infinitive form in Arabic; again the infinitive is expressed as a second simple verb, with or without *that*.

> **I want (that) I go out.*
> *(*)It is necessary that I go out.*

It follows that Arab learners will have not only the usual problems of making the correct choice between gerund and infinitive, but also basic problems of form and concept for both.

The active and passive voices

There are active and passive forms for all tenses in Arabic, but they are virtually identical to the active forms, differing only in the pronunciation of the (unwritten) short vowelling. A passive verb in a text is therefore only recognisable as such from its context and is used far less frequently in Arabic writing than in English, and hardly at all in everyday speech. Thus while the concepts of active and passive should readily be understood, the forms and uses of the passive will cause problems.

The preposition for the agent in Arabic is bi, which facilitates the use of *by* in English.

This is often overused, giving rise to:
> *He was stabbed by a knife.*
> *The letter was written by a pen.*

Common errors arise from the use of active verb forms for passive:
> *He hit by a stone.*
> *The bill paid by the government.*

Another common circumlocution is simply to make the passive verb active:
> *The bill, the government paid it.*

Articles

There is no indefinite article in Arabic, and the definite article has a range of use different from English. The indefinite article causes the most obvious problems as it is commonly omitted with singular and plural countables:
> *This is book. Or even *This book. (for *This is a book.*)
> *He was soldier.*

When the English indefinite article has been presented, it tends to be used wherever the definite article is not used:
> *These are a books.*
> *I want a rice.*

There is a definite article form in Arabic, though it takes the form of a prefix (al-). It is used, as in English, to refer back to indefinite nouns previously mentioned, and also for unique references (*the sun, on the floor*, etc.).

The most common problem with the definite article arises from interference from the Arabic genitive construction:

English	Arabic
John's book. (or *The book of John.*)	*Book John.*
A man's work. (or *The work of a man.*)	*Work man.*
The teacher's car. (or *The car of the teacher.*)	*Car the teacher.*

Most errors of word order and use of articles in genitive constructions are interference of this kind:
> *This is book the teacher.*
> *This is the key door.*

It follows that Arabic speakers have great difficulties with the English 's genitive construction.

The cases in which English omits the article, e.g. *in bed, at dawn, on Thursday, for breakfast*, etc. usually take the definite article in Arabic:
> *At the sunset we made the camp.*
> *What would you like for the breakfast the Sunday?*

All days of the week, some months in the Muslim calendar, and many names of towns, cities and countries include the definite article in Arabic, which is often translated, appropriately or not:

We lived in the India.
We had a flat in the Khartoum.
We travelled to the Yemen.

Adjectives and adverbs

Adjectives follow their nouns in Arabic and agree in gender and number. This may cause beginners to make mistakes:

He (is) man tall. (for He is a tall man.)

Adverbs are used less commonly in Arabic than in English and, except for adverbs of time, do not have a fixed pattern. Adverbs of manner are often expressed in a phrase: *quickly* is expressed as *with speed*, and *dangerously* as *in a dangerous way*. There is frequent confusion between the adjective and adverb forms in English, and the adjective form is usually overused:

He drives very dangerous.

Gender and number

Arabic has two genders, masculine and feminine, which are usually evident from word ending or word meaning. Plurals of nouns not referring to human beings are considered feminine singular:

'Where are the books?' *'She is on the table. I gave her to the teacher.'*

Plurals of nouns in Arabic are very often formed by internal pattern changes (as with *mouse – mice* in English). The addition of an *-s* suffix for the plural seems almost too easy for Arabic speakers, and it is often omitted:

I have many book.

For nouns following numbers above ten, it is the rule in Arabic to use a *singular* form, and this is often transferred:

I have ten brothers and sixteen uncle.

Prepositions and particles

Arabic has a wealth of fixed prepositions and particles, used with both verbs and adjectives. Many of these do not coincide with their direct English translations:

*to arrive to	*afraid from	*angry on
*a picture from (for of)	*near from	*to look to (for at)
*to be short to	*in spite from	*an expert by
*responsible from		

Some prepositions have verbal force.
- The equivalent of *on* can express obligation:
  It is on me that I pay him.
- The equivalents of *to* and *for* can express possession:
  This book is to me / for me. (for *This book is mine.*)
- The equivalent of *with* can express present possession:
  With me my camera. (for *I have my camera with / on me.*)
- The equivalent of *for* can express purpose:
  I went home for (I) get my book. (for *I went home to get my book.*)

There are no phrasal verbs in Arabic and this whole area is one of great difficulty for Arabic speakers. Defence mechanisms may involve selecting alternative but regular verbs to avoid using phrasal verbs altogether, or the misuse or omission of the preposition or particle.
  I search my keys.
  I look my keys.
  I dress me.
  I put my clothes (off).

As prepositions in Arabic are always followed by or linked to a noun or pronoun, preposition-stranding patterns in English (*Who did you buy it for? That's the woman I was talking about.*) will usually be avoided in favour of the Arabic patterns, which are often similar to more formal English. For example: *For whom did you buy it?* or *For who you bought it? That's the woman about whom I was talking.* Or, more often, *That's the woman I was talking about her.* (The addition of the redundant pronoun is necessary in Arabic syntax – see also 'Subordinate clauses' below.)

Confusion of it and there

The expressions *there is/are* are expressed in most colloquial Arabic dialects by the preposition fee (*in*), but this is not commonly carried over into English. In more formal Arabic the concept is expressed by a passive of the verb *to find*, meaning *to exist*:
  It exists a horse in that field.
  A horse is found in that field.

Since the verbs *to exist* or *to be found* are not known to early learners, they are usually replaced by the verb *to be*:

Arabic speakers

*It is a horse in that field.
The word *there*, when encountered, is usually understood as a positional marker. *There is a horse in that field* would be understood more as *Over there (there) is a horse in that field.*

It follows that the distinction between the use of *it* and *there* in such expressions needs careful grounding.

Question tags

There are question tags in common use in all Arabic dialects, usually some unchanging form along the lines of '*Is that not so?*'

The problems, therefore, with question tags are not conceptual, but syntactic, and Arab learners, like most others, are bewildered by the multitude of changing forms in English question tags.

Subordinate clauses

A. Purpose

Clauses introduced by *in order that* are introduced in Arabic by a conjunction loosely translated as *for* and followed by the subjunctive (present) tense:
I went to the shop for (I) buy some shoes.

B. Relative

The relative pronoun (*which, who, that*) makes a distinction in Arabic according to gender, but not human and non-human. There is, therefore, confusion in the choice of *who* or *which*.

In Arabic it is *necessary* to include the object of a verb in a relative clause, which in English must be omitted:
This is the book which I bought it yesterday.
The hotel, which I stayed in it last year, was very good.

C. Conditional

Arabic has two words for *if*, which indicate the degree of likelihood of the condition. In conditional sentences which in English use conditional verb forms, Arabic uses the simple past in both main and conditional clauses:
If he went to Spain, he learned Spanish. (for *If he went to Spain, he would learn Spanish* and *If he had gone to Spain, he would have learned Spanish.*)

208

Vocabulary

The acquisition of vocabulary is particularly difficult for Arab learners. They have virtually no positive transfer: only a minimal number of words in English are borrowed from Arabic. A small range of mainly technical words, such as *radar, helicopter* and *television*, have been taken into Arabic, but these are common to most languages. Arabic speakers have very few aids to reading and listening comprehension by virtue of their first language, and they should not be expected to acquire English at anything like the same pace as European learners.

The following English words sound similar to vulgar words in Arabic, and sensitive teachers should avoid them if possible: *zip, zipper, air, tease, kiss, cuss, nick, unique.*

Culture

Literacy is highly regarded in the Arab world and the teacher is usually a respected figure. The approach to learning varies greatly between countries but, in general, it could be said that teaching is much more reliant on rote learning and the receiving of information than it is in the western world. Systems of teaching in which ideas and answers are elicited and discussed may be rejected as unsound, since it is for the teacher to know and impart all knowledge. Tests and examinations, too, frequently require only the reproduction of rote-learned notes, and tasks requiring original thought or the expression of personal opinions may be considered unfair.

The written language is revered and a good writer admired. Colloquial language has little status or value and English lessons concentrating on 'everyday colloquial English' may not be popular.

Add to this the difficulties which adult Arab learners have in coping with an informal teaching approach, in which the teacher uses first names and acts as an equal rather than a superior (though TEFL methodology in Arab schools is being up-dated rapidly) and you have a situation in which lesson content, methodology and teacher may be rejected as useless. If in doubt, teachers should err on the side of formality and always be prepared to explain where there is confusion.

Teachers, male and female, should always dress carefully and keep arms and legs reasonably covered. What the students are exposed to in the streets and on the beaches is another matter: the teacher has a status to maintain. It should be remembered that in many Arab countries schools are strictly segregated at all levels, and men and women are not permitted to mix socially at all outside the immediate family circle. The casual mixing of the sexes in a typical UK language school can produce emotional turmoil. Above all, teachers (of either sex) should maintain a firmly professional relationship with Arab learners. Once a female teacher has reached an age which bestows on her the mature 'mother' image, rather than the 'sister' image, she will have fewer problems.

The cultural changes in many Arab countries brought about by contact with the west (as regards such matters as the role of women, diet, dress and marriage customs) seem to be swinging back in many countries towards Islamic tradition and orthodoxy under the strong influence of Islam. It must be accepted that, in many areas of the Arab world, western values, politics and influences are very unpopular. There is a long history of distrust and many Arab nations are very defensive in their attitudes to the USA and Britain in particular. Teachers should be aware of history and Islamic culture and make every effort not to offend unwittingly.

Written samples of Arabic

Type-written Arabic

في قلب لندن تقع ساحة واسعة تسمّى ترافلغار سكوير أو ، إذا أردنا أن نستعمل

لها إسمها العربي الأصلي ، ساحة الطرف الأغر · هذه الساحة المقصود منها إحياء ذكرى

تلك المعركة التي إنتصر فيها اللورد نلسون ، على نابليون غربي شبه جزيرة أيبريا · ويتوسط

هذه الساحة عمود مرتفع يعتليه تمثال اللورد نلسون، · وبجانب هذه الساحة المعرض الوطني

للصور الزيتية المشهورة وكنيسة القديس مارتن ·

A direct transliteration

fee qalbi lundun taqa' saaHa waasi'a tusummee traafulghaar skweer aw, idha aradnaa an nasta'mil lahaa ismhaa al-'arabee al-aSlee, saaHat aT-Taraf al-agharr. haadhi-s-saaHa al-maqSood minhaa iHyaa' dhikra tilka l-ma'raka intaSar feehaa al-loord nilsoon 'ala naabulyoon gharbee shibh jazeerat eebeeryaa. wa-yatawassaT haadhi-s-saaHa 'amood murtafi' ya'taleeh timthaal il-loord nilsoon. wa-bijaanib haadhi-s-saaHa al-ma'raD al-waTanee li-S-Suwar az-zeeteeya al-mashhoora wa-kaneesat il-qadees maartin.

A word-for-word translation

in heart London she-stands square broad she-is-called Trafalgar Square or, if we-wanted that we-use to-her name-her the-Arabic the-original, square the-headland the-beautiful. this the-square the-intended from-her commemoration memory that the-battle which he-was-victorious in-her the-lord Nelson on Napoleon westwards resemblance island Iberia. and-he-centres this the-square column high he-surmounts-it statue the-lord Nelson. and-beside this the-square the-gallery the-national for-the-pictures the-oiled the-famous and church the-saint Martin.

An idiomatic translation

In the heart of London there is a broad square called Trafalgar Square or, if we want to use its original Arabic name, the Square of Taraf Al-Agharr (the Beautiful Headland). This square was designed to perpetuate the memory of that battle in which Lord Nelson won a victory over Napoleon, west of the Iberian Peninsula. Standing in the centre of this square is a tall column on top of which is a statue of Lord Nelson. Beside the square is the National Gallery of famous oil paintings and St Martin's Church.

Printed Arabic

(This extract is from the catalogue of the Qatar National Museum. The English translation from the same source is beside it.)

قطر في العهد الاسلامي
كان سكان شبه جزيرة قطر من اول
الاقوام التي اعتنقت الدين الاسلامي .
وتاريخ المنطقة منذ ذلك الحين يشمل
نمو وازدهار تجارة اللؤلؤ التي لعبت قطر
فيها دورا على غاية من الأهمية .
ويصف هذا القسم من المتحف ايضا
ظهور اسرة ال ثاني في القرن التاسع عشر
لتتبوء زعامة الدولة ورجالها الافذاذ الذين
خدموا البلاد كحكام للدولة .

Qatar in the Islamic Era
The people of the Qatar peninsula were amongst the first in Eastern Arabia to embrace Islam. The history of the region since then includes the growth of the pearl trade, in which Qatar played a particularly important role.
This section of the Museum also describes the emergence, during the 19th century, of the al-Thani family's leadership of the State and the remarkable men who have served the State as Rulers.

A direct transliteration

qatar fee-l-'ahd il-islaamee
kaan sukkaan shibh jazeerat qatar min awwal il-aqwaam allatee a'tanaqat
ad-deen al-islaamee. wa-taareekh il-minTaqa mundhu dhaalik al-Heen
yashmal numoow w-izdihaar tijaarat il-lu'lu' allatee la'ibat qatar feehaa
dawran 'ala ghaaya min al-ahamiyya. wa-yaSif haadha al-qism min al-matHaf
aiDan DHuhoor usrat Al-Thaanee fee-l-qarn at-taasi' 'ashar li-tatabbu'
za'aamat ad-dawla wa-rijaalhaa al-afdhaadh alladheen khadamoo al-bilaad
ka-Hukkaam li-d-dawla.

A word-for-word translation

it-was inhabitants resemblance island qatar from first the-peoples which
she-embraced the-religion the-islamic. and-history the-area since that
the-time he-includes growth and-flourishing trade the-pearl which she-
played qatar in-her role on extreme the-importance. and-he-describes
this the-part from the-museum also appearance family Al Thani in the-
century the-ninth ten for-she-occupies leadership the-state and-men-her
the-unique who they-served the-country as-rulers for-the-state.

Handwriting difficulties: samples written by two Arabic-speaking beginners

My country is, Sauide Arabie, and everyone know that S.A is a big a country it's about one mullone K/M square. Almost of it is a desiartes, so everboday in S.A like the desiarte. You can amayen how it is beautpul in the naight, watechisg the stares in the sky lying on the sand and lecitniny, to the anmails sound. In the spring the desiarte

Turkish speakers

Ian Thompson

Distribution

TURKEY, NORTH CYPRUS, Eastern Bulgaria. The Azeri language of northwestern Iran is largely co-intelligible with Turkish.

Introduction

The Turkic languages are scattered over a wide area from Turkey eastwards to northwestern China and into Siberia, yet there is great homogeneity within the family, which is related neither to the Indo-European tongues nor to the Semitic. Turkish is therefore fundamentally different from both Farsi and Arabic, though it has in the past borrowed heavily from both, as well as from French. Since 1928, Turkish has been written in a modified version of the Roman script.

Turkish is often taken as a copybook example of the agglutinative type of language, where numerous endings are tacked on to simple roots. For instance, küçümsenmemeliydiler (= *they shouldn't have been belittled*) can be analysed as follows:

    küçük = *small* (final *k* disappears here)
    -mse- = *regard something as*
    -n- = passive/reflexive
    -me- = negative
    -meli- = *should*
    -ydi- = past
    -ler = *they*

Turkish shares with Korean and Japanese a word order based on two principles: (a) modifier stands before modified, i.e. adjective before noun, adverb before verb; and (b) the finite verb stands at the end of the sentence. Here is an example from a popular science magazine:

> Yeraltı   suyundan   düşük dereceli ısı
> *Ground-under-its water-its-from low   degree-d heat*
>
> çıkartan   ısı   pompalarından   banliyölerdeki
> *get-out-ing heat pump-s-its-from suburb-s-in-being*

214

bahçelerde kârlı   bir biçimde yararlanılabilir.
garden-s-in profitable one form-in benefit-passive-passive-can.

or more freely:

> *Heat pumps that extract low-grade heat from underground water*
> *can profitably be made use of in suburban gardens.*

In popular speech, however, word order varies widely for rhythm, emphasis and good discourse flow; the case and possession suffixes anyway make it clear who does what to whom, regardless of word order. Turkish speakers therefore find English word order less alien than a glance at the passage might suggest, but it is nevertheless a major stumbling block in long, complex sentences.

Phonology

Vowels

1. /iː/ as in *key* is often pronounced like the diphthong /ɪə/, or in a closed syllable as /ɪ/ – the Italian error in reverse: /kɪə/ for *key*; *kip* for *keep*. The Turkish word giy contains a good approximation to English /iː/.
2. /e/ as in *bed* is often far too open before *n*, approaching /æ/: *man* for *men*.
3. /æ/ as in *back* plagues Turkish-speaking learners, lying as it does between their /e/ and /æ/. They often substitute /e/: *set* for *sat*.
4. /ɔː/ is often pronounced as /oʊ/, leading to confusion between pairs such as *law* and *low*. Turkish speakers can pronounce /ɔː/ successfully if they lengthen Turkish /o/.
5. /uː/ tends to become /ʊə/ when final and /ʊ/ in closed syllables: /dʊə/ for *do*; *'pullink'* for both *pooling* and *pulling*. Turkish speakers are able to pronounce the sound successfully after /j/, as in *few*.
6. /ə/ finds a nearish equivalent in Turkish ı, which is however higher and tenser. Under the influence of spelling, Turkish speakers often give unstressed vowels their stressed value: /ɪnkonwɪnient/ for *inconvenient*; /eddɪʃonal/ for *additional*.
7. When the diphthongs /eɪ/, /aɪ/ and /ɔɪ/ occur in final position, /ɪ/ may be devoiced and pronounced with friction (rather like German *ch* in ich, or the sound at the end of French oui, or the *h* in *human*: /bɔɪç/ for *boy*; /deɪç/ for *day*).
8. /eə/ as in *care* usually becomes /eɪ/.
9. /əʊ/ is often heard as /oʊ/, with a fully back first element. This is generally more acceptable to English speakers than the 'posh' fronted version /əʊ/ or /œʊ/ at which some Turkish speakers aim.

10. Between *s* and a consonant, /ɪ/ and /ə/ may become devoiced or disappear altogether: /stɪə/ for *city*; *sport* for *support*, /beɪsk/ for *basic*.

Consonants

1. /θ/ and /ð/ do not occur in Turkish, and they give a great deal of difficulty. Learners often replace them by over-aspirated /t/ and /d/, so that, for example, *through* becomes /tʰruə/ instead of /θruː/.
2. Turkish /b/, /d/ and /dʒ/ lose voice when final, and /g/ does not occur finally: *bet* for *bed*; *'britch'* for *bridge*.
3. Turkish /v/ is much more lightly articulated than the English equivalent, and with back vowels is close to English /w/. The Turkish alphabet doesn't contain the letter *w*, and loan words containing *w* are written with *v*. Therefore students find the two sounds very confusing: *'surwiwe'* for *survive*; *'vait'* for *wait*.
4. /ŋ/ only occurs before /g/ and /k/ in Turkish: *'singgingk'* for *singing*.
5. Standard Turkish has three varieties of /r/, none of them very like standard British /r/. R is pronounced wherever it is written.
6. Turkish has both 'clear' /l/ (as in *let*) and 'dark' /l/ (as in *tell*). However, their distribution is not the same as in English, and mistakes can be expected before vowels ('dark' /l/ instead of 'clear' /l/ in some cases) and before consonants ('clear' /l/ instead of 'dark' /l/ in some cases).
7. When /p/, /b/, /m/, /f/ and /v/ are followed by /æ/ or /ɑ/, a glide (like a /w/) is inserted: /bwaɪ/ for *buy*; /fwɑn/ for *fun*.
8. Final /m/, /n/ and /l/ tend to be pronounced very short and devoiced. This makes them difficult to perceive, and may lead to intelligibility problems.

Consonant clusters

The Turkish consonant system does not allow initial clusters in native words, and clusters of more than three consonants in any position are unusual. Although some loan words have an initial easing vowel (e.g. istasyon = *station*), the tendency when speaking English is to insert the vowel after the first consonant: *'siprink'* for *spring*; *'filute'* for *flute*.

Rhythm, stress and intonation

The rhythmic pattern of English, with its stretched-out stressed syllables and hurried unstressed syllables with their reduced vowels, is alien to and difficult for Turkish speakers. Sentences like *There was considerable confusion over them*, where only *-sid-* and *-fu-* are fully stressed, need much practice.

Word stress exists in Turkish. Most words are stressed on the final syllable, but many verb-forms – particularly negative ones – have an earlier stress. Adverbs and proper names also tend not to be finally stressed. Sets like *'photograph / pho'tographer / photo'graphic* are, quite predictably, troublesome.

Remarkably often English and Turkish agree on which word is to carry the main stress in a sentence, but *wh*-question words (such as kim = *who*, ne = *what*, niçin = *why*) are usually stressed in Turkish, whereas they are only stressed in English for special emphasis or when standing alone. Turkish speakers therefore tend to say *'**Where** are you going?* for *Where are you '**going?**

In declaratives and orders, stress is expressed as a fall in pitch on the stressed syllable, together with slight lengthening and an increase in loudness – much as in English. But an English characteristic not found in Turkish is the rising pitch on repeated, afterthought or otherwise secondary material *after* the main stress, as in:

There's a badger in the garden.
Oooh – I've never seen a badger.
Ssh! He'll run away if we make too much noise.

Also unfamiliar is the fall–rise with its connotations of warning, incompleteness and partial congruence of information:

Can you lend me a pen?
Well, I can lend you a red one.
That'll do fine. Don't let me run off with it.

Many Turkish speakers – particularly men – find this pattern embarrassing. Falling–rising patterns do occur in Turkish, but mainly to give shape to strings of clauses, the final clause taking a fall. This pattern is often carried over into English. Note the lack of conjunctions, too:

I went to bus-station, I searched my brother, I couldn't see, I went to home.

Punctuation

Turkish makes use of most of the punctuation marks available to Latin-script languages, but in its own way:

1. A comma is usually written after the topic of a sentence, which often happens to be the subject:

   **My father, works in a factory.*

2. Subordinate clauses are not usually marked off with commas:

   When you get back please remember to telephone me.

217

Sentences opening with the equivalent of *He said, I imagine, It's obvious* and similar expressions use a comma *after* the particle ki (= *that*), which gives rise to:

*He told that, his passport at home office.

3. A comma often separates two co-ordinate clauses:

She has a good voice, she enjoys singing.

4. Sentences opening with Çünkü (= *because*, explaining what has gone before) normally stand after a full stop.

She was tired. *Because worked very hard.

Otherwise the use of the full stop and paragraphing conventions are much as in English.

5. Colons are used as in English, but are usually followed by capital letters. Semi-colons are little used.

6. Quoted speech is found between English-style inverted commas, between « and », or unmarked. Often a quoted single word or phrase is enclosed in parentheses ( ); parenthetic material may be found between « and », and emphasis – where English might underline or use bold type – is shown by capital letters or even inverted commas.

Grammar

Word order

Turkish is a 'subject–object–verb' language, where qualifier precedes qualified, topic precedes comment and subordinate precedes main, but departures from this ideal are common in speech and lively writing. All adjectivals, however long, precede their substantive. The equivalent of English prepositions follow the noun, and the equivalent of subordinating conjunctions follow their clauses. Modal verbs follow lexical verbs.

Students quickly learn the fundamentals of English word order as it applies to simple sentences, but continue to have difficulty in more complex structures. The position of pronoun objects with phrasal verbs is a problem:

*I saw that the light was still on, so I turned off it.

Structures with 'preposition-stranding' also cause trouble: learners have trouble understanding and producing sentences like:

How many people did she go with?
That's the hospital I was in.

Verbs: general

The Turkish verb shows person, number, tense, aspect, voice, mood, modality and polarity, and students will therefore be prepared for these concepts to be expressed through changes in verb forms, though the English forms themselves cause great difficulty. The object is not expressed within the verb; nor is gender.

To be

There is no independent verb *to be* in Turkish. The simple copula use usually goes unexpressed.
> *My uncle farmer.*

The Turkish equivalent of *there is* can be used (unlike the English structure) with definite subjects:
> *There was not the driver in the bus.* (for *The driver wasn't in the bus.*)
> *Yesterday I looked you from telephone, but there wasn't you.* (for *Yesterday I tried to phone you, but you weren't at home.*)

To have

To have, in its various uses, does not have direct Turkish equivalents. (For instance, the Turkish for *I've got a car* translates literally as *'Car my there is'*.) So this verb presents beginners with some serious learning problems.

Questions and negatives

Yes/no interrogatives and negatives are constructed in Turkish by inserting particular particles into the verb. Learners find both inversion and the use of *do* difficult:
> *You are tired?*
> *I not think we can finish it today.*

The Turkish equivalent of English question tags is a simple invariable expression:
> *You're not very well today, isn't it?*

Time, tense and aspect

Differences in the coverage of Turkish and English verb forms result in the following difficulties:

219

1. Students may use the present progressive inappropriately with stative verbs such as *know* and for habitual actions:
   I am knowing her. I am seeing every day.
2. A present tense is used in Turkish to say how long things have been going on. And Turkish does not have separate equivalents for *since* and *for*:
   I learn English since three years.
3. Students have predictable difficulty with the multiplicity of structures that exist in English for referring to the future. For instance, the simple present may be used instead of the *will* future, especially in requests, offers and promises, and when referring to conditions and inevitable outcomes:
   'Will you bring one?' '*Yes, I do.*'
   Don't drop it – it breaks!
   Ask Gülay; she tells you.
4. The past progressive and the *used to* construction may be confused:
   I was often going to the mountains when I was younger.
5. Learners tend to overuse the past perfect, substituting it for the simple past in cases where a past event is seen as being separated from the present by a long time lapse, a delay, or intervening events:
   This castle had been built 600 years ago.
   I had written to you last month, but I couldn't receive any reply till now.

Modal verbs

Turkish has a comprehensive set of modal verbs which express similar meanings to the English modals, including separate forms corresponding to structures such as *I was able to go / I could have gone*, or *We had to do it / We should have done it*. Students are therefore broadly familiar with the meanings expressed by the English modals (though the differences between *should*, *must*, *have to* and *have got to* cause difficulty). The sheer mechanics of the English forms, however, with their contractions and neutralised vowels, cause a great deal of trouble.

Conditionals

All the above is true of conditionals, with the added complication that Turkish uses the *past* unreal form even for present unreals if they really are unfulfillable:
   If I had been English I would have missed the sun. (for *If I were English I would miss the sun.*)

The passive voice

Passives present no conceptual difficulties, but structurally the English passive strikes Turkish speakers as clumsy, and the triple role of *be* as progressive auxiliary, passive former and modal is a source of difficulty, leading students to confuse such structures as *was taking, was taken, was to take, was to be taken*.

> *My house was building in 1920.*

Complex forms like the present progressive or present perfect passive cause particular difficulty:

> *Nothing is doing for poor people.*
> *My uncle has hurt in a car crash.*

Turkish is often more specific than English as to passive and active:

> *This tea is too hot to be drunk.*
> *It's easy to be written.*

Overlapping the active–passive opposition is that of transitivity. English has a number of verbs which can be used both transitively (with the agent as subject) and intransitively (with the patient as subject), as in *I broke the window / The window broke; She burnt the wood / The wood burnt; I couldn't start the engine / The engine wouldn't start.* In cases like these Turkish uses separate verbs; students may therefore find it confusing to use the same verb in both cases. A common mistake:

> *When will school be opened?*

Participles and subordinate clauses

English participle and clause structures are organised very differently from their Turkish equivalents, and present a serious learning problem. Each of the following expressions corresponds to a single complex participial verb form in Turkish:

> *write and . . .*
> *who writes/wrote*
> *when someone writes/wrote*
> *unless it is/was written*
> *while they are/were writing*
> *as if it had been written*
> *without writing*
> *by not writing*
> *because we couldn't write*
> *of the things you write/wrote*

Since the Turkish forms do not show tense, students may have difficulty getting tense right in English subordinate clauses (e.g. in indirect speech constructions).

> *I told him that I am lost and I asked him how I can find my hotel.*

Relative clauses

The most common Turkish equivalent of an English relative clause is a participle construction placed before the noun. There is no relative pronoun or relativising conjunction.

> Çalıştığımız günler . . . *The days on which we work . . .*
> Çalıştığımız mesele . . . *The problems we're working on . . .*
> Çalıştığımız yer . . . *The place we work in . . .*

English relative structures are therefore difficult for Turkish learners. They may avoid using them altogether, or make various kinds of mistake:

> *Do you know the people which I was talking to them?*
> *I went to visit my friend lived in Paris.*

Nominalised clauses

English has a variety of ways of nominalising clauses, so as to use them as subjects, objects or complements. Turkish students find the use of structures such as the following difficult and unpredictable; they tend to overuse the possessive structure in such cases:

> *I advised her **to go**.*
> *I suggested **she went**.*
> ***Her going** was a good thing.*
> *It was a good thing **she went**.*
> ***The fact that she went** was a good thing.*
> *It was a good thing **for her to go**.*
> *I approved of **her going**.*

Nouns

Turkish nouns are genderless, but they show number, possession and case. The plural is less used than in English – particularly when a noun is indefinite or generic, and after number-words. Mistakes resulting from this take a long time to eradicate:

> *In the Turkish, tomato too cheap.*
> *I spend the evenings writing letter.*
> *We saw a few animal.*
> *three week ago*

Formation of nouns from other parts of speech is highly regular in Turkish, and students have predictable trouble with English word formation.

Pronouns

Personal pronouns are much less used than in English: the subject pronoun is expressed only for emphasis, contrast or to introduce the subject as a topic, which are uses normally distinguished in English by changes in stress and intonation. Object pronouns are used even less. Possessives are also normally unnecessary, since the 'possessed' form of the noun makes the relationship clear:
> *When my father had finished breakfast, went out.*
> *Tramp asked some money, for this reason I gave.*
> *John is having trouble with car.*

Turkish has only one third-person pronoun, so *he*, *she* and *it* are commonly confused, as are *him* and *her* and the possessives *his* and *her*:
> *Mary changed his job because he didn't like the boss.*

Articles

Turkish has an indefinite article, which is sandwiched between adjective and noun. As in many European languages, it is not used for professions or in negative existentials:
> *I am student.*
> *There wasn't bus.*

The choice between *a/an* and *some* is difficult for Turkish speakers, since the line between countable and uncountable is less sharply drawn than in English. Students tend to overuse *some*:
> *I asked some policeman, he told you will see some bridge.*

Turkish has no definite article, but direct objects are different in form according to whether or not they are definite in meaning. This encourages learners to put *the* with all definite direct objects, leading to mistakes such as:
> *Librarian controlled the my ticket.*
> *I like the Cambridge.*

Adjectives

Comparatives are not always marked in Turkish:
> *She is old than you.*

Quantifiers

The 'negative/positive' distinction in *few / a few* and *little / a little* is observed in Turkish, whereas the uncountable/countable distinction in *few/little* is not.
> **I eat few butter.*

The differences between *much, many* and *a lot; long* and *a long time*; and *far, a long way* and *distant* are difficult for Turkish-speaking students as for other learners.

Too and *very* are commonly confused:
> **Teacher, you are too beautiful.*

Adverbs

Adverbs that modify verbs are usually identical in form to adjectives in Turkish:
> **He generally works slow.*

Here and *there* can be nouns in Turkish:
> **Here is boring place.*
> **Do you like there?*

Intensifiers are a problem area: çok soğuk represents, according to context, *very cold, colder* or *too cold*, causing students to confuse the English forms.

Conjunctions

Among the conjunctions that cause special difficulty for Turkish speakers are *even if, however* and *whether . . . or*. Often the same Turkish word corresponds both to a conjunction and to a preposition in English, leading to confusion between, for instance, *although* and *despite; as far as, until* and *by; before, ago* and *earlier; after, next, afterwards, in . . .'s time* and *later*.

Other groups of words which may have single Turkish equivalents (causing confusion in certain contexts in English) are: *and* and *whether; and, also, either* and *even; because* and *in order to*.

Co-ordinate clauses are often juxtaposed without a conjunction in spoken Turkish, leading learners to drop *and, so* or *but*:
> (*)*We looked, they had gone.*
> (*)*I ran, I caught the ferry.*

Prepositions

Prepositions that cause confusion include *at/in/on*; *than/from*; *with/by*; *to/for*; *until / as far as / as much as / up to / by*; *with / near / up to*.

> **in Saturday *for learn English *by pencil *until the bank*
> **I must get back until Monday.*
> **I am living near my landlady.*

Students sometimes leave out the preposition altogether, even at an otherwise good intermediate level.

> **He came near me and asked me my name.*
> **She went Newcastle.*

Vocabulary

The only lexical common ground between English and Turkish is a body of borrowings from French, such as enflasyon (= *inflation*), kalite (= *quality*). Some of these words are false friends – for instance sempatik (= nice), kontrol (= *check*). Available dictionaries range from abominable to very good. Turkish lacks equivalents for many English abstract nouns, and groups of not-quite-synonymous English words, such as *shorten*, *abbreviate*, *abridge*, often have one Turkish counterpart. Some especially common confusions:

> *mind/idea/opinion/thought*
> *tell/say*
> *definitely/exactly/completely*
> *cut/kill*
> *turn/return*
> *finish/leave/graduate from*
> *food/meal*
> *nearly/about*
> *pass/go on*
> *already/before*
> *still/yet*
> *now/no longer*
> *always/every time*
> *win/earn/pass (exam)*

In Turkish you *pull* trouble and photographs; you *give* decisions; you *stay* (fail) in an exam; you *throw* a swindle and your victim *eats* it; you *see* education, work and duty; it *comes* (seems) to me that . . .; you *become* an illness, injection or operation.

225

The language classroom

Society and its institutions have traditionally been fairly authoritarian in Turkey. In many teaching environments, what the textbook and the teacher say are expected to be right, and learners expect teaching to be prescriptive rather than descriptive. There is often a good deal of rote learning, sometimes with insufficient attention to meaning, and little emphasis may be put on oral production. Turkish learners in general are by no means meek, passive students, though. They tend to have a strong awareness of language, are not usually shy and are often resourceful in expressing a lot even with little language. Communicative approaches to language teaching may come as a surprise, but are usually entered into enthusiastically when their purpose becomes apparent. Turkish students tend to voice their opinions openly and attach little importance to compromise. Occasionally they may criticise aspects of their home-land and its politics, but the teacher should not join in the criticism, for the Turks have enormous national pride and are highly sensitive to the world's opinion of them. They warm immediately to anyone who shows an interest in the nation and its language.

Given the great differences between the two languages, most students learn to speak English, and to understand spoken English, remarkably well. Reading material with much abstract vocabulary presents difficulty. Written composition is often dreaded, since here one must use complex constructions that can be deftly sidestepped in speech, and because composition may not have been 'studied' at home.

Speakers of South Asian languages[1]

Christopher Shackle

Distribution

INDIA, PAKISTAN, BANGLADESH, NEPAL, SRI LANKA, MALDIVES, Arabian Peninsula, East Africa, Mauritius.

Introduction

Some sixteen major languages are spoken in the countries of the Indian subcontinent. The four languages of South India (Tamil, Malayalam, Kannada, Telegu) are members of the independent Dravidian family. The others are all Indo-Aryan languages, members of that branch of the Indo-European family which derives from Sanskrit. They include the national languages of India (Hindi), Pakistan (Urdu), Bangladesh (Bengali), Nepal (Nepali), Sri Lanka (Sinhala) and the Maldives (Divehi), besides many important regional languages of India and Pakistan (Gujarati, Marathi, Oriya, Assamese, Kashmiri, Sindhi, Panjabi). Several of these languages have been spread by emigration to other parts of the world, and the United Kingdom now has large communities of speakers of Bengali, Gujarati, Panjabi (many of these are also fluent in Urdu), and Tamil.

As a result of the long period of British rule, English has become very firmly established in South Asia. Even those with no direct command of English will have been exposed to its indirect influence through the very numerous loanwords which have entered all South Asian languages. At the other end of the spectrum, English continues to be used as a natural medium of expression by those with the highest level of education, for whom the most prestigious variety of the language remains standard British English spoken with 'received pronunciation'. In between these two groups lie those who have varying degrees of command over 'Indian English'. Chiefly distinguished by the presence of features drawn from South Asian languages, this South Asian English is current with a remarkable degree of uniformity throughout the subcontinent and

---

[1] The focus in this chapter is on the Indo-Aryan languages of South Asia. See the following chapter for the problems of speakers of Dravidian languages.

among immigrants in Britain (though inevitably with some regional variation, especially of accent), and in its educated form has achieved the status of a separate standard, on a par with American or Australian English. Many of the distinctive features of South Asian English are common to most or all of the Indo-Aryan languages, and many are also found in Dravidian. They are most conveniently described by referring to the typical example of Hindi, which is here taken to include the colloquial Hindustani that is the most widely used *lingua franca* of the subcontinent, besides its officially fostered literary varieties, the High Hindi of India and the Urdu of Pakistan.

Given the long-established position of English in the schools of the subcontinent, the problems encountered by learners are likely to be mainly determined by their educational rather than their particular language background. This chapter deals principally with the general problems that speakers of South Asian languages (whether in the subcontinent or in Britain) may encounter if they choose to adopt standard British English as a target model. (The less significant features which may cause problems for speakers of only one particular South Asian language approaching this variety of English cannot properly be dealt with in a chapter of this limited size.) References to typical learners' mistakes should be seen in this framework, and are not intended to imply that standard British English is in some way superior to South Asian English: in some cases a form that is incorrect in one variety may be perfectly correct in the other.

Apart from Urdu and the other Pakistani languages which are written in variants of the Arabic script, almost every South Asian language has its own script, written from left to right, to record both consonants and vowels. Although the Roman alphabet is not normally used to write any major South Asian language, the English writing system poses no general problems for most South Asian learners.

Phonology

General

The phonological systems of South Asian languages and English differ in important respects, notably in the very different prominence given to distinctions between vowels and distinctions between consonants. While English has 22 vowels and diphthongs and 24 consonants, Hindi has only ten vowel phonemes but distinguishes over 30 consonants. Sets of aspirated and unaspirated consonants are carefully distinguished in Hindi, and in place of the English alveolar series /t/, /d/, there is both a series of dentals produced with the blade of the tongue behind the teeth,

/t/, /tʰ/, /d/, /dʰ/, and the typically South Asian retroflex series produced with the tip of the tongue curled back behind the alveolar ridge, /ʈ/, /ʈʰ/, /ɖ/, /ɖʰ/.

Among the features of South Asian languages which give rise to a 'South Asian accent' in English are:

– Tenser articulation than English, with vowels produced further forward, leading to the loss of some distinctions between different vowels.
– The pronunciation of the voiceless consonants /p/, /t/, /tʃ/, /k/ without aspiration in all positions.
– The pronunciation of the English alveolar consonants /t/ and /d/ as the heavier retroflex consonants /ʈ/ and /ɖ/.
– A different intonation system from English (see below).

Vowels

iː	ɪ	e	æ	eɪ	aɪ	ɔɪ
ɑː	ɒ	ɔː	ʊ	aʊ	əʊ	ɪə
uː	ʌ	ɜː	ə	eə	ʊə	aɪə / aʊə

Shaded phonemes have equivalents or near-equivalents in most South Asian languages, and should therefore be perceived and articulated without serious difficulty, although some confusions may still arise. Unshaded phonemes may cause problems. For detailed comments, see below.

1. /e/ and /æ/ are often confused: *said* and *sad*.
2. /ɒ/ and /ɔː/ are generally confused with /ɑː/, and the same vowel /ɑː/ is typically heard in pronunciations of such sets of words as *lorry, law, laugh*.
3. The diphthong /eɪ/ is usually pronounced as the close monophthong /eː/: /meːd/ for *made*. The diphthongs /aɪ/ and /ɔɪ/ are both liable to be realised as /aːɪ/: *tie* for *toy*.
4. The diphthong /əʊ/ is usually pronounced as the close monophthong /ɔː/: /kɔːʈ/ for *coat*.

Consonants

p	b	f	v	θ	ð	t	d
s	z	ʃ	ʒ	tʃ	dʒ	k	g
m	n	ŋ	l	r	j	w	h

Shaded phonemes have equivalents or near-equivalents in most South Asian languages, and should therefore be perceived and articulated without serious difficulty, although some confusions may still arise. Unshaded phonemes may cause problems. For detailed comments, see below.

1. The voiceless consonants /p/, /t/, /tʃ/, /k/ are pronounced without aspiration in all positions; the /p/ in *pit* having the same value as that in *spit*.
2. The fricative consonants /θ/ and /ð/ are replaced by the aspirated dental /tʰ/ and the unaspirated /d/ respectively: /dem/ for *them*. /f/ is often replaced by the aspirated /pʰ/: thus /pʰɪt/ for *fit*, as opposed to /pɪt/ for *pit*.
3. The alveolar consonants /t/ and /d/ are regularly replaced by the retroflex consonants /ʈ/ and /ɖ/: thus /ɖen/ for *den*, as opposed to /dem/ for *them* (see above).
4. There is only one South Asian phoneme in the area of /v/ and /w/, and the distinction between these two sounds is a major difficulty for learners: *vet* and *wet*.
5. In many South Asian languages /z/ is an allophone of /dʒ/, and words like *bridges* may be tongue-twisters for some learners.
6. Most South Asian languages lack the phoneme /ʒ/, which may be variously realised as /z/, /ʃ/, /dʒ/ or even /j/ in such words as *pleasure*.
7. The 'dark' *l* as in *fill* is generally replaced by the 'clear' *l* as in *light*.
8. /r/ is pronounced as a tap or fricative in all positions where it is written (see below), without affecting the quality of the preceding vowel.
9. Some South Asian languages have only one phoneme in the area of /s/ and /ʃ/, and many speakers of, for example, Bengali or Gujarati find it difficult to distinguish between these two sounds, confusing pairs of words like *self* and *shelf*.

Influence of spelling on pronunciation

South Asian scripts are for the most part phonetic, so that spelling is largely an accurate guide to pronunciation. Learners' pronunciation of English words is consequently over-faithful to the written forms:

1. /r/ is pronounced wherever *r* is written, including positions where it comes before a consonant or silence, as in *market, officer, order*. The quality of the preceding vowel is not affected as in RP, and some common false rhymes are created, notably /diːər/ for *there*, rhyming with *here*.
2. A written *h* may be interpreted as indicating one of the South Asian voiced aspirate consonants and pronounced as such in words like *ghost, which*.
3. The written *-ed* of the regular past tense is often pronounced as it is written, even after stems ending in a voiceless consonant, as in /ḓeveləpeḓ/ for *developed*, or /ɑːskeḓ/ for *asked*.
4. The written *-s* of the plural may be pronounced as /s/, even after a voiced consonant, as in *walls*, or a long vowel, as in *fees*, where it should be pronounced /z/.

Consonant clusters

The range of consonant clusters occurring at the beginning and end of English words is much wider than in South Asian languages. Many such clusters are simplified:

1. Initial two-segment clusters beginning with /s/ may be prefixed by /ɪ/: *'istation'* for *station*, *'istreet'* for *street*, etc.
2. Initial clusters of most types are liable to be broken up by the insertion of the short vowel /ə/ to assist the pronunciation: *'faree'* for *free*, *'salow'* for *slow*, etc.
3. Final clusters may be similarly broken up, or simplified by the omission of a consonant: *'filam'* for *film*, *'toas'* for *toast*, etc.
4. A final /l/ or /n/ following a consonant, as in *little, button*, etc., is pronounced as a complete syllable with a clear vowel /ə/ before the /l/ or /n/.

Rhythm and stress

As distinct from English, which is a stress-timed language in which word stress is both heavily marked and not always predictable, South Asian languages are syllable-timed, and stress is secondary to the rhythm, which is based primarily upon the arrangement of long and short syllables. Word stress in them accordingly tends to be weakly realised, and is always predictable.

The appropriate stressing of syllables in English words and compounds is therefore an area of great difficulty for speakers of South Asian languages.

1. The variation in stress in sets of related words may not be properly realised, producing for example *ne'cessary*, following *ne'cessity*. Incorrect stressing of the initial syllable is particularly common, as in *'development*, *'event*.

2. The grammatical contrast between nouns with stress on the first syllable and verbs with second syllable stress is lost in favour of a weak stress on the second syllable for nouns as well as verbs, as in *re'cord*, *trans'port*. There is a similar confusion between noun–noun combinations and free combinations of adjective with noun, so that a *'toy factory* is not distinguished from a *toy 'factory*.

3. Full vowels tend to be retained, even in unstressed syllables, so that both the *e* of cricket and the second *o* of *Oxford* retain their value. Many common words normally pronounced as reduced 'weak forms' in English, like *and*, *but*, *than*, *as*, *is*, *has*, *was*, *will*, *would*, similarly keep their full 'strong form' values in all positions, and receive a relatively strong stress.

Intonation

This naturally varies greatly in detail over the vast speech area covered by the South Asian languages. The most notable difference from English lies in the use of substantially raised pitch, without heavier articulation, to indicate emphasis. This prominent contrast with the normal English pattern contributes further to the 'sing-song' impression of South Asian English that derives primarily from the syllable-timed character of the languages of the region.

The typical rising intonation of questions in English is reserved for expressions of surprise in most South Asian languages. Their characteristic interrogative pattern, in which the end of a question is marked by a rise-fall in the intonation, is quite unlike the English norm, and can easily cause misunderstanding. Particularly in polite requests, an unfortunate impression of peremptoriness is liable to be created.

Intonation, rhythm and stress are all particularly likely to cause problems for speakers of South Asian languages, especially in the production of weak forms and in the production and recognition of contrastive stress used to emphasise particular elements within a sentence.

Juncture

Given the preference for avoiding the use of elided weak forms, the general evenness of stress, and the tendency to simplify complex consonants, this is not a feature of English likely in itself to cause special problems.

Orthography and punctuation

There is no direct influence on learners of English from the rather different alphabetical systems used to record South Asian languages. Semi-phonetic spellings are encountered with the usual frequency, and there is sometimes some uncertainty in the use of capital letters, which are not distinguished in any South Asian script.

South Asian scripts possessed only the equivalent of the full stop before the introduction of English typography. The whole battery of commas, colons, question marks and the like are now freely used in writing these scripts, although not always very systematically. A similar uncertain use of punctuation may be detected in South Asian learners of English, who have particular problems in the use of inverted commas. Since true reported speech is not a construction characteristic of most South Asian languages, it is quite common to find punctuation of this type:

*She said that 'Rakesh was not feeling well'.

Grammar

General

The following section has been compiled on the basis of the contrasts between English and Hindi, as the most prominent representative of the Indo-Aryan languages. For those concerned with speakers of the South Asian languages most prominently represented in the United Kingdom, it may be observed that what is said about Hindi applies equally to the virtually identical Urdu, and almost without exception to the very closely related Panjabi. Much will also hold true of Gujarati, though rather less of Bengali, which has evolved many independent patterns. It should be understood that the Dravidian languages of South India have a quite different grammar (see the following chapter).

The 'parts of speech' of English and Hindi are broadly similar. Hindi is, however, a much more highly inflected language, which in European terms may be compared with Spanish. It has singular and plural noun forms; adjectives placed before nouns; a generally regular system of verb conjugation, which includes simple and progressive, active and passive forms; auxiliary and modal verbs; and past, present and future tenses (mostly indicated, as in English, by periphrastic compounds involving the use of auxiliary verbs).

Unlike English, Hindi distinguishes masculine and feminine nouns, has common (gender-neutral) forms for all pronouns, lacks markers for the comparative and superlative forms of adjectives, has no word class corresponding to the English articles, prefers postpositions placed after a noun or pronoun to prepositions, and has as its normal word order one in which the verb is placed finally in a sentence. Some of these differences, as well as some of the apparent similarities, frequently cause problems for South Asian learners of English.

Questions and negatives; auxiliaries

1. There is no equivalent of the auxiliary *do* in Hindi. Where no specific interrogative word is used, a question is marked only by its intonation – of a different pattern from English – and word order is unaltered:
   * When you came to India?
   You like our Indian food?
2. Negatives are formed by putting a negative marker (which corresponds to both *not* and *no*) before the verb:
   * You no(t) like curry?
   The Hindi idiom is to answer *yes/no* questions by signalling assent or dissent. Assenting to negative questions in the affirmative can cause confusion:
   'You have no objection?' *'Yes.' (= *I have no objection.*)
3. There is a common question tag or reinforcer for all questions, irrespective of the subject, like German nicht wahr?:
   * You have met Mohan, isn't it?
   This is realised in contemporary British Asian English as *innit?*
4. The principal Hindi auxiliary verb is the equivalent of *to be*. There is no Hindi verb corresponding to *to have*, and its use is often avoided by learners of English:
   * Your book is lying with him. (for *He has got your book.*)

Time, tense and aspect

A. Past time

Besides a simple past tense, Hindi also distinguishes the past habitual, past progressive and past perfect, though usage is not completely identical in Hindi and English.

1. With the small group of common stative verbs including *believe, hear, know, understand, want* which are rarely used in progressive forms, the English past progressive may be used inappropriately by analogy with the Hindi past habitual, formed with the present participle and past auxiliary:

    **We were wanting to go to England.*

2. The simple past may be used where English would prefer the present perfect:

    **She cooked the food just now.* (for *She has just cooked the food.*)

3. The past perfect in Hindi is used to refer to past time regarded as separate from the present, without the reference back from one point of time to another implied in English:

    **They had gone to Delhi this year.* (for *They went . . .*)

4. There is no true reported speech in Hindi, which usually preserves the original tense after past reporting verbs:

    **He asked that if we are doing this.* (for *He asked if we were doing this.*)

B. Present time

Besides a simple tense, Hindi also distinguishes the present progressive and present perfect. Two common areas of confusion concern the wrong use of the present progressive in English.

1. With stative verbs rarely used in progressive forms, the present progressive may be used inappropriately by analogy with the Hindi simple present, formed with the present participle and present auxiliary:

    **We are not understanding what she means.* (for *We don't understand what she means.*)

2. The present progressive in Hindi is used to say how long a present state of affairs has been going on:

    **How long are you living in England?*
    **She is studying English since six years.*

C. Future time

There is a full set of future tenses in Hindi, and these are used much more freely than in English to express the notion of probability:

> *You will be knowing him.* (for *You must know him.*)

Conditionals

Learners typically use a future tense instead of the present tense in the conditional clause, by false analogy with the Hindi future or present subjunctive:

> *If he will come, then we may go.* (for *If he comes . . .*)

In remote conditions, *would* may be used instead of the simple past in the conditional clause as well as the main clause:

> *If he would again come, then we would come.* (for *If he came . . .*)

Modal verbs

Hindi has either direct equivalents to most English modal verbs or quite closely analogous constructions, but there are frequent mismatches in South Asian English, in particular through extensions in the usage of *could, would, may*. Thus *could* is used to indicate past attainment:

> *We could succeed because of hard work.* (for *We were able to succeed . . .*)

The frequent choice of *could* in preference to *can* is governed by an underlying sense of greater politeness inherent in the former, analogous to that of a Hindi present subjunctive:

> *Let us leave so that we could meet him in time.* (for *so that we can meet . . .*)

Similarly, *would* is preferred to *will*:

> *We are hoping that you would come.* (for *We hope you will come.*)

Courtesy is also frequently marked by the use of *may* in place of *should*:

> *He may be instructed to attend.* (for *He should . . .*)

But an unfortunate contrary expression of brusqueness may be conveyed when *may* is used for *will* in requests unmarked by interrogative word order:

> *You may kindly come tomorrow.* (for *Will you please come tomorrow?*)

Compare:

> *I may go now.* (for *May I go now?*)

Verbs of wishing are a double problem to many South Asian learners, who instead of the English infinitive often substitute the Hindi pattern of a subordinate clause, and reproduce the Hindi present subjunctive by inappropriate use of *should*:

> **I want that I should come.* (for *I want to come.*)
> **I wanted that she should intervene.* (for *I wanted her to intervene.*)

Non-finite forms

English has both *to do* and *doing* to express the idea of a verbal noun, where Hindi has only a single infinitive. Confusions between the two English forms are particularly common in expressing the idea of purpose, where the Hindi model – of the infinitive followed by a postposition equivalent to *for* – may be imitated:

> **He went to college for improving his English.* (for . . . *to improve his English*)

Conversely, the English infinitive is frequently used in place of an *-ing* form:

> **She showed great interest to study.* (for . . . *in studying*)
> **We prevented him to speak.* (for . . . *from speaking*)

Reflexive verbs

Learners may drop reflexive pronouns in cases where these do not have a mother-tongue counterpart:

> **'Please enjoy.' 'Oh, yes, we will enjoy.'*

Word order

Although most South Asian languages differ from English in having postpositions rather than prepositions, and place the verb at the end of the sentence, this is not an area of especially serious confusions, except in direct and reported questions (see above).

Articles

The use of the English articles is one of the most difficult points for learners to grasp. Like other South Asian languages, Hindi has no equivalent of the definite article, and only the number 'one' to cover some uses of the indefinite. Confusions are consequently very frequent in English, where learners often omit the articles, especially *the*, or substitute *one* for the indefinite article.

Gender, number and case

Hindi nouns are grammatically either masculine or feminine; except where natural sex is concerned, the classification has little relation to meaning. The form of a noun often shows its gender, and adjectives and verbs may also differ in form ('agreement') according to the gender of their governing noun. Both nouns and pronouns have varying forms, supplemented by postpositions, to show their syntactic role (subject, object, etc.) in a sentence. Pronouns are not distinguished for gender, and the third person pronouns – the equivalents of *he*, *she* and *it* – are represented by demonstratives, also meaning *that* or *this*.

Generally speaking, neither gender nor case is a serious problem in English for South Asian learners. But difficulties in distinguishing gender in the third person singular pronouns may be resolved by indiscriminate use of the masculine:

I know this car and his problems. (for . . . its problems)

The English possessive case is closely analogous to the Hindi pattern of oblique case followed by possessive postposition. The main problem for South Asian learners is in learning not to generalise the possessive case where English prefers *of* with reversed order of complex elements:

this grave situation's two very important causes (for *two very important causes of this grave situation*)

Plurals of nouns are formed by the alteration of the final vowel or by the addition of endings. But a large group of masculine nouns makes no change in the simple form of the plural, and this may account for the occasional dropping of *-s* from English plurals.

There are also some differences between Hindi and English in their ideas of what constitutes a plural noun, and this may cause confusions in English. Words like *scissors* and *trousers* are singular in Hindi, whereas some other nouns, uncountable in English, are treated as plural:

The rice are not very well cooked.

Her hairs are very long.

Plural pronouns are often used in Hindi to refer to a single person. When used as actual plurals, the equivalent of *people* is often added to them:

We people are very lazy. (for We are very lazy.)

238

Adjectives and adverbs

Adjectives precede the nouns they qualify, in Hindi as in English, and the two languages have comparable sets of simple adverbs. A few common points of confusion do, however, arise:

1. Hindi has no special forms for the comparative and superlative of adverbs, using instead a simple construction of the type:
    The boy is clever from the girl.
    There is consequently some confusion as to the use of the English comparative and superlative forms, and double forms are common:
    He is the most cleverest boy in the class.
2. Hindi does not make the same distinctions between intensifying adverbs as are drawn by the English *more, very* and *too*:
    I like this music too much. (for . . . *very much*)
3. Both adjectives and adverbs are very frequently repeated in Hindi to give a sense of distribution or emphasis, or both:
    He cut the bread into little, little pieces. (for . . . *lots of little pieces*)
    Please speak slowly, slowly. (for . . . *rather slowly* or . . . *very slowly*)

Prepositions and particles

Considerable difficulties are caused for most speakers of South Asian languages by all forms of preposition stranding, including those associated with suppressed relative pronouns (*That's the woman I was talking about*) and with passive phrasal verbs (*He's just been operated on*). Many of their most common errors occur at the simpler level of using the wrong preposition, by analogy with the postposition that would be used in a language like Hindi in a comparable expression. Only a few of the most common confusions can be indicated here:
    I was angry on him. (for . . . *angry with him*)
    They were sitting on the table. (for . . . *at the table*)
    She is studying English since six years. (for . . . *for six years*)
Many verbs having a direct object in English are supplied with a preposition:
    We reached to that place.
    Tell to that boy that he is a cheater.
    I asked from him that he should come.
The final element of phrasal verbs is also liable to confusion:
    He left off one important point. (for *He left out* . . .)

> **He has built up a house for himself.* (for *He has built himself a house.*)

Subordinate clauses

South Asian languages are generally less fond of complex subordinate clauses than English, preferring simple parallel constructions. Difficulties are therefore usually experienced by learners of English in handling the more complex types of subordination, including not only indirect speech and the other constructions illustrated above, but also relative clauses, where Hindi favours the construction:

> **Which people lived there, they were all very poor.* (for *The people who lived there were all very poor.*)
> **All that he was doing, that we liked very much.* (for *We very much liked all that he was doing.*)

Vocabulary

English loanwords are present in large numbers in all South Asian languages, especially in areas connected with modern institutions or technology. This is naturally a great help to learners of English, who will inevitably know a good deal of vocabulary to start with.

Not all such loanwords are, however, immediately transferable back into English, either because their pronunciation has been significantly changed, or because they are now obsolete in British English, or because they represent distinctively local extensions of meaning or fresh coinages. A few examples will demonstrate the types of difficulty which may arise. The names of the months are all borrowed from English, but their pronunciation has often been significantly altered: *'farvari'* for *February*; *'a'prail'* for *April*; *'a'gast'* for *August*; *'ak'toober'* for *October*, etc.

Similarly, a hotal is not the simple equivalent of the English *hotel*, but also includes cafés and restaurants. A furlong, now restricted to the race track in Britain, may be used to indicate a short distance anywhere, for instance, down the road to the next crossing i.e. *crossroads*. The roof of a room is its *ceiling*, and the back garden of a house is where one is invited to go by one's host with the words 'Now I will show you my back side.'!

Culture

In spite of changes in recent times, and the influence of the cultures of the surrounding societies upon communities of speakers of South Asian languages settled outside the subcontinent, the traditional Eastern respect for the teacher and for the written word is still a prominent characteristic of learners from India and the neighbouring countries. An emphasis on formal discipline and written work is the one best calculated to meet preconceived attitudes, which may find it harder to cope with the necessary emphasis on everyday colloquial usage. Teachers may find it hard to elicit responses from female learners, unless they are in an all-female class.

Samples of Hindi and Urdu

A passage of Hindi printed in the Nagari script

एक दिन बेगम साहृबा के सिर में दर्द होने लगा । उन्होंने लौंडी से कहा — जा कर मिर्ज़ा साहृब को बुला ला । किसी हृकीम के यहाँ से दवा लायें । दौड़, जल्दी कर । लौंडी गयी तो मिरज़ाजी ने कहा — चल, अभी आते हैं । बेगम साहृवा का मिजाज गरम था । इतनी ताब कहाँ कि उनके सिर में दर्द हो और पति शतरंज खेलता रहें । चेहरा सुर्ख हो गया । लौंडी से कहा — जा कर कह, अभी चलिए, नहीं तो वह आप ही हृकीम के यहाँ चली जायेंगी ।

A direct transliteration and word-for-word translation

ek   din begam sāhabā ke sir   meṅ dard hone lagā.
One day Begam Sahiba -'s head in   pain to-be began.

unhoṅne lauṇḍī se   kahā – jā-kar   mirzā sāhib ko
Her-by maid from said   'having-gone Mirza Sahib to

bulā lā.   kisī hakīm ke yahāṅ se   davā
call bring. Some doctor -'s house from medicine

lāeṅ.   dauṛ, jaldī kar.   lauṇḍī gayī to
(he) may-bring. Run, haste make.' Maid went then

mirzājī ne kahā – cal abhī   āte haiṅ. begam
Mirzaji by said 'Go, just-now (we) come.' Begam

241

sāhabā kā mizāj   garm thā. itnī   tāb   kahāṅ
Sahiba -'s temper hot was. So-much patience where

ki   unke sir   meṅ dard ho aur pati   shatranj
that her head in   pain be and husband chess

kheltā   rahe.   cehrā surkh ho gayā. lauṇḍī se
playing remain. Face red   became. Maid from

kahā – jā-kar   kah, abhī   calie,   nahīṅ to
said 'Having-gone say, "Just-now let-him-go, not   then

vah ap hī   hakīm ke yahāṅ jāeṅgī.
she her*self* doctor -'s house will go."'

An idiomatic translation

One day Begam Sahiba started to have a headache. 'Go and call Mirza Sahib,' she told the maid, 'and ask him to get me some medicine from a doctor's. Run along, hurry!' When the maid went to him Mirzaji said, 'Off you go, I'm just coming.' Begam Sahiba was furious. How could she put up with having a headache while her husband went on playing chess? Her face flushed. She told the maid to go and tell him to leave straight away, otherwise she'd go to the doctor's herself.

(From *The Chess Players* by Prem Chand)

A passage of Urdu in Perso-Arabic calligraphy

اب سوال یہ اٹھتا ہے کہ اگر وہ سب کچھ ٹھیک ہے جو اردو والے ہندی کے متعلق اور ہندی
والے اردو کے متعلق سوچتے ہیں ، اور اگر ان دونوں زبانوں کی بنیاد مصنوعی اور غیر فطری ہے ، تو پھر
اس کا کیا سبب ہے کہ ان دونوں زبانوں کی دن بدن ترقی ہو رہی ہے اور ان کی مقبولیت عوام میں
بڑھ رہی ہے ؟

A direct transliteration and word-for-word translation

ab   savāl   ye uṭhtā hai ki   agar vo sab kuch   ṭhīk hai jo
now question this arising is that if   that all   something right is which

urdū vāle   hindī ke muta'alliq aur hindī vāle   urdū ke muta'alliq
Urdu wallahs Hindi -'s about   and Hindi wallahs Urdu -'s about

socte   haiṅ, aur agar in   donoṅ zubānoṅ kī bunyād   masnūī
thinking are, and if   these both languages -'s foundation   artificial

aur ghair-fitrī hai, to   phir is   kā kyā   sabab hai ki   in   donoṅ
and unnatural is,   then so   this -'s what reason is   that these both

zubānoṅ   kī din ba-din taraqqī   ho   rahī hai aur in   kī
languages -'s day by-day development happen -ing is   and these -'s

maqbūliyat avām   meṅ baṛh   rahī hai?
popularity people in   grow -ing is?

An idiomatic translation

The question now arises that if all that the Urdu supporters think about
Hindi and the Hindi speakers about Urdu is correct, and the basis of
both these languages is artificial and unnatural, then what is the reason
that both languages are developing day by day and that their popularity
among ordinary people is growing?

(From *Hindi and Urdu since 1800*, C. Shackle and R. Snell)

Speakers of Dravidian languages: Tamil, Malayalam, Kannada, Telugu

Sita Narasimhan

Distribution

SOUTH INDIA, SRI LANKA, SINGAPORE, Malaysia, Indonesia, East and South Africa, Mauritius, Burma, Vietnam, Guyana, the Caribbean; there are Tamil-speaking communities in many other parts of the world.

Introduction

Many of the problems faced by speakers of Dravidian languages when they learn English are shared with speakers of other South Asian languages. For details of these, see pages 227–243. However, Dravidian languages are agglutinative languages, like Turkish; they differ radically in their phonology, morphology and syntax from the Indo-European languages of the subcontinent, and have correspondingly less in common with English than these languages. Speakers of Dravidian languages therefore encounter a number of additional problems when learning English. This chapter deals with the English of Tamil-speaking learners, but the points made are generally valid for speakers of other Dravidian languages.

Phonology

Vowels

The Tamil vowel system consists of five pairs of short and long vowels: /ʌ/, /ɑ/; /ɪ/, /iː/; /e/, /eː/; /o/, /oː/; /u/, /uː/.

All the vowels are undiphthongised, though raised or lowered in context. The two vowels /o/ (a pure close rounded short vowel) and /oː/ (the long equivalent) have no close counterparts in standard British English, though similar vowels occur in Scottish, Irish and other regional varieties.

There are two diphthongs: /aɪ/ (like the vowel in *buy*) and /aʊ/ (like the vowel in *cow*).

Common problems:
1. English diphthongs tend not to be accurately perceived, and are mostly pronounced as two short vowels with interpolated glides, as in *paint* /pe(y)int/ and *pound* /pʌ(w)ʊnd/.
2. Vowels may be shortened or lengthened in accordance with Dravidian pronunciation patterns. A popular chain-store called 'Foodworld' is pronounced /pʰʊdˌvʌrˌd/; *vegetable* is commonly pronounced /ʋedʒɪʈʈeːbuḷ/.
3. Learners find it especially difficult to distinguish and produce the vowels in *cot*, *caught* and *coat*, which have no close Tamil equivalents; the vowel in *pat* may also be confused with that in *pot* or *part*.

Consonants

1. Tamil consonants can all be pronounced with retroflexion – that is to say, with the front of the tongue curled up and back to touch the top of the hard palate. This is an often-imitated feature of an 'Indian accent', but is particularly striking in Tamil speakers.
2. Dravidian languages do not have aspirated consonants. This means that English initial /p/, /t/ and /k/, which are normally aspirated, are hard for learners to produce correctly; they typically substitute retroflex consonants. Hearers may interpret these as /b/, /d/ and /g/ respectively, hearing *pear*, *ten* and *could*, for example, as *bear*, *den* and *good*.
3. The fundamental English distinction between voiced consonants (e.g. /b, d, g, z/) and their unvoiced equivalents (e.g. /p, t, k, s/) has no counterpart in Tamil, where all consonants can be voiced in certain positions. This leads to predictable confusions.
4. Tamil consonants are 'geminated', or doubled in certain positions, so that a 'single' consonant may be fully pronounced twice (as if *Duchies* were pronounced like *Dutch cheese*). Carried over into English, this can help to make learners hard to understand.
5. /θ/ and /ð/, as in *think* and *then*, cause great difficulty, since the approximate Tamil equivalents are dental rather than interdental. Learners' pronunciation may come close to /t/ and /d/.
6. There is no /z/ in Tamil; *maze* may sound like *mace*.
7. There is no /f/ in Tamil; learners may pronounce English /f/ as an aspirated /p/, leading to confusion between, for example, *full* and *pull*.
8. /ʒ/ does not exist in Tamil, and /ʃ/ is substituted in words such as *occasion*.
9. Final nasal consonants as in *him*, *thin* are heavily pronounced. Final /ŋ/ as in *thing* is geminated to /ŋg/: 'thingg'.

10. The systematic English distinction between initial 'clear' /l/ as in *look* and final 'dark' /l/ as in *full* is difficult for Tamil speakers; Tamil has a variety of different consonants in this area, but they are not distinguished in this way.

Syllable structure; consonant clusters

Tamil has far more consonant clusters than, for instance, Hindi, so Tamil-speaking learners do not have very serious trouble with this aspect of English. However, Tamil words do not usually end in consonants, and learners may add a weak /ʊ/ at the ends of some English words to facilitate pronunciation.

Stress and rhythm

The problems are largely similar to those of speakers of other South Asian languages. Note, however:

1. Tamil has a distinctive stress pattern in which, to generalise, syllables with long vowels and closed syllables ending in geminated consonants bear the stress.
2. Speakers who have learnt English largely from studying written texts may tend to pronounce each word as a separate unit, so that no sentence rhythm emerges.

Morphology and syntax

General

Tamil morphology is 'agglutinating' or 'concatenating'. That is to say, grammatical and semantic elements are 'stuck on' in sequence as suffixes to a word stem:

> அழித்தார்கள்
>
> [azhitta:rgal]
>
> destroy – past suffix – plural suffix
>
> = *They destroyed.*

The notion of 'word' does not therefore have the same status in Tamil and English: a Tamil word may contain elements that in English would be expressed by several different words belonging to different parts of speech, and the boundaries between parts of speech themselves are somewhat fluid in Tamil. Learners may have considerable difficulty in grasping concepts and distinctions that are commonplace in the grammar of Indo-European languages, such as aspect, modality, auxiliary, adjective, adverb, preposition; and in understanding the ways in which English words are structured into clauses and sentences.

Word order and sentence structure

Modifiers precede modified elements (but see 'Relatives' below). Verbs come at the end of Tamil sentences, and main verbs precede auxiliaries, which can lead beginners to make mistakes.

A Tamil sentence can be formed without a finite verb, or without an expressed subject or object. There is a marked cultural preference for impersonal structures, and for avoiding specifying agency when reporting an action. (See the text at the end of the chapter for examples.) All of these features may be reflected in learners' English.

Complex sentences

Complement clauses precede main clauses in Tamil. Relationships such as co-ordination, contrast and condition, which tend to be expressed by conjunctions in English, may be indicated in other ways in Tamil syntax. Learners may not therefore always make these relationships explicit. Conditional structures cause particular problems.

Distinctions between finite and non-finite forms are not always clear-cut. A Tamil sentence, however complex, only has one finite verb at most; all other verbs will appear in participle-like forms. Learners may carry this over into English, using *-ing* forms instead of finite verbs in subordinate clauses.

Indirect speech

English indirect speech structures are very different from their Tamil equivalents, and learners may find them difficult to get used to.

Relatives

Tamil does not have relative pronouns. The Tamil equivalent of an English relative structure involves putting a clause before the noun (on the lines of *'living next door people'* or *'foreign returned people'* for *'the people who live next door'* or *'people who have returned from abroad'*).

247

Learners therefore find English relative structures difficult, and may avoid using them.

Interrogatives and negatives

Students find the English use of auxiliaries for questions and negatives, and inverted word order for questions, hard to learn. (Questions are marked in Tamil by intonation and an interrogative particle.) Question tags may be replaced by a single negative marker: *You will come, no?*

Tenses

Tamil has a complex system of tenses, with meanings that do not always correspond closely to those of their nearest English equivalents. For example the 'future tense' can express habituality, conjecture or wishes, among other things.

> *In young age I will play a lot. (for When I was young I played a lot.)*
>
> *Next year he will come back home. (for Next year he may come back home.)*
>
> *Tomorrow I will win a prize. (for I wish I could win a prize tomorrow.)*

Articles

Tamil lacks what we call articles, though demonstratives are used in ways corresponding to some of the uses of English articles. Predictably, learners find the article system difficult. Typical mistakes involve using *one* instead of *a/an*, and leaving out *the* except in demonstrative and emphatic contexts.

Emphatic and reflexive pronouns

Tamil has various emphatic and reflexive markers, leading learners to overuse their English equivalents.

> *When he was young itself he lost his father.*
> *There itself I ate my lunch.*
> *It was he himself who stole the book.*
> *The book belongs to myself.*
> *She only stole the jewel, not her sister.*

Adjectives and adverbs

These may be confused with each other, or with nouns or verbs (see remarks above on parts of speech).

Tamil expresses comparative and superlative meanings by special particles, not by changes in the adjective.

Adjectives and adverbs are typically repeated for emphasis.

Hierarchy and honorifics

Tamil has various linguistic devices for indicating the relative status of speaker and hearer. Learners may feel uneasy at not knowing how to do this in English, and may assume that they are missing something.

Speech and writing

The gap between the spoken and written varieties is great in all Dravidian languages. This may lead learners to favour an over-elaborate or over-formal style in written English.

A literal translation of a Tamil text, with a normal English gloss

இது ஒரு மனிதனின் ஒரு நாளைய வாழ்க்கை.

This one man-of one day-of (adj.) living.
This is one day of a man's living.

You (hon.) having-dared-being-if having-done-being-able small-nesses,
The pettinesses that you might have committed if you had dared,

compel-being-forced-being-if having-shown-being-able daring,
the daring you might have displayed if you had been forced to,

having-wished-being-if having-received-being-able diseases,
the diseases you might have got if you had desired,

having-touched/taken-being-if attained-being-possible disrepute/shame,
the shame you might have achieved if you had allowed yourself to be touched,

these-indeed that-man life.
these indeed are that man's life.

That-man-that next day (acc.) about we knowing taking need-not.
There is no need for us to find out about his next day.

Why-asked-if that-man-to-also – us-among many-to like-indeed –
Because, for that man too – as for many among us –

tomorrow   different-one day-indeed!
tomorrow is another   day.

(G. Nagarajan)

Reference

Thomas Lehmann, *A Grammar of Modern Tamil*. Pondicherry, 1989.

Speakers of West African languages

Philip Tregidgo

Introduction

The languages of West Africa are too numerous and diverse for detailed regional listing. Within each state many different mother tongues are spoken, often unrelated one to another and mutually quite unintelligible. Even those which have achieved some status as a *lingua franca* within a given area tend to have more than one dialect, and any written literature will be of recent origin. Many languages are spoken only within very small areas, and many have never been written down at all.

From an English language teaching point of view, it is more useful to classify the states of West Africa according to their official second language (English or French). The second language is the language of government and, to a large extent, of education, subject to local policy. It is also the medium of a growing African literature, since French, and particularly English, command greater prestige and a far wider market than any of the mother tongues. For these reasons, the choice of English or French as an official second language tends to have a stronger influence on English teaching materials and methods than the mother tongue of pupils or teacher.

A large proportion of the population are of limited education, and understand only a few words of English, or none at all. Those who have had an elementary education may use English only occasionally, and with severely limited competence. Even the highly educated elite do not necessarily speak it in the home, and may seldom read it, except in the press and at work.

The status of pidgin English is controversial. Each anglophone country has its own dialect of pidgin, used to some extent as a popular *lingua franca*, and pidgins in general are attracting increasing attention academically. But pidgin English is strongly opposed by most West African intellectuals, and it has little official recognition. It will not be considered here, though it will be reflected in many of the features of pronunciation and grammar to be referred to. (Note that much of the strangeness of written pidgin derives from its spelling, which is adapted to suit the pronunciation.)

The anglophone states of West Africa include Nigeria, Ghana, Sierra Leone, and Gambia (all former British colonies), and also Liberia, which has historical links, now tenuous, with the USA. In Cameroon, English has, in theory, equal status with French, but in practice only two of its five provinces (about 25 per cent of the population) are anglophone.

The francophone states (apart from Cameroon) comprise Mauritania, Mali, Niger, Chad, Senegal, Guinea, The Ivory Coast, Burkina Faso, Togo and Benin. Here the education system shows a strong French influence, and English, learnt by some as a third language, tends to be spoken with a French accent. These anglophone and francophone countries cover the whole of West Africa except for Guinea-Bissau. Arabic is not learnt except to some extent for religious purposes among Islamic peoples, chiefly in the sub-Saharan areas.

The most important of the mother tongues in anglophone West Africa (apart from English in Liberia) are as follows:

- *Nigeria*: Hausa and Fulani in the north, Yoruba in the southwest, Ibo in the southeast. Hausa is probably the most important and highly developed of all West African languages. It has been strongly influenced by Arabic, and has a long literary tradition. It is Ibo speakers, however, who have contributed most to modern Nigerian literature in English.
- *Ghana*: The Akan group of languages (mainly Twi and Fante) in Ashanti and the south, Ga in the area of Accra, Ewe (usually pronounced *evay*) in the southeast, Dagbani and others in the north.
- *Sierra Leone*: A little English in Freetown, but mainly Krio in the west, Temne and others in the north, and Mende (= Mande, Mandingo) in the south.
- *Gambia*: Mende, Wolof and others.
- *Liberia*: a little English in Monrovia, but mainly a variety of other languages.

Although the influences of these many first and second languages are very diverse, it is possible to talk about typical West African problems for learners who adopt standard British English as a target model. These problems may be partly due to the interference of certain broad features that are common to many West African languages, such as tonality and a comparatively simple vowel system, partly also to the development of an African variety of English as a *lingua franca*, and partly to common cultural features. The ensuing analysis applies particularly to Nigeria and Ghana, which (especially the former) make up the heavy nucleus of West African English teaching.

Phonology

General

West African languages tend to have fewer vowels than English, and fewer final consonants and consonant clusters. Thus many English vowels are not differentiated by West Africans, and many mid and final consonants sound indistinct. In addition, most West African languages are both tonal and syllable-timed. These features tend to give West African English a jerkiness, both in timing (with unnaturally regular syllables, and not much variation of emphasis) and in intonation (with ups and downs, but not much overall pattern).

Vowels

1. /iː/ and /ɪ/ often sound identical, both being pronounced short, and sometimes further confused with /eɪ/: *ship* for *sheep*, or sometimes *shape*.
2. /e/ and /ɜː/ are very often identical: *bed* and *bird*. The /ɜː/ phoneme causes particular problems, and may be further confused with /ɑː/: *bird* and *barred*.
3. /æ/, /ɑː/ and /ʌ/ are confused: *cat*, *cart* and *cut*. In some areas /æ/ and /ʌ/ are confused with /e/: *bat* and *but* with *bet*.
4. /ɒ/, /ɔː/ and /əʊ/ are confused: *rod*, *roared* and *road*.
5. /ʊ/ is confused with /uː/: *pull* and *pool*.
6. /ə/, like /ɜː/, causes great difficulty, not only in itself, but also (more especially) because West Africans do not generally weaken the vowels of unstressed syllables. As a result they tend to pronounce English words as they are spelt, making a clear difference, for example, between *policeman* and *policemen*, *-ence* and *-ance*, etc. The indefinite and definite articles are pronounced approximately /ɑː/ and /de/, and *-er* endings are pronounced /ɑː/.
7. No distinction is made in vowel length. All vowels tend to be pronounced short. This increases the confusion between voiced and voiceless consonants, as in *write* and *ride*.

Consonants

1. /θ/ and /ð/ are usually pronounced /d/ and /t/: *day* for *they*; *tin* for *thin*; *tree* for *three*, etc.
2. /ŋ/ is commonly pronounced /n/ or /ŋg/: '*singin*' for *singing*.
3. In some areas /l/ and /r/ are confused: '*rolly*' for *lorry*, and there may

253

be widespread confusion between, for example, *grass* and *glass*; *play* and *pray*, etc.

4. Voiced final consonants tend to be devoiced and the preceding vowel shortened: *write* for *ride*; *rice* for *rise*; *rope* for *robe*; *picks* for *pigs*, etc.

5. Consonant clusters cause difficulty, especially where final, when some consonants tend to be omitted: *nest* for *next*; *knees* for *needs*; *fat* for *fact*, etc.

6. Final clusters such as *film, months, asked, helps*, etc. cause special problems, and the same sort of difficulty occurs at junctures, as in *five big towns*. For these reasons there is often a general indistinctness in the consonants of continuous speech, which hinders comprehension more than inaccurate vowel pronunciation.

Influence of spelling on pronunciation

As has already been mentioned, vowels that should be pronounced weak are very commonly given the full form implied by the spelling. It may also be the influence of spelling that causes such words as *tongue, among, money, stomach, love, other* and *touch* to be pronounced with /ɒ/ or /ɔ:/ instead of /ʌ/. Pronunciation faults also affect spelling, of course, especially following the successful use of direct method teaching in primary schools: *the order one; in other that; the sun bent my skin*, etc.

Rhythm and stress

West African languages are typically syllable-timed, which strongly affects the rhythm of West African English. Stress-timed speech is totally unfamiliar. Contrastive stress, as in *I **did** it* v. *I did **it*** or *Did you say the **green** book or the **red** book?* also needs special attention.

Intonation

West African languages are typically tonal, i.e. each lexical item, even of a single syllable, will have a fixed tone or sequence of tones, irrespective of its context. Thus the concept of a particular tone applying to a whole utterance, and being capable of variation for the sake of emphasis or attitude, is quite strange. The intonation of West African English is largely limited to a rise for *yes/no* questions and for pauses within the sentence, and a final fall for statements and *wh*-questions. Other patterns are rarely heard except among the highly educated. A further difficulty arises when an African name with its fixed intonation has to be fitted into an English sentence, since it is almost impossible to avoid distorting either the English intonation pattern or the pronunciation of the name.

Punctuation

The hyphen and the dash are not well understood and are often confused. In some areas a comma is often used incorrectly before reported speech:
> *He said that, he doesn't want to come.*

Other common mistakes, e.g. overuse of capitals or commas between complete sentences (often incorrectly linked with *also, however*, etc.) are, of course, not confined to West Africa.

Grammar

General

It would be difficult even for a specialist to make valid and useful generalisations about the grammar of West African languages, but every teacher of English in West Africa quickly notices the recurrence of certain types of mistake. The following selection is very widespread, though the part played by mother tongue interference is not always clear, and regional variations are certainly found.

Verbs

1. The regular endings and the use of auxiliaries in the simple present and past cause frequent problems:
   > *She want to speak English, but she don't know how.*
   > *He doesn't goes to school.*
   > *He didn't came back.*
2. Mistakes are common when verb phrases are reduced after conjunctions:
   > *I didn't see anything or heard anything.*
   > *He made me sit down and told him about it.*

   Either/or questions produce similar errors:
   > *Do you make it by hand, or you use a machine?*
3. The infinitive form after *make, let, see* and *hear* causes problems:

> **He makes me to do it.*
> **He makes me does it.*
> **I saw him did it.*

4. Choice of an appropriate tense form causes many problems. Progressive forms may be wrongly selected with certain stative uses of e.g. *have, think* and *see*:
> **I was having no money.*
> **I am thinking you are wrong.*
> **I am not seeing anything.*

5. The present perfect is frequently misused or not used:
> **I have seen him yesterday.*
> **I am a teacher since 1980.*

6. The past perfect, too, is not generally understood, and tends to be used in place of *used to*:
> **In the old days we had travelled on foot.*

Used to itself is often used in the present for habitual action:
> **That boy use to tell lies.* (for *That boy tells lies.*)

7. *I will* and *I am going to* (or in pidgin *I go*, e.g. *I go kill him*) tend to be overused when the contracted form *I'll* would be more apt.

Modal verbs

Modal verbs and related forms are used fairly well on the whole, though epistemic uses (e.g. *That must/may/can't be true*) are not well understood:

Must and is to tend to be overused at the expense of *have to*:
> **I can't come as I must take an exam.*
> **Nowadays all children are to go to school.*

Needn't is often followed by *to*:
> **You needn't to say that.*

Nouns, articles and determiners

1. The difference between countable and uncountable nouns is not well understood, and many uncountables are wrongly classified:
> **We had a rain this morning.*
> **He gave me some informations.*

Similar mistakes occur with other nouns: e.g. *firewood, food, luggage, advice, furniture, news, equipment, help, dress, property, land, luck, permission.*

2. Other mistakes with articles may or may not be related to countability:

This is goat. (Names of animals in particular tend to be treated as proper nouns.)
   This instrument is called thermometer.
   He has written some book.
3. *Some* often occurs after negatives:
   I don't want some.
4. The definite article is often wrongly used or omitted with names and titles:
   Do you want to speak to Minister?
   He goes to Roman Catholic school.
   *The South Africa   *The Tema Harbour*
5. Expressions of quantity are often misused, e.g. *much*:
   They don't have much children.
   Yes, I can eat much.
   It is much interesting.
6. *Little* and *few* are also confused, and the negative effect of omitting *a* is not understood:
   There are a little eggs.
   Give me few more oranges.
   There are a few mosquitoes, so we do not suffer from malaria.

Intensification and comparison

1. *Too* may be confused with *very*:
   This stew is too good!
   He ran too fast to catch the bus.
2. *Enough* is often not understood:
   The roads are bad, so there are enough accidents.
3. *So* is often used inappropriately in a formal non-emphatic style to mean *very*:
   In the southwest there is so much forest.
4. Comparatives may be used instead of positive forms:
   The library contains more books. (for *The library contains quite a lot of books.*)

Pronouns

1. *He* and *him* are often used for human females and for animals:
   I greeted my sister when he came.
2. Reflexive pronouns are often used instead of *each other*:
   They greeted themselves.
3. In continuous writing there is a tendency to avoid pronouns (and

other anaphoric devices) in an effort towards completeness and clarity, and the result often sounds wordy and repetitive.

Subordinate clauses

A. Conditional

Tense forms in conditional sentences cause problems:
> *If I tell him, he would beat me.*
> *If it would not have happened, he would not be killed.*

B. Time clauses

These have similar tense form problems, and *if* is commonly used incorrectly for *when*, in referring to the future:
> *If the sun sets this evening the meeting will begin.*

C. Indirect speech

Sequence of tense rules in indirect speech are not well understood:
> *Jesus told them he will die.*
> *I didn't know you are here.*
> *I hope you would come.*

Indirect questions are not distinguished from direct ones:
> *I want to know how do you do it.*
> *He asked her that, will you marry me.*

D. Concessive

Though clauses tend to be followed by *but* in the main clause; and *however* clauses cause word order difficulties:
> *Although it is difficult, but I can do it.*
> *However it is difficult, I will do it.*

E. Relative

Relative clauses commonly cause problems, especially the repetition of pronouns:
> *That is the man I saw him.*

Vocabulary and culture

Where English is a second language as opposed to a foreign language, it becomes to some extent the property of the non-native user; it is adapted to his or her own purposes, and reflects his or her own culture. Africans themselves have often resisted this notion, especially in the presence of a British teacher, and claim to want to learn standard British English. The fact remains that in West African countries English has already been adapted in certain characteristic ways; in pronunciation, in vocabulary and general expression, even in certain marginal points of grammar; and many teachers will find difficulty in deciding how far to go in 'correcting' certain features in order to make them conform to the British norm. Should one, for example, accept a *storey-building*; *He has travelled far* (for *He is away*); *We are tight friends*; *They were making noise*, etc., all of which are commonly used in West African English? Should one try to reduce the degree of formality in letter writing, or in greetings, which is ingrained in West African culture? Such questions remain highly debatable.

West African languages are rich in proverbs and colourful sayings. Africans tend in consequence to be unduly attracted to English proverbs and sayings, and to mistake them for idioms, to be used as often as possible.

The reading of fiction and biography for pleasure is comparatively rare. Most reading is done for educational or self-improvement purposes, at a very slow pace, and with excessive use of the dictionary. Books chosen tend to be very dry and didactic. Choice of suitable fiction is not easy. African students are often totally unfamiliar with European objects, attitudes, interests, worries and conventions, and from this point of view, twentieth century fiction is often less suitable than, say, Dickens. The rapid expansion since the 1950s of a genuinely African literature in English suggests a possible solution, but the language of much of it is too difficult at junior secondary level, and the content is sometimes controversial.

Swahili speakers

Neville Grant

Distribution

TANZANIA, KENYA, UGANDA, MOZAMBIQUE, ZAIRE, Comoros, Somalia, Rwanda, Burundi, Oman, Zambia.

Introduction

Swahili is the most important language in East Africa, with at least 60 million speakers. Only a minority speak Swahili as their mother tongue: most speak it as a second, third, or even fourth language. Swahili is the national language of Tanzania, one of the four African national languages of Zaire, and the official language of Kenya. It plays a very important role as a *lingua franca* in Eastern and to some extent Central Africa, where it is very widely used both in local trade and international broadcasting. It is used in a number of newspapers, and has a growing literature.

Recent research indicates that Swahili was emerging as a separate language as early as the ninth century, and that it probably originated from around the Tana River estuary in Kenya. But as trade developed, the language spread both up and down the East African coast, and into the interior. The name Swahili comes from the Arabic word sawāḥil, meaning *coasts*, and the language contains a number of words of Arabic origin. However, the language is essentially African.

Swahili belongs to the Bantu family of languages, which are spoken by most Africans south of a line drawn roughly from Douala in Cameroon in the west, eastwards to the north of Lake Victoria; and from the east of Lake Victoria across to Brava in Somalia. Swahili is not completely typical of Bantu languages (see below), but it is the most widely spoken language in black Africa, and it shares with the other Bantu languages all their most outstanding structural and morphological characteristics. Because of this, many if not most of the observations made about Swahili in this chapter may be applied, *mutatis mutandis*, to other Bantu languages.

Bantu languages share *inter alia* the following characteristics:

1. *Noun class system*   In any Bantu language almost all noun forms consist of a prefix plus stem. The prefix will act as a marker, indicating what class the noun is in:

   mtu = *person*   watu = *people*
   kiko = *a pipe*   viko = *pipes*

   The number of noun classes varies slightly from one Bantu language to another. Swahili has some fifteen noun classes, rather fewer than most other Bantu languages.

2. *Concord*   In Bantu languages the noun dominates the sentence. The other words in the sentence are brought into concordial relationship with the noun by means of affixes called *concords*. Two examples of Swahili will suffice:

   Kisu kile kikubwa kimevunjika. (lit. *knife – that – big – is broken*) = *That big knife is broken.*

   Visu vile vikubwa vimevunjika. (lit. *knives – those – big – are broken*) = *Those big knives are broken.*

3. *Agglutination*   All Bantu languages have an agglutinating morphological structure (words may contain various grammatical particles). Here is a Swahili example:

   wameshindwa
   wa = *they*
   me = tense/aspect marker
   shinda = stem of the verb kushinda *to conquer*
   w = passive marker
   (meaning *They have been conquered.*)

4. *Sound systems*   Bantu languages have a very similar sound system:
   – Most Bantu languages are tonal: however, tonality is virtually absent from most dialects of Swahili.
   – Phonemically the Bantu languages are also remarkably similar. Most of them have the same five vowel phonemes (see below), and no diphthongs. The consonant systems are also very similar, except that some of the southern Bantu languages have borrowed some Khoisan 'click' sounds, and Swahili has borrowed some Arabic sounds for words of Arabic origin.

These then are some of the salient defining characteristics of Bantu languages. It will be seen that the main differences between Swahili and the other Bantu languages lie in the few words of Arabic origin it has borrowed, together with some consonants, its lack of tonality, and in the smaller number of noun classes that it contains. In all other respects, Swahili may be regarded as a typical Bantu language, and the comments that follow about Swahili speakers' difficulties in learning English will therefore be applicable to a very large extent to speakers of other Bantu languages as well.

Phonology

General

The main differences between Swahili and English are as follows:
- Swahili has only five vowels, in contrast to the 22 of English.
- English has 24 consonants; Swahili has 28.
- Swahili speech alternates vowels with consonants, and contains virtually no consonant clusters.
- In Swahili, all utterances and syllables end in a vowel sound.
- The two languages have very different systems of word stress.
- The intonation patterns are somewhat different.

Vowels

The vowel sounds represent the biggest single problem area for Swahili speakers learning English. The five vowels of Swahili are as follows:

/i/ ⎫
/e/ ⎬ These are slightly higher than their nearest equivalents in English.
/u/ ⎭

/a/   This sound is shorter, higher and further forward than its nearest English equivalent.

/o/   This sound is somewhere between the English /ɒ/ and /əʊ/.

Virtually all English vowel and diphthong sounds may therefore cause problems. The tendency is for Swahili speakers to deploy the Swahili sound that they perceive as being nearest to the target English sound, and this problem is compounded by the notoriously misleading orthography of English. The problem may be summarised conveniently by this diagram:

Swahili phonemes	English phonemes (RP)	Key words
/i/	/iː/	*bead*
	/ɪ/	*bid*
	/ɪə/	*beard*
	/eɪ/	*bayed*
/e/	/e/	*bed*
	/eə/	*bared*
	/ʌ/	*bud*
	/æ/	*bad*
	/ɜː/	*bird*
/a/	/ɑː/	*bard*
	/aʊ/	*bowed*
	/aɪ/	*bide*
	/ɒ/	*bod*
/o/	/ɔː/	*board*
	/əʊ/	*bode*
	/ɔɪ/	*buoyed*
	/ʊ/	*bull*
/u/	/ʊə/	*boor*
	/uː/	*booed*

The author is indebted to Dr H. F. Grant for a version of the diagram above. Another version (featuring General American) appears in Polomé (1967).

The English phoneme /ə/ is omitted from this diagram, as it has no equivalent in Swahili and requires special attention. In practice Swahili speakers tend to assign to it the sound value most strongly implied by the orthographic symbol that represents it, e.g. *again* might be pronounced /ægeɪn/.

Specific sound contrasts causing difficulties include:

/iː/ and /ɪ/	*leave* and *live*
/æ/ and /e/	*band* and *bend*
/æ/ and /ʌ/	*rag* and *rug*
/æ/ and /ɑː/	*hat* and *heart*
/ɑː/ and /ʌ/	*heart* and *hut*
/ɪ/ and /e/	*bit* and *bet*
/ɜː/ and /ʌ/	*bird* and *bud*
/e/ and /ɜː/	*lend* and *learned*
/ɒ/, /ɔː/ and /əʊ/	*cot*, *caught* and *coat*
/e/ and /eɪ/	*edge* and *age*
/ʊ/ and /uː/	*full* and *fool*
/æ/ and /ɜː/	*tanned* and *turned*

Swahili speakers

Consonants

All the English consonants have their rough equivalents in Swahili, except /r/, which in Swahili is an alveolar trill, not unlike a rolled Scottish /r/. In addition there is a certain amount of dialectical variation in Swahili, which can cause problems that are not easily predictable. There may also be influences on the speaker's English from his or her first language, if this is not Swahili. Predictable problems include:

1. /l/ and /r/ are often confused by those who speak Swahili as a second or third language: *load* for *road*.
2. /h/ is sometimes dropped: *eat* for *heat*.
3. /θ/ and /ð/ occur in Swahili words derived from Arabic, but not in other Bantu languages. Such words and sounds are avoided in some dialects: the sounds /t/ or /s/ may be used for /θ/, and /d/ or /z/ for /ð/: *useful* for *youthful*; *breeze* for *breathe*, etc.
4. The following sound contrasts are not made in some dialects of Swahili and other Bantu languages, and confusion can arise:
   /g/ and /k/: *engaged* and *encaged*
   /b/ and /p/: *bride* and *pride*
   /dʒ/ and /tʃ/: *judge* and *church*
   /t/ and /d/: *train* and *drain*
5. /s/ replaces /ʃ/ in some dialects of Swahili, which can carry over into English: *sew* for *show*.
6. In Zairian Swahili and in other Bantu languages, /g/ is devoiced to /k/, and /z/ to /s/: *lock* for *log* and *peace* for *peas*.
7. Also in Zairian Swahili, /d/ and /l/ may be used in free variation, as may /l/ and /r/; even sometimes /b/ and /w/.

Syllabic intrusion and addition

Consonant clusters are much rarer in Swahili than in English, and Swahili speakers therefore tend to separate out the consonants in a cluster with 'intrusive' vowel sounds. In addition, Swahili speakers tend to add an extra vowel to utterances ending in a consonant:
/ekɪsplaneɪʃon/ for *explanation*
/sɪtɪrenɪθɪ/ for *strength*

Influence of spelling on pronunciation

Since there is a regular correspondence between sound and orthographic symbol in Swahili, the unwary learner is easily misled by the irregularities of English spelling. The problems are fairly predictable:

1. Silent letters may be pronounced, e.g. in *honour* and *sign.*
2. Incorrect sound values will be assigned to words that are oddly spelt, e.g. *'orainge'* for *orange,* *'biskwit'* for *biscuit,* etc.

Rhythm and stress

Swahili is a syllable-timed language, whereas English is a stress-timed language. In consequence, Swahili speakers tend to give every syllable in English almost equal stress.

Weak forms in English tend to be overstressed, and may be given their strong pronunciation.

Swahili, in common with all other Bantu languages, stresses the penultimate syllable of a word. Carried over into English, this can lead to distortions in words like *photo'graphy, hospital'ity, ci'garette,* etc.

Intonation

In Swahili the typical intonation pattern is a low fall, which is carried over into English even where English uses a rise. As a result it is not always clear if a Swahili speaker is, for example, asking a question in English.

Grammar

General

From the description of Bantu languages above, it will already be apparent that there are radical differences between the grammatical systems of English and Swahili. The noun class system, noun dominance, and agglutination have already been referred to. Swahili also has a number of extremely economical inflectional devices for signalling a great variety of grammatical meanings.

Aliweka kalamu mezani. (= *He (or she) put the pen on the table.*)

A	li	weka	kalamu	meza	ni
third person sing. pronoun marker	simple past tense marker	verb: *put*	noun: *pen*	noun: *table*	location marker

Swahili does not have anything quite like the English auxiliary verb system for asking questions, indicating tense and modality, etc. In Swahili there are no articles, and there is no gender marking. English prepositions have no exact equivalent in Swahili, which uses locative forms attached to the noun, as in the example above (mezani), various class concords, and a variety of multi-purpose prepositional inflections and particles.

Word order – S-V-O, S-V-IO-O – is more or less the same (in statements, but not in questions), but in Swahili, as in all Bantu languages, aspect is at least as important as tense, and this leads to a wide variety of confusions in using verbs in English.

Questions and negatives; auxiliaries

1. The auxiliary *do* has no equivalent in Swahili, and tends therefore to be misused, or omitted:
   He not leave yesterday.
   He leave yesterday?
   Why the boys hid behind the trees?
2. Sometimes *do* is used unnecessarily:
   Every morning I do get up and I do have my breakfast.
3. *Yes/no* questions are marked only by a change of intonation, and orthographically by the question mark:
   The work it is finished?
4. Questions with a question word follow either the pattern 'statement + interrogative', or the pattern 'interrogative + statement':
   He arrived when?
   Why you are late?
5. *No* and *not* tend to be used interchangeably:
   He is no going to the mosque today.
   There is no any rice in the market.
   (See also the section 'Articles and determiners'.)

Time and tense

Time is indicated by the following tense markers (infixes):

1. -na-: Present time
   Watoto wanasoma. (= *The children are reading. / The children read.*)
   Swahili uses adverbials to differentiate between present progressive and simple present, and the two tenses are thus confused in English:
   They are going to school every morning.

Also affected are verbs of perception, and non-conclusive verbs, such as *know, like, have,* and *understand*:

> **I am seeing many different colours in that khanga.*
> **I am having no news from home.*

Another very common error is the omission of the *-s* on the third person singular form of the simple present:

> **The boy love to play football.*

In subordinate clauses -na- can also be used as a marker to indicate the present time in the context. When carried over into English, this results in many tense errors, in direct and reported speech:

> **The students realised that the school is on fire.*
> **One day she was told that her mother is ill.*

2. -li-: Past time

> Nilikwenda mjini jana. (= *I went to town yesterday.*)

It will be observed that the stem of the verb – in this case kwenda – remains unchanged, and this too results in error when carried over into English:

> **I go to town yesterday.*

Sometimes the auxiliary *did* is seen as equivalent to the tense marker -li-, and an unnecessary auxiliary intrudes:

> **I did go to town yesterday.*

Other problems in using the simple past in English include:

– Use of the regular suffix for irregular verbs:
> **leaved* for *left*
> **finded* for *found*, etc.

– Inflecting question and negative forms:
> **Did they went to town?*
> **The man did not died.*

– Using the simple past instead of the present perfect:
> **We finished the exercise.* (for *We have finished the exercise.*)

– Using the simple past instead of the past perfect, which does not exist in Swahili:
> (*) *He said he never saw a plane before he came to Nairobi.*

– Using the present instead of the past for the 'unreal past':
> **You have better go soon.*
> **It is time we return to school.*

Problems also arise from the use of Subsecutive -ka-:

> Nilikwenda mjini nikamwona Moyo. (= *I went to town, I then see Moyo.*)

The infix -ka- indicates that one action follows another, and is part of a sequence of actions. Attempts to transfer this convention to English lead to further tense errors, as well as either the omission of the conjunction *and* or, alternatively, the failure to commence a new

267

sentence. What may be perceived as a punctuation error is often, more seriously perhaps, an attempt by the writer to superimpose Swahili syntax on English:

> *I went to the market I buy some fruit.*

3. -ta-: Future (in relation to the time of reference)
Nitakwenda mjini kesho. (= *I shall go to town tomorrow.*)
The *shall/will* future forms tend to be used in English as direct equivalents of this infix -ta-, including occasions when these future forms are not used in English:

> *Don't go until he will come.*
> *Unless he will come soon, he will miss the bus.*

The -ta- infix is also used in Swahili in contexts that in English require *would*:

> *I wish he will hurry up.*
> *Mwajuma said she will tell the manager next day.*

Note here that the tense marker stays the same in reported speech. It should be added that Swahili conventions in using reported speech lead to other errors in English, too:

> *He said that, I shall go to town tomorrow.* (for *He said he would go to town the next day.*)

Note that the intrusive comma as well as the unchanged person and tense forms are all results of direct translation from Swahili.

Aspect

Arguably, aspect plays as important a part in verb formation as time, and this can lead to a number of problems. Like other Bantu languages, Swahili uses different markers to indicate the way an action is visualised. Among these markers are:

1. -me- This infix indicates an action that has been completed, the results of which are still relevant, and thus may be seen as parallel to one use of the present perfect in English:
Wanangu wamefika. (= *My children have arrived.*)
However, its use does not correspond exactly with the English usage:
Chumba kimechafuka. (= *The room is untidy.*)
Tumesikia. (= *We understand. / We have heard.*)
This may account for Swahili speakers occasionally using the present perfect tense instead of the simple present tense in such contexts.

Conversely Swahili speakers very frequently fail to use the present perfect in sentences like *He has worked there since 1980.* The Swahili convention is to use the -na- infix:

> *He is working there since 1980.*

Another common error is the confusion of *since* and *for*:
> *He has worked there since six years.* or *He is working there since six years.*

2. -ki- In contrast with the -me- infix, the -ki- infix indicates an action happening simultaneously with another action, but not completed:
> Tuliwaona watoto wakisoma. (lit. *We saw them the children they reading.*)

Attempts to make parallel constructions in English lead to errors such as:
> *The women pounded the grains and sifting them.*
> *He walked slowly and carrying a heavy basket.*
> *He slept meanwhile his sister was working.* (where *meanwhile* may be an attempt to convey the sense of the -ki- infix).

-ki- is also used as a conditional marker:
> Mungu akipenda. (= *If God wills.*)

Since there is no equivalent in English, Swahili speakers may use a variety of different tenses in conditional clauses. Typical mistakes include:
> *If I went to town I will see Mwajuma.*
> *If I will go to town, I will see Mwajuma.*
> *If I have gone to town, I would see Mwajuma.*

Modal verbs

Modality is usually expressed by means of verb inflection, and a number of errors are made including:
– The use of *can* and *will* for *could* and *would*:
> *Ali promised he can help them the following week.*
– Faulty construction:
> *I can be able to help.*

Other verb forms

1. The verbal noun form in Swahili is the same as the infinitive form. This leads to many problems:
> *They succeeded to finish the work.*
> *They stopped to talk.* (for *They stopped talking.*)
> *They made him to work hard.*
2. Verbs that are transitive in English may be intransitive in Swahili:
> *At the party they enjoyed very much.*
> *She needed some rice, so she went to the market and bought.*

3. Verbs of prohibition, prevention and denial in Swahili must be followed by a verb with a negative inflection:
   He prevented him not to go.
   He denied that he did not know him.

4. In Swahili verbs may be transferred into the passive by means of inflection:
   kupiga = *to beat*
   kupigwa = *to be beaten*

   The Swahili convention is so different from English that many problems arise:
   A school is hoped to be built.
   Our school is difficult to be reached.
   This water is good to be drunk.

5. Question tags are very commonly misused. Swahili has a simple tag sivyo? (= *not so?*):
   You have seen the headmaster, didn't you?

6. Answers to negative questions can also lead to a complete break-down in communication. The Swahili words ndiyo and siyo are often roughly translated as *yes* and *no*. More accurately, they signal assent and dissent: *It is (not) as you say.* So the answer to a negative question might be misleading:
   'So you don't want to go to the dance?' 'Yes.' (= *Yes, I don't want to go.*)

Non-verb sentences

These are common in Swahili, e.g. location markers may be taken to imply predication:
   Kikapu kiko jikoni. (lit. *Basket – it – there – kitchen – in/at*) = *The basket is in the kitchen.*

Often phrases with *to* + infinitive or present participles are used as sentences:
   The bus left for town. The supporters being too late to catch it.
   The committee reached no firm decision. Each case to be considered on its merits.

Miscellaneous

All the following errors are attributable to Swahili interference:
   I forgot my book at home.
   It was last week when I came to Tabora.
   Clinics are not enough. (for There are not enough clinics.)
   In my family we are many. or *We are many in my family.*

Articles and determiners

There are no definite or indefinite articles in Bantu languages, and there are many problems as a result:
1. The omission of articles:
    Where is pen I gave you?
2. The use of the wrong article:
    Please close a door.
3. Confusion of *a* and *an*:
    That is an useful book.
4. Misuse of the definite article with proper nouns:
    the President Nyerere
    River Tana is long.

Common errors with other determiners include:
1. Confusion of *few / a few, little / a little*:
    Because of the rain, there were a few at the match.
2. Use of *all* for *both*:
    All my parents come from Mombasa.
3. Confusion of *much/many, few/little*:
    She has much clothes.
    There is few rice in the basket.
4. Confusion of *no* and *not*:
    There is no any / no enough food.
5. Confusion of *some* and *any*:
    Has he some petrol?   *He hasn't some petrol.*

Nouns

Bantu language noun class systems are so different from English that many problems arise, including:
– Misuse of uncountable nouns:
    *informations, *equipments, *breads, *a cattle, *an advice*, etc.
– Using a plural verb form with a singular noun:
    This news were good.
– Using plural nouns in the singular:
    *a trouser, *a scissor*, etc.
– Failure to use or misuse of the -'s genitive, which does not exist in Swahili:
    *the door's handle   *the house of my friend*
– Confusion of nouns and adjectives (often through faulty phonology):
    wealth/wealthy, difficult/difficulty, etc.

Pronouns

The biggest single problem is the failure to distinguish between masculine and feminine forms, which are not marked in Swahili or other Bantu languages:

> *She loved his husband.*

Another major problem is the redundant use of pronouns, a feature of Swahili:

> *Kukubo he has brought the food.*
> *Have you brought it the food?*

The reply to this question sometimes omits the object pronoun infix, leading to such errors as:

> *I have brought.*

Emphatic forms are sometimes used inappropriately:

> *Myself I have arrived.*
> *Myself travelled to Mombasa.*

Adjectives and adverbs

Adjectives, or descriptives, follow the noun in Swahili, and the order of adjectives in English can cause problems. But the main problem areas are in complex adjectival patterns involving comparison:

> Mtoto wangu ni mrefu sawa na wako. (= *My child is tall as yours.*)

There is no inflection for comparative and superlative forms, which are signalled by words like kuliko or kupita, and this leads to many errors:

> *This house is very big than that one.* (The intensifier sana is used as the equivalent of *more*.)
> *This house is more bigger than that one.*
> *He was the very interesting man I have met.*
> *This is the best book than all the others.*

Apart from the difficulties with adverb particles, noted below, other problems with adverbs include:

1. Omission of adverbs:
> *'Are they coming later?' *'I don't think.'* (so omitted)
> *I worked as I could.*

2. Faulty comparative constructions, as with adjectives:
> *They are walking slowly more than me.*
> *I am working hard as you.*

3. Faulty adverb formation:
> *They ran away cowardly.*

Other similar errors include *fastly, hardly* (for *hard*), *quick* (for *quickly*), *loudly* and *aloud* being used interchangeably.

Prepositions and particles

The systems used in Swahili are very different from English and therefore cause great problems.

1. Omission:
    She explained them the exercise.
    He arrived ten o'clock.
    She replied me that she doesn't know.
2. Use of unnecessary prepositions:
    They requested for help.
    What time did you reach at Tanga?
3. Use of incorrect prepositions. One major problem is that Swahili has a locative suffix (ni), the meaning of which varies according to the context. As a result English prepositions of location are likely to be confused:
    mezani (= *at, to, on, by, from the table*)
    nyumbani (= *at, to, in, by, from the house*)
    mwituni (= *at, to, in, by, inside, from, near the forest*)

There are other problems, one of the more significant being the multipurpose preposition katika, which can mean *in, into, out from, up into, up from, on,* and *while*. It also has other idiomatic uses.

Another multi-purpose preposition is kwa, which can mean *with, on, to, from, for, as a result of,* and *during*:
    kwa miguu (= *on foot*)
    kwa kisu (= *with a knife*)

Among the many common errors are:
    to arrive to school
    to drive with a car
    to be full with water
    to meet at London
    to look to the board
    to walk till the college
    to stay to evening
    to enter for the hall
    to go for leave

All English phrasal verbs are likely to cause problems. Their nearest equivalent in Bantu languages are the 'prepositional verbs' which, by inflection, express a wide and subtle variety of relationships that are in some ways comparable to, but not coincident with, the prepositional and adverbial particles used in English. Many errors result:
    They put off the fire.

Other verbs are given unnecessary particles:
    They accompanied with his sisters.
    We discussed about politics.

Subordinate clauses

A. Relative

The equivalent of the English relative pronoun in Swahili is the connective amba, which inflects to show concordial agreement:

> Hiki ni kikapu ambacho nilikinunua. (= *Here is the basket which I bought.*)

One feature of this structure is that the subordinate clause includes the object pronoun infix -ki-, so that the literal translation of the sentence is *This is the basket which I bought it.* The inclusion of the subject or object pronoun is consequently a common error:

> *The girl who I married her is very beautiful.*
> *The people that they came from Lesotho settled in Zambia.*
> *The man I married him is very lazy.*

B. Co-ordination and subordination

The main conjunction in Swahili is na (= *and*), which is used mainly as a connective in phrases. Also common are co-ordinating conjunctions such as juu ya hayo (= *in addition*), kwa hivyo (= *because of this*). Their equivalents in English are sentence connectors rather than conjunctions, and this leads to sentences like:

> *She missed the bus therefore she was angry.*
> *The pupils did the exercise meanwhile the teacher was marking.*
> *She was exhausted. Even though she continued to work.*
> *He worked hard because of this he was made a prefect.*

Patterns of subordination can also cause problems. The all-purpose intensifier sana is translated directly into English to produce sentences like:

> *The chest is too heavy that I cannot lift it.*
> *The chest is very heavy that I cannot lift it.*

The equivalents of *although* (ingawa) and *but* (lakini) are both used in a concessive sentence:

> *Although it was late but they went on working.*
> *Despite they were cold, but they worked hard.*

Vocabulary

The following tend to be confused or misused, either because they each have only one equivalent in Swahili, or because of semantic overlap, or for other reasons:

to borrow / to lend	to rest / to have a holiday
to rise / to raise	to see / to find
to rob / to steal	to send / to bring
to stay with / to keep	to leave / to give up
to escort / to see someone off	to wear / to put on (clothes)
to bath / to bathe	to cheat / to deceive / to tell
to refuse / to deny	lies
to like / to love	to follow / to accompany
to prefer / to like	to meet / to find / to discover
to do / to make	to hurt / to pain
to reach / to arrive	to lay / to lie
to discover / to invent	to say / to tell
to learn / to teach	to take place / to take part
to think / to hope	to convince / to persuade
to wound / to hurt /	to attend / to attend to
to injure /to damage	to win / to beat
to refuse / to forbid	to take off / to put off
newspaper/magazine	every time / all the time
fault/mistake	wonderful/strange
arm/hand	leg/foot
very/too/so	all/both
job/work	in time / on time

The following examples of East African idiomatic English are in common use, though many are of arguable acceptability:

on my side . . . (= *in my opinion . . .*)
on the side of . . . (= *as regards . . .*)
somehow (= *rather*)
to school (vb), e.g. *I schooled in Moshi.* (= *to go to school*)
brotherisation (= *nepotism*)
menu (= *programme*)
to foot (= *to walk*)
to help myself (= *to urinate*)
today morning (= *this morning*)
yesterday night (= *last night*)

Culture

Anyone who has taught in Africa will agree that the students are a pleasure to teach. They want to learn, and if this chapter may seem to imply that they find it hard to do so, or make many errors, then such an inference is completely wrong. Africans are born linguists: they may well have to know several African languages (and not all of them Bantu), before they learn English, and their success in learning English,

275

given the many difficulties, is quite remarkable. The visiting teacher who hopes to teach in Africa would do well to remember the following points:

1. The good teacher is also a good learner, of both the culture of the host country and one of its languages. If students and fellow members of staff form the impression that you are anxious to learn, they will be that much more welcoming. Even if you regard yourself as a poor linguist, do try to learn whatever the main local language is. It is enjoyable, it helps you to teach more effectively, and above all, it helps you to form worthwhile relationships with people from the host country.

2. Find out as quickly as possible about local etiquette. Note particularly how people greet each other, and take leave of each other, and try to act in a similar way. It is widely felt that Europeans tend to be far too preoccupied with the job in hand to bother to observe basic rules of courtesy. For example, in Britain or the USA it would not be considered unusual to start a conversation: 'Hello. Look, about that timetable. When . . . ?' In such a situation the main focus of interest is the timetable, not the person being addressed. In many parts of the world, including Africa and the Middle East, such a brisk approach would be seen as very rude. It is very important to start off any such conversations with enquiries about the person's health, family, etc., in a manner that shows you are really interested.

3. Many gestures and mannerisms acceptable in European societies are considered rude in many African countries. For example, in many African societies, greeting a person with a strong handshake and a steady gaze may be thought offensive. On the other hand, shaking hands is much more common than it is in Britain, even with someone whom one sees fairly often. Most finger gestures should be avoided, particularly the vertical 'come here' beckoning with the forefinger.

4. A visitor who sits down uninvited is showing normal courtesy, not undue familiarity. Unexpected visitors should always be welcomed, no matter how pressing one's prior engagements. This may partly explain why guests at a party often arrive late, although it should be added that in many African societies guests are not expected to arrive on time.

5. Find out about local attitudes to dress. On the coast, or in Muslim areas, great care should be taken to avoid causing offence. For example, women should dress carefully and arms and legs should be reasonably covered. Men too need to exercise some care. There is a common belief among young European males that very casual dress indicates informality, and therefore friendliness. Often, however, it has the opposite effect. Except on very informal occasions, shorts are usually considered distasteful at best. Short shorts are definitely

unacceptable. In a few countries, notably Tanzania, shorts are actually forbidden.

A sample of written Swahili with a word-for-word translation

Hapo kale   paka hakukaa   katika nyumba za watu; alikaa
Here formerly cat   did not stay place houses   of men; he stayed

mwituni   au maguguni tu.   Paka mmoja alikuwa rafiki   ya sungura
in forest or in bush   only. Cat   one   he was friend of hare

wakatembea   pamoja, na   paka akastaajabia   werevu   wa
and they wandered together, and cat   and he admired cleverness of

rafiki   yake; lakini siku moja funo   akagombana   na
friend his;   but   day one   duiker and he argued together with

sungura akamwua   kwa   pembe zake. Sasa   kwa   kuwa rafiki
hare   and he him killed with horns   his.   Then of   to be friend

yake amekufa   paka akafuatana   na   yule   funo.
his   he is dead cat   and he accompanied with this (the) duiker.

An idiomatic translation

A long time ago the cat did not live in men's houses: he lived only in the forest or in the bush. A certain cat was the friend of a hare and wandered about with him; the cat admired the cleverness of his friend, but one day, a duiker quarrelled with the hare and killed him with a thrust of his horns. Since his friend was dead, the cat began keeping company with the duiker.

(From *An Introduction to Languages and Language in Africa* by
Pierre Alexandre)

Acknowledgement

The author would like to thank Said El-Gheithy of the Centre for African Language Learning, London, for his comments on an early draft of this paper.

Bibliography

Alexandre, Pierre (1972) *An Introduction to Languages and Language in Africa*. Translated by F. A. Leary. Northwestern University Press and Heinemann Educational Books.

Ashton, E. O. (1944, 13th impression 1966) *Swahili Grammar*. London: Longman.

Greenberg, J. H. (1966, 2nd edn) *The Languages of Africa*. The Hague: Mouton.

Myachina, E. N. (1981) *The Swahili Language*. Translated by G. L. Campbell. London: Routledge and Kegan Paul.

Russell, Joan and D. V. Perrott (1996) *Teach Yourself Swahili*. London: Hodder and Stoughton

Whitely, Wilfred H. (1969) *Swahili (The rise of a national language)*. London: Methuen.

Malay/Indonesian speakers

Janet Y. Yong

Distribution

THE REPUBLIC OF INDONESIA, THE FEDERATION OF MALAYSIA, THE REPUBLIC OF SINGAPORE AND THE SULTANATE OF BRUNEI; southern and western coasts of Borneo, southernmost provinces of Thailand, Mergui Archipelago of Burma. Malay-based creoles are found not only among the originally Chinese-speaking inhabitants of the old Straits Settlements of former British Malaya, but also in various ports of eastern Indonesia and on Christmas Island and the Cocos Islands in the Indian Ocean.

Introduction

The Malay or Malay/Indonesian (M/I) language belongs to the western Austronesian group of languages. A variety of Malay is an official language in four Southeast Asian countries: Indonesia, Malaysia, Singapore and Brunei, and some sort of standard formal Malay exists or is being developed by official bodies in these countries. Standard Malay in Malaysia and Indonesia serves as a means of communication for administration and political integration and as a mark of national identity in these two countries; it is used for academic, philosophical and professional communication as well as in literary writing. Most commonly, Malay/Indonesian is considered to constitute either a single language, or else two very closely related languages. Despite some marked differences between the two varieties in lexicon, pronunciation, grammatical choices and features of discourse organisation, the standard forms are mutually intelligible. As Malaysian and Indonesian students are schooled in Standard Malay in both countries, the linguistic problems they may encounter in learning and using the English language are quite similar.

Phonology

General

The Malay/Indonesian and English phonological systems are very different. English has 22 vowels and diphthongs and 24 consonants. Indonesian has only six vowels /i, e, a, ə, o, u/ and three diphthongs, while Malay has an additional three vowels /ɛ, ɔ, ɜ/ for certain speakers. M/I has 19 native consonants. (Arabic and English loan sounds /f, v, θ, ð, ʃ, z, x, ɣ/ have been assimilated into the sound system of modern M/I and given variant renderings similar to existing sounds in the language.) Some of the features of M/I which give rise to a 'Malay/Indonesian accent' in English are covered below.

Vowels

iː	ɪ	e	æ	eɪ	aɪ	ɔɪ
ɑː	ɒ	ɔː	ʊ	aʊ	əʊ	ɪə
uː	ʌ	ɜː	ə	eə	ʊə	aɪə aʊə

All vowels may cause problems to some extent. However, shaded phonemes have equivalents or near equivalents in M/I and should therefore be perceived and articulated without great difficulty. Unshaded phonemes may cause more serious problems.

The following are the most common confusions:

1. All vowels with the exception of /ə/ are pronounced with more or less comparable length: *bit/beat, pill/peal, full/fool, cot/caught*.
2. Conflation of /æ/ and /e/ into /e/: *hat* → /het/; *ankle* → /enkəl/; *grammar* → /gremə(r)/.
3. Pronunciation of /ɒ/ (as in *hot* or *knock*) with noticeable lip-rounding.
4. English diphthongs may be realised as pure vowels uttered sometimes long and sometimes short and with no appreciable glide.

Consonants

p	b	f	v	θ	ð	t	d
s	z	ʃ	ʒ	tʃ	dʒ	k	g
m	n	ŋ	l	r	j	w	h

Shaded phonemes have equivalents or near equivalents in M/I and should be perceived and articulated without great difficulty, although some confusions may still arise. Unshaded phonemes may cause more serious problems. For detailed comments, see below.

1. The glottal stop /ʔ/ (like the cockney pronunciation of *tt* in *butter*) is a distinct phoneme in M/I, and may occur inappropriately in students' pronunciations.
2. The same is true of the palatal nasal /ɲ/ (like the *ni* in *onion*). English /nj/ may be realised as /n/ or /ɲ/.
3. /p, t, k/ are always unaspirated, which can make them sound close to /b, d, g/ to an English ear; in initial position this can lead to confusion between, for instance, *pin* and *bin*, *tile* and *dial*, *cot* and *got*. In post-vocalic and final position they are unreleased or omitted, resulting in pronunciations such as '*jum*' (*jump*), '*saajan*' (*sergeant*), '*as*' /asʔ/ (*ask*) – in many dialects final /k/ is pronounced as a glottal stop at the end of a closed syllable.
4. M/I words cannot end in voiced stops /b, d, g/, the fricatives /v, z, ʃ/ or the affricates /tʃ, dʒ/. Learners are likely to drop these sounds at the ends of English words, especially after other consonants: '*bul*' (*bulb*), '*oul*' (*old*), '*haan*' (*hand*), etc.
5. /f/ in any position is frequently replaced by /p/ by less proficient speakers: '*preper*' (*prefer*), '*pavour*'/'*papour*' (*favour*), '*piləm*' (*film*).
6. /v/ is very rare in M/I; when used it occurs before vowels only. Students are likely to replace /v/ by /f/ or /p/, especially at the ends of words.
7. Learners generally pronounce /θ/ as /t/: *tin* for *thin*, *tot* for *thought*, '*tousan*' for *thousand*. /ð/ is realised as /d/: '*dat*' for *that*; '*dere*' for *there*.
8. The affricates /tʃ, dʒ/ are sometimes realised as alveolar fricatives: *ship* for *chip*, *leisure* for *ledger*. /ʃ/ may be pronounced /s/: *sip* for *ship*.
9. Indonesian speakers tend to pronounce post-vocalic /r/ (as in *car park*), realising it as a rolled alveolar sound with a pronounced trill.

Malay speakers generally drop /r/ at the ends of words, but lengthen the preceding vowel: '*caa*' for *car*, /peɪpəː/ for *paper*.

10. In producing /h/, the glottis is held wide open, giving the sound a rather different quality from English /h/. Some speakers do not use /h/; some use /ʔ/ instead.

11. Relatively few consonant clusters are permitted in M/I in word-initial and word-final positions; the most frequently occurring syllable structure in simple M/I words is consonant-vowel-consonant. Students are likely to simplify clusters in English words: '*stan*' for *stand*, *talk* for *talked*, or to insert a schwa vowel, as happens in many loan words: '*səkərip*' for *script*, '*filəm*' for *film*, '*pərojek*' for *project*, '*kəlinik*' for *clinic* etc.

Spelling and pronunciation

Malay/Indonesian words are usually spelt the way they are pronounced; thus English words where the spelling does not match the pronunciation can cause problems. English words corresponding to loan words in M/I are frequently misspelt: *ekonomi* (*economy*), *risiko* (*risk*), *prinsip* (*principle*), *talipon* (*telephone*), etc.

Rhythm and stress

Word stress in one variety of Indonesian is penultimate, while that of Malay is final; M/I speakers tend to transfer these patterns to their pronunciation of English words. Most varieties of M/I have a syllable-timed rhythm, and the difference between various degrees of stress tends to be small; when carried over into English, this creates an impression of monotony or flatness. Function words are almost never reduced, so that students tend to give English auxiliary verbs, prepositions, etc. their full 'written' pronunciation. M/I learners reading English aloud will often avoid contracted forms and elisions, and read with a slow and staccato rhythm.

Intonation

Questions, suggestions and offers are marked by a general rise ending, while the imperative tune shows overall a high initial and a low final pitch. The equivalent features in English should not pose problems.

Orthography and punctuation

Malay/Indonesian is written in the Latin (romanised) script, so hand-writing is not a problem for students of English. M/I writers of English tend to avoid long and complex sentence constructions; when they do use them, punctuation can be non-existent or erratic.

Grammar

Word order

Malay/Indonesian word order is similar to that of English: subject–verb–object. In casual speech, however, the subject may be dropped and the word order reversed. This may be reflected in students' mistakes in English.

Number

M/I nouns are not inflected for number. They can be made plural by reduplication (kucing-kucing = *cats*), though this does not happen after numerals. M/I speakers have problems both with English plural endings and with third-person verb agreement; plural endings are particularly likely to be dropped after numbers or plural quantifiers:
> *She have three sister and two brother.*
> *a number of boy*
> *one of the man*
> *a few doctor*

Reduplicated verbs indicate repeated action:
> *He beat and beat the dog many times.*

Singular and plural forms of quantifiers and demonstratives are not always correctly used:
> *The teacher gave too much corrections.*
> *a lots of types of stones*
> *this pictures*
> *these bicycle*

Countability

Less proficient learners may pluralise English mass nouns:
> *two milks   *three bags of flours   *many furnitures*
> *a lot of butters*

283

Malay/Indonesian speakers

Abstract nouns which can be mass or count produce errors like:
> *some works to do   *five year experiences
> *very good educations

Gender

Gender is not expressed grammatically in M/I. One word, dia (*he/she/ it*), is used for third-person singular subject, object and sometimes possessive pronouns:
> *John sat for exam and passed. She cannot believe got five distinction. Her parents very happy.

Personal pronouns

M/I speakers often use repeated noun phrases where English would drop repeated elements or use anaphoric pronouns:
> *Many students work very hard. Many of them work all day in the library. Is sad many students cannot pass the English test.

Genitive and possessive pronouns

Possessive relations in M/I can be shown by a bound pronoun -nya or by the free personal pronouns dia (*he/she/it*) and mereka (*they/them/their*). Students have difficulty with the very different English system. Typical errors:
> *my wife friend
> *my father name Jaid bin Omar
> *yours school bag
> *the book of them
> *their's houses
> *the cat's tails

Relative pronouns

Malay/Indonesian has only one relative word yang, which corresponds to the English *wh*-pronouns, *that* and zero. Errors such as these are common:
> *People which live in town are rich.
> *The flower that red is hibiscus.

Relative pronouns may be duplicated by personal pronouns:
> *the letter that I haven't received it yet*

Reflexive pronouns

The literal translation of the reflexive *self* is diri in M/I; learners find the English system complicated. Typical mistakes:
> *Ali hurt heself.*
> *They cook for theirselves.*
> *We must listen to ourself.*
> *Me, myself do all the work.*

Topicalisation structures

M/I speakers of English frequently emphasise ('topicalise') certain constituents by placing them at the beginning of sentences, as typically happens in M/I:
> *This kind we don't have.*
> *Ten per cent off we give our customers.*
> *Cantonese I can speak quite well.*
> *From school I learn English.*
> *My homework I have to do first.*

A related feature is pronoun copying, where the subject or object of the sentence is stated as a noun and then repeated in the sentence in pronominalised form:
> *Some Europeans, they like to eat here.*
> *My mother, she wants me to help her cook.*
> *My sister and me, we always fight.*

It *and* there

English structures with the dummy subjects *it* and *there* are difficult for learners. The equivalent M/I structure uses the word ada (*got/has/is*):

> Ada   sebatang   pen di atas meja.
> *Got/Has/Is a* (classifier) *pen on top table.*

Errors such as these are common:
> *Was an examination last week.*
> *A few people in the room.*
> *Is nice to play football.*

Articles/determiners

The complexity of the English article system presents an awesome task for Malay and Indonesian learners.

1. M/I does not have articles, although the demonstratives ini (*this*) and itu (*that*) can overlap in function and assume the meaning of 'the'. This use is often optional, and learners consequently tend to drop the definite article in English:
    *How was exam?
2. Demonstratives are used with M/I reduplicated plurals, which may lead learners to use an inappropriate article with an English plural:
    *It have the four legs.
3. Learners tend to drop the indefinite article particularly before nouns relating to concepts of mass and quantity, and other abstract nouns:
    *number of schools
    *change for the worse
4. Alternatively, learners may overuse the indefinite article:
    *My hobbies is a sleeping when I have a problems.
5. The definite article may be used instead of the indefinite and vice versa:
    *They have to deal with a economic recession. (meaning . . . the current economic recession)
    *They include the secondary school and a kindergarten.

Verbs

M/I verbs are not marked for person, tense or number; auxiliary elements are used to indicate tense and aspect. Even the most proficient Malay and Indonesian speakers have difficulty in mastering the complexity of the English verb phrase.

Time, tense and aspect

A. Past time

Sudah/telah/pernah indicates an action completed at the time of speaking, but M/I has nothing corresponding to the English distinction between simple past and present perfect. Learners have considerable difficulty with English past and perfect verb forms. Typical errors:
    *I write the letter yesterday.
    *I was write yesterday the letter.
    *I finished written the letter.

*Last week I have wrote to her.
*I already finish write the notes.
*I already inform him and he agree.

B. Present time

M/I uses the temporal adverb sekarang (*now, at this moment*) before or after a verb to signify an action unfinished at the time of speaking:
*Now he swim.
*He is swim at this time.
*He swim right now.

C. Future time

The aspectual particle akan in M/I indicates future time. Students have problems using and distinguishing the various English forms:
*This book will we read.
*Tomorrow you come.
*They will to market on Sunday.

D. Progressive/continuous

Malay/Indonesian expresses durative aspect ('in-the-process-of') by using sedang/semasa/sewaktu/sementara with a verb to describe an on-going action or event. Learners use the English *-ing* form as an equivalent, but tend to drop the auxiliary:
* They eating their dinner tonight.
* They coming back late tomorrow.
* They waiting here since 2 o'clock past.
* They playing chess yesterday when the phone was ringing.

To be

Berada, adalah and ialah correspond to the English copula *to be*; they are frequently optional.

Adiknya   (berada) di rumah.
Younger sister/brother his/her is/was   at home.
Fatimah (adalah/ialah) guru   sekolah.
Fatimah is/was   teacher school.

The copula is dropped in a sentence that expresses a condition or state of existence:

Yusoff sangat gembira.
Yusoff very   happy. (Yusoff is/was very happy.)

Malay/Indonesian speakers

Mother-tongue interference and confusion over which form is correct results frequently in the omission of forms of *to be*, or in errors in their use:

> *His sisters very clever too. / *His sisters was very clever too.*
> *Their parents not happy. / *Their parent is not happy.*
> *They hardworking farmers. / *They was hardworking farmers.*

Non-finite forms

Gerunds and infinitives do not exist in M/I, and the various forms are often confused by learners:

> *To running very good for your health.*
> *My mother like to cooking not to sewing.*
> *Without money, I can't to continuing my studies.*
> *Mother is going clean the room.*
> *I shall to go to market early.*

Modal auxiliary verbs

Malay/Indonesian speakers have problems using *can*, *may*, *shall* and *will* and their special past forms (*could*, etc.). The complex modal auxiliary system of standard English is drastically reduced in M/I to two main modals, *can* and *must*, with *can* in particular taking on a wide range of uses, some of which must be regarded as institutionalised in M/I English. Some typical utterances:

You can borrow my book.	– permission
You can drive, isn't it?	– ability
Can you lend me your car or not?	– willingness
She can lend you her car.	– agreement
*'How the movie?' *'Can do.'*	– mild approval
You go with me, can or not?	– affirmation
He can't be sleeping all this time.	– improbability
Cannot be he so rich as this.	– impossibility
Must be he is sick.	– certainty
You must be hungry by now.	– certainty
You must go see your professor.	– obligation/compulsion

Learners may also avoid modals altogether, using adverbs or ordinary verbs to express the modal meanings:

> *Maybe Ahmad calling on the phone. / *I think that Ahmad . . .*
> *(for That will be Ahmad calling on the phone.)*
> *I think Samy joking. / *Maybe Samy joking. (for Samy could be joking.)*

*Surely that Fatimah. / *(I'm) sure that Fatimah. (for That has to be Fatimah.)*

*Maybe expensive to shop here. / *I think not cheap to shop here. (for It can be expensive to shop here.)*

*My father normally not home now. / *I don't think he at home now. (for My father wouldn't be home at this hour.)*

Active and passive

Old Malay and Indonesian literary writing uses passive forms more frequently than the modern language, which has a strong preference for active forms. In spoken Malay and Indonesian the passive form is generally avoided. For this reason, and because passives are formed very differently in the two languages, M/I speakers find English passives difficult:

That car drives by Amin.

The door is open by me.

For Sarimah the coffee make by me.

Question forms and question tags

In simple *wh*-questions, M/I allows three different types of structures: *in situ* questions, fully-moved questions, and focus questions. Common errors involve direct translation from M/I into English:

Ali buy what?

What Ali buy?

Why you so angry?

Want to go where you?

What that Ali buy?

Question tags in English tend to be reduced to only two forms, *isn't it?* and *is it?*:

She will remember, isn't it?

They don't know you, is it?

Negatives

Malay/Indonesian speakers use the negative particles *no, not, never* and *not yet*, etc. indiscriminately:

I said no to do it again.

She no understand my problems.

The teacher never come to class today.

Malay/Indonesian speakers

> *I not want to be a teacher after I graduate.*
> *He not yet finish his homework.*

Complex sentences

Malay/Indonesian writers tend to avoid complex sentences. When learners use them, they may not structure them well, and may fail to differentiate between dependent and independent clauses. Conjunctions and linking expressions may be duplicated. Some typical errors:

> *Education although expensive but is valuable for a good future.*
> *I failed my exam as a result because I didn't study hard.*
> *I was late for school and suddenly I got up and with quick I brush my teeth.*

Structures with *and* and *or* may be unbalanced:

> *When I have time I like to watching TV and read the story book.*

Prepositions

Errors occur in the use of the correct preposition after a verb, adjective or noun in expressions like *add to, attend to, allow for, hope for, conscious of, based on.* Learners also have difficulty choosing the right preposition in fixed expressions like *with great courtesy, in anger, by the back door, on the radio, by train.* Many prepositions in English do not have equivalents in Malay and their functions are performed by other types of word. Some typical mistakes:

> *He don't work at Monday.*
> *I have to attend for my garden.*
> *He shouted in angry his mother.*
> *He roundabout his house with bicycle.*

Similar problems may arise with adverbial particles:

> *Please don't on and off the light.*

Adjectives and adverbs

Learners may substitute adverbs for adjectives and vice versa, often under the influence of the mother tongue:

> *You sit quiet there.*
> *Ali dress smart every day.*
> *In recent we have the steadily increase of tourists.*
> *The students study hardly.*

Confusion with other parts of speech also occurs:
> *He write with well.*
> *a luxury life*
> *. . . consist of agriculture land*

Common errors with adjectives describing degrees of comparison point to direct translation from Malay/Indonesian:
> *My sister as clever your sister.*
> *His cousin is very bravest soldier.*
> *His house less smaller than your house.*
> *In my village, Pak Toha most richest than all people.*

Vocabulary and style

Range and choice of vocabulary

Even advanced M/I learners may use a relatively reduced range of vocabulary, avoiding idiomatic or less common expressions in favour of more basic forms of expression: *very very proud* (for *putting on airs*); *to pass very well / have a good result* (for *to pass with flying colours*); *very good food* (for *a delicious / excellent meal*), etc. This contributes to a tendency to long-windedness: *after I finish doing the course* (for *after I graduate*); *I will further my studies to specialise* (for *I will specialise*); *my mother stays at home only and doesn't go to work* (for *my mother is a housewife*).

Tautology is commonly used to show emphasis in M/I, and this may be reflected in students' use of English:
> *You just merely cycle along.*
> *the short cut way home*

Transfer

Lexical transfer or borrowing, especially of technical terms, takes place from English to M/I in varying degrees, involving loanwords, blends and substitutions. Students may be misled by the M/I spelling of words like talipon, bankrup, ekonomi, industri, psikologia.

Confusions

M/I learners have considerable problems distinguishing pairs of English
words that have a single M/I equivalent. Examples:

live/stay	**I've stayed in my village since I was born.*
tell/ask/say	**They tell (ask) me where is the canteen.*
	*They say to me to shut the window.
open/start	**Matt and his wife start the shop early.*
take/send/pick up	*She sends (takes) her children to school every day.*
	*She takes her son after school.
can/could	**We are happy if you could help us.*
will/would	**Will you mind if I smoke?*
at/in	**We cannot play at class.*
borrow/lend	**Borrow me two dollars.*
find/look	**I found everywhere for the cat.*
hear/listen	**I listened a sound in the dark.*
follow/accompany	**You want to follow me to market?*

Culture and language

In Malaysia and Indonesia, English is very important because a knowledge of English gives added prestige as well as a means of personal
advancement in the professional and academic fields. Thus the English
teacher is a very respected figure. In the classroom, teachers are
expected to maintain a firmly professional and formal relationship with
learners. Female teachers should always dress carefully and keep arms
and legs reasonably covered.

Foreign teachers will find the Malay language easy to master: its
phonological system is simple, and the grammar has no inflexions and
does not mark tense, case, gender or number. The prevalence of vowels
and liquids in the words, the infrequency of harsh combinations of
unvoiced consonants and the word chimes in reduplications make
Malay a smooth and sweet-sounding language.

Foreigners may regard Malay speakers as excessively gentle or non-
assertive.

There is a high percentage of Malay/English bilinguals in Malaysia as
Malay and English are the two predominant languages used in school
and for inter-ethnic communication. However, while Malay/Indonesian
students at schools and universities acquire textbook Malay and
English, outside those learning environments a localised variety of
English and home-Malay are used. Foreign-educated speakers and
foreign-trained teachers whose English sounds too native-like are
considered affected or westernised.

Since standard Malay has become the sole language of instruction in Malaysia, its use is on the increase and a time will come when the sociolinguistic situation in Malaysia will be similar to that of Indonesia, where people use the national language as their main means of communication. In the official language policy of both countries, only standard Malay is allowed to be used at meetings and government functions. However, English is also allowed at international conferences. Switching between English and M/I is common, as is dialect switching within M/I.

A sample of Malay with a word-for-word translation

This is an article from a local university newsletter in Malaysia. The English translation from the same source is given below.

Internet telah mengubah wajah   perpustakaan dan bagaimana
Internet have change   appearance library   and how

pustakawan bertugas hari ini.   Perpustakaan tidaklagi   terbendung
librarian   work   day this. Library   no more is confine

oleh empat dinding. Ia telah berkembang ke ruang siber.
by four   wall.   It have extend   to space cyber.

Ramai pustakawan telahpun masuk ke dalam ruang siber   untuk
Many librarian   have   go   to in   space cyber for

mendapatkan sumber   dalam talian.   Sesetengah pustakawan
to get   resource in   on line. Half of   librarian

pula telah membantu menyusun sumber   melalui   home page
also have help   organise resource through home page

masing-masing. Pengguna perpustakaan kini dapat melawat
at same time.   User   library   now can   visit

ke perpustakaan yang   terkenal   di seluruh dunia.
to library   which very famous in whole world.

Mereka boleh membuat carian pengarang, tajuk ataupun
They   can do   search author,   title or

subjek   dalam internet. Semuanya ini   dapat dibuat dengan selesa
subject inside internet. All   this can be make with   comfort

dari   rumah atau pejabat dengan mengklik butang tetikus
from house or   office with   to click button mouse

Malay/Indonesian speakers

ataupun menaip pada papan kekunci komputer.
or   to type on   board key   computer.

Apakah antara   perpustakaan dalam talian?   Apakah antara   buku
What   among library   in   on line? What   among book

yang   terdapat di dalam Internet?   Apakah pustakawan akan menjadi
which is find   in inside Internet? What   librarian   will become

pustakawan siber? Ini   adalah antara   perbincangan artikel di bawah.
librarian   cyber? This is   among discussion   article in below.

The Internet has changed the appearance of libraries and how librarians work today. The library is no longer confined to the four walls of a building. It has, instead, extended into cyberspace. Many librarians have gone into cyberspace to locate on-line resources. Some librarians have also helped organise the materials via their home pages. Library patrons are now fortunately able to visit famous libraries around the world. They can also make an author search, title search or subject search on the Internet. All these can be done in the comfort of the home or office at the click of a mouse or tapping on the keyboard keys. What are some of the on-line libraries? What are some of the books available on the Internet? Are librarians becoming cybrarians? These are among the highlights of the article below.

A sample of student's writing

About myself.

My name is Wan Azura binti Wan Awang. I was born at Kota Bharu, Kelantan in 1977. I'm 21 years old. My mothers name is Wan Hasnah binti Awang. My fathers name is Wan Awang Wan Jusoh. But now, he passed away 11 years ago. When my mothers borned me, she are very young. I like my mother because she is very loving me.

I have six sibling and I a second daughter. I have one brother and four younger sister. I love them because they can give me inspiration. My primary school at Sekolah Rendah Kebangsaan Tengku Mahmud until class six. And then I get UPSR exam. I'm very happy because I get good results. I'm very proud because I can make my family success.

Japanese speakers

Ian Thompson

Distribution

JAPAN, Korea, Hawaii.

Introduction

Japanese is probably related to Korean, and possibly to Manchurian, Mongolian and Turkish too. It is not related to Chinese. In modern Japan everybody understands and can speak an approximation to the standard language, though wide dialectal variety exists.

Japanese and English speakers find each other's languages hard to learn. One reason for this is that the broad constituents of sentence structure are ordered very differently in the two languages. The following fragment from a Japanese magazine, translated word for word into English, illustrates the learner's problem:

> Listener called one as-for, midnight at waking study doing be expectation of person (focus-particle) nucleus being reason is-probably.

or, less exotically:

> It must mean that the audience consists of people who are presumably staying up studying late at night.

In addition to the difficulties posed by great grammatical, lexical and phonetic disparity, Japanese speakers' attitudes to language in general are heavily coloured by aspects of their own language. Firstly, 'respect language' is so finely graded that an out-of-context fragment of dialogue can tell the eavesdropper a great deal about the age, sex, relationship and relative status of both speakers: even a transcript bereft of such vocal clues as voice quality and articulation reveals a sensitive choice of vocabulary and grammar in this respect. Students of English are therefore anxious about whether they are being sufficiently (or excessively) polite, and many cannot bring themselves to say *you* to strangers, or to call their teacher by name. Secondly, Japanese has enormous numbers of words which are pronounced the same but written differently – sometimes twenty in a group – so that the Japanese speaker trusts eyes before ears. It is worth noting, also, that eloquent, fluent speech is not highly rated in Japan; indeed, it is often distrusted. Tentativeness is preferred to assertiveness, hesitancy to momentum. Japanese abounds in what are to European ears 'unfinished' utterances, and the Japanese have an amazing ability to hear the unspoken word and to sense changes in atmosphere and human relationships.

Given these striking differences between Japanese and English attitudes to language, it takes the student a good while to tune in. An added barrier to adaptation is the tension associated in Japan with language learning – though women find it easier to relax in the language class than men.

Phonology

General

Japanese has a rather limited phonetic inventory, both in number of sounds and in their distribution. There are only five vowels, though these may be distinctively long or short. Syllable structure is very simple (generally vowel + consonant or vowel alone). There are few consonant clusters. Japanese learners therefore find the more complex distinctions and sound combinations of English very hard to produce, and they may have even greater difficulty in perceiving accurately what is said. Often a student can say quite a complicated sentence with faultless grammar and choice of words, yet would be unable to understand the same sentence if it was said to him or her. In order not to embarrass the speaker, Japanese listeners often nod sagely even when they understand scarcely a word.

In Japanese speech, lip and jaw movement tend to be minimised, and many social situations demand soft speech. Many speakers prefix utterances with an indrawn hiss as a sign of modesty. These features may be carried over into English.

Vowels

Some of the most noticeable problems for Japanese learners are:
1. /ɔː/ and /əʊ/ are both pronounced as a long pure /oː/, causing confusion in pairs like *caught* and *coat*, *bought* and *boat*.
2. /æ/ and /ʌ/ are both pronounced as /a/, causing confusion in pairs like *lack* and *luck*, *match* and *much*.
3. /ɜː/ becomes /aː/: *tarn* for *turn*.
4. /ə/ becomes /aː/, or else is replaced by the short vowel suggested by the spelling: /kɒmpoːzaː/ for *composer*.

297

5. Diphthongs ending in /ə/ are pronounced with /ɑː/ instead: /ðeɑːfɑː/ for *therefore*.
6. /ɪ/ and /ʊ/ are devoiced (whispered) in some contexts, making them difficult for an English listener to hear.
7. /uː/ is unrounded. Practice may be needed in words like *who, too, unusual*.

Consonants

Some of the most noticeable problems are:
1. /l/ and /r/ are both pronounced as a Japanese /r/ (a flap almost like a short /d/), causing confusion in pairs like *glamour* and *grammar*, *election* and *erection*.
2. /h/ may be pronounced as a bilabial f /ɸ/ before /uː/: 'foo' for *who*. Before /iː/, /h/ may sound almost like /ʃ/ (so that *he* and *she* are confusingly similar).
3. Conversely, /f/ may be pronounced almost like /h/ before /ɔː/: *horse* for *force*.
4. /θ/ and /ð/ do not occur in Japanese. They may be pronounced as /s/ and /z/ or /ʃ/ and /dʒ/: *shin* for *thin*; *zen* for *then*.
5. /v/ may be pronounced as /b/: *berry* for *very*.
6. /g/ may be pronounced /ŋg/ between vowels: 'binger' for *bigger*.
7. /n/ after a vowel may disappear (with nasalisation of the vowel), or may become /m/ or /ŋ/, depending on context: *sing* for *sin*.
8. /t/, /d/, /s/ and /z/ often change before /ɪ/ and /iː/ as follows:
    /t/ becomes /tʃ/: 'cheam' for *team*.
    /d/ becomes /dʒ/: *jeep* for *deep*.
    /s/ becomes /ʃ/: *she* for *see*.
    /z/ becomes /dʒ/: 'jip' for *zip*.
9. /t/ and /d/ often change before /ʊ/ and /uː/ as follows:
    /t/ becomes /ts/: 'tsoo' for *two*.
    /d/ becomes /dʒ/ or /z/: 'dzoo' for *do*.

Syllable structure and word-linking

English consonant clusters are difficult for Japanese learners, and they often tend to break them up by inserting short vowels, which also serve to 'round off' final consonants. So for instance *table* may be pronounced /teburu/, or *match* /matʃi/. Students find it hard to shed this 'rounding-off' vowel and to link when a vowel begins the following word: this is particularly noticeable when the final consonant is /n/ or linking /r/. A good deal of practice may be required in this area.

Rhythm, stress and intonation

The Japanese are very good at hearing and repeating stress and intonation patterns, but there are only limited parallels between the prosodic systems of the two languages. Japanese does not have the equivalent of 'weak' unstressed forms of words like *was*, *can*, *have*, and learners may fail to perceive these or other unstressed syllables.

Prosodic near-universals common to both languages include:
- raising the whole pitch-range of the voice when embarking on a new topic of conversation and lowering it to signal a coming end;
- broadening the pitch-range to show interest and involvement.

Japanese questions, both *wh-* and *yes/no*, usually have a rise on the utterance-final question particle ka; the question-tag particle ne tends to rise to show uncertainty and fall to show confirmation and agreement.

Many of the attitudinal colours painted by English intonation patterns find expression in Japanese by adverbials and particles. And Japanese does not share the English use of intonation to highlight information structure (for instance, to distinguish information which speaker and listener share from information which is new to the listener).

English intonation and sentence-stress patterns therefore have to be consciously learnt and practised, but Japanese students are particularly receptive to clear explanations of how these features work. They quickly learn word stress, though problems may occur with compound nouns, and with words borrowed into Japanese with an accent pattern that conflicts with the English stress pattern, such as rekoodo (*a 'record*).

Summary

The following transcription will give some of the flavour of the vowels, consonants, syllable structure and word-linking features of a Japanese accent:

> *The team who usually win have lost this year. They'll have to make a bigger effort in future.*

[//za tʃiːmu ɸɯː jɯːdʒɯari ˀwiĩ habu rosto dʒisu ˀjiaː//zeiru habu tsuː meiku a biŋɑː ehoːto iĩ çɯːtʃɑː//]

Orthography and writing

Japanese learners do not generally have great difficulty with English spelling or handwriting, perhaps because of the training involved in mastering the Japanese writing system (which combines Chinese-derived ideograms with syllabic characters). And Western script is familiar to most Japanese, even those who have learnt no English, from its frequent use in 'rōmaji' transliterations, which are common for instance in advertisements and shop signs.

Grammar

Word order

Japanese is a 'subject–object–verb' language. Qualifier precedes qualified, topic precedes comment and subordinate precedes main. What correspond to English prepositions follow the noun, and so do particles meaning *too, either, only* and *even*. Subordinating conjunctions follow their clause; sentence particles showing interrogation, affirmation, tentativeness and so on follow the sentence. Modal verbs follow lexical verbs. All adjectivals, however long, precede their substantive. Some illustrations:

> kore wa   nan   desu ka?
> *this speaking-of* [topic particle] *what is   question particle*
> (= *What's this?*)

> watashi wa   kore o   kakimashita[1]
> *I   speaking-of this object particle wrote*
> (= *I wrote this.*)

> ano hito   wa   se   ga   takai desu
> *that man speaking-of stature subject-particle tall   is*
> (= *That man is tall.*)

> Tookyoo wa   Nippon no   shuto   desu
> *Tokyo   speaking-of Japan genitive particle capital is*
> (= *Tokyo is the capital of Japan.*)

Japanese learners quickly get used to the basic word order of English sentences. Points which continue to cause difficulty include pronoun objects with phrasal verbs:

> **She didn't know the word, so she looked up it.*

and structures with 'preposition-stranding': learners have trouble understanding and producing sentences like:

> *What did you mend it with?*
> *That's the shop I told you about.*

---

[1] This and the two following examples are quoted from George L. Campbell's *Compendium of the world's languages* (Routledge 1991).

Topicalisation

It is common for the topic of a Japanese sentence (which may not be the subject) to be announced separately at the beginning – rather as happens in spoken English in sentences like *That car – we've had nothing but trouble with it.* This can lead to mistakes, especially in written English, and especially if a subject pronoun is dropped as well:

> *Those people do not understand at all.* (Meaning *I do not understand those people at all.*)

Attempts to topicalise verbs can lead to inappropriate use of introductory *it*:

> *It should be opened more places at the university.*

Verbs

The Japanese verb is a very self-contained entity: except for the copula da (= *be*) every verb can stand as a sentence on its own, requiring neither subject nor object to be expressed.

> Wasureta. (= *I've forgotten it.*)

This can lead students to leave out pronoun subjects and objects in English.

> '*Did you get the bread?*' *'Yes. Went to supermarket and bought.*'

The copula *be* is often dropped (see 'Adjectives and adverbs' below):

> *I terribly bad at English.*

Like English, Japanese expresses tense, voice and other meanings through changes in the form of the verb. However, Japanese has one-word verb forms, with no auxiliary verbs, so that students find English verb phrases difficult to construct. Confusion in this area often causes learners to use auxiliary *be* inappropriately:

> *I was opened the door.*
> *We are write to each other in English.*

The Japanese verb does not change for person or number, so students easily forget the English third-person singular -*s*.

> *She usually go to country at weekend.*

The use of *do* in questions and negatives causes problems. (Japanese questions of all types are marked by clause-final ka, with no change of word order; negation is shown by a change in the verb form.)

> *You want a drink?*
> *This is not mean what you think.*

Learners find question tags complicated, and may settle for one invariable form:

> *You're tired, isn't it?*
> *This is yours, no?*

Prepositional verbs are found complicated, and the preposition is often dropped:

> *I can communicate many people. Now I want to speak native speaker.*

Students may have special difficulty with embedded questions such as *It depends whether . . .* or *It's a question of how far . . .*

Tenses

Broadly speaking, Japanese students have the same difficulties as other learners with the complex English tense/aspect system. Mistakes encouraged by Japanese grammar include the use of the present for the future:

> *I see her tomorrow.*

and occasional confusion between progressive and perfect forms.

Indirect speech maintains the tense of the original, leading to mistakes in English:

> *She said she cannot write it.*

Conditionals

Unreal conditionals (e.g. *If I had known . . .*) are not formally distinct from real conditionals in Japanese, and herein lies a major problem for students, for even when they have mastered the mechanics of forming unreal conditionals and wishes in all their complexity, the problem of concept remains: there is no neat Japanese peg to hang it on. So learners will need careful explanations of the meanings involved in structures such as these. Typical mistakes:

> *If I know you are here, I would come sooner.*
> *We can go swimming tomorrow if we got up early.*

Passives

Japanese has a suffixed passive, but its range of use differs from English. Difficulty in constructing English passives leads to errors such as:

> *Usually the house of Japan makes in wood.*
> *I speak badly because I have never taught pronunciation.*
> *In 19th century many modern countries establed.*
> *My purse stolen on bus.*
> *The exhibition will be visit by people from many countries.*

Inanimate subjects take a passive verb less readily in Japanese, so students may find it difficult to construct sentences like *Our house was built 200 years ago* or *The parcel was sent last week.* On the other hand, a Japanese passive can be used in some cases where it is not possible in English (for instance, the passive subject can refer to a person who is affected by the action, but who would not be the direct or indirect object of the equivalent active sentence).

> *He was stolen his money.* (for *He had his money stolen.*)
> *She was died her husband.* (for *Her husband died.*)

Learners often drop the preposition from the passive of an English prepositional verb:

> *I was waited by my mother after school.*

A difference in the way underlying voice is expressed in English and Japanese leads to mistakes with the expressions *easy to* and *difficult to*:

> *I'm easy to catch cold.*
> *This pen is difficult to write.*

The passive is also used in a wholly active sense to show respect and reserve:

> *When were you come to Japan?*

Complementation

Verbs and clauses are nominalised in Japanese in a very simple way, by placing after them one of the particles koto or no. The Japanese, no less than any other nationality, find confusing the choice exemplified in:

> *I'd like **you to go**.*
> *I object to **your going**.*
> *I'm surprised at **the fact that you're going**.*
> *It's a good idea **for you to go**.*

Relatives

Relative pronouns do not exist in Japanese. Nouns (and pronouns) may be modified by complex phrases which come before the noun or pronoun, rather on the following lines:

> *there in visible house living people* (= *the people who live in the house you can see over there*)
> *twenty years ago together school-to went friend* (= *a friend I went to school with twenty years ago*)
> *Tokyo in born I* (= *I, who was born in Tokyo, . . .*)

This means that learners have serious difficulty in using English relative pronouns and constructing relative clauses, and they often simply avoid using them. Misunderstanding of relatives also leads to *which* being used as a general-purpose connector:

> *This story reminds me of my memory which I was in the elementary school.*
> *Nobody could understand my feeling which I looked forward to this day.*

Nouns

A large class of Japanese nouns of Chinese origin can also function as adjectives and adverbs (depending on the following particle). This can lead to mistakes in English:

> *Tokyo is very safety city.*
> *We should eat more nourishment diet to avoid ill.*

Nouns compound freely, placing the elements in much the same order as in English: the tendency of Romance-language speakers to split and link (*scheme of insurance of employees of bank*) is not shared by the Japanese.

The English stylistic taboo against repeating nouns does not hold in Japanese:

> *My sister's friends sometimes telephone my sister early in the morning.*

Number and the use of articles

Many nouns referring to people may take one of a number of plural suffixes (depending on degree of respect), but if the context makes plurality clear the noun goes unmarked, as do virtually all nouns not referring to people. Therefore, as no element in the Japanese sentence regularly shows plurality, and since the distinction between count and mass (countable and uncountable) is not recognised, number and countability pose major problems. Many Japanese learners achieve really creditable proficiency in all aspects of written English except for articles and the number-countability problem:

> *In Japan, industrial product is cheap. Because we have an economic growth. But vegetable is so expensive. Because we Japanese have a few lands.*

Surprisingly little material exists for teaching plurals and articles. It is a difficult area, and perhaps a tedious one, but many Japanese feel inhibited in speaking because they have not been trained to make instinctive choices of article and number. Typical article errors at an elementary level are:

We used to live in the big house in suburb of Fukuoka. A house was built of the wood.
I usually spend Sunday by a river; the people who work in office need to relax in some countryside.

Pronouns

English personal pronouns have various equivalents in Japanese. For instance, *you* is anata, kimi, omae, kisama, the addressee's name or title, or a kinship term, among other forms of address. Each word carries precise implications of age, relationship, status and attitude, and the lack of choice in English often embarrasses the Japanese.

Typical errors of pronoun choice in English include using *he* or *she* about a person present, instead of the name, and addressing somebody by their name plus a third-person verb. Examples of other problems:

'Do you get a lot of snow in Hokkaido?' *'Yes, I do.'*
To make omelette, first I crack two eggs . . .
'Do you ever write poetry?' *'Yes, I wrote it yesterday.'*

Possessive pronouns, unless emphasised or contrasted, can go unexpressed in Japanese:

She washed face and cleaned teeth.

English indefinite pronouns involve the same difficulties (in particular, the choice between *some* and *any*) as for other learners.

We didn't have some food in the house.

Adjectives and adverbs

Japanese has a class of 'adjectives' which behave largely like verbs: they can be inflected to show tense and condition:

yokatta (= *was good*)
yokattara (= *if it's good; if you like*)

This can lead students to treat English adjectives like verbs, at least to the extent of omitting the copula *be*:

That film good.
We should not afraid the failure.

Many of these Japanese adjectives are 'subjective', referring to the speaker's or hearer's feelings. So a Japanese learner may ask *Is Japanese food delicious?* meaning *Do you find Japanese food delicious?* To take another example, the Japanese adjective kowai tends to mean *I/you/we are afraid* or *You are frightening*; with a third-person subject it will mean, not *he/she is afraid*, but *I/you/we are afraid of him/her*. This naturally leads to confusion in students' use of parallel English adjectives.

Japanese speakers

The grammar of Japanese nouns can lead to the misuse of English nouns as adjectives, as mentioned above:

This is democracy country.

A number of English verbs can be followed by adjectival complements (for instance *look*, *sound*, *turn*). The Japanese equivalents have adverbial complements:

It looks tastily.

It sounds strangely.

It turned bluely.

Japanese does not distinguish between gradable and non-gradable adjectives, so students may use adverbs of degree and emphasis inappropriately:

It was very enormous.

I'm absolutely tired.

Comparative and superlative inflections do not exist in Japanese. A common mistake is:

I intend to work hard more than last term.

Words answering the questions *Where?* and *When?* are nouns in Japanese; *top* and *up* are the same word; mae means *the front* or *ago*:

I like here.

She is in upstairs.

Japanese has an impressive inventory of devices for injecting vagueness and tentativeness into utterances, which gives rise to overuse of *perhaps*, *rather*, *a little* and *such*.

Determiners

Troublesome pairs of quantifiers include *whole/all*, *all/every*, *several / any number of*, *far / a long way*, *long / a long time*, *much / a lot of*, *much/many*, *a bit / quite a bit*, *far/distant*.

Infelicitous collocations can also arise:

I have quite many English friends.

Much/many and *little/few* in Japanese can be predicative:

Mountain is many. So vegetable field is few.

Conjunctions and complex sentences

English and Japanese conjunctions do not always have simple one-to-one equivalents. *And*, for instance, corresponds to at least eleven different Japanese forms, depending on whether they connect nouns, adjectives, verbs or clauses. Taking one common *and* equivalent, namely Japanese to, and turning it back into English, we find *and*, *with*, quotation marks, *when, if, whenever, as, to* and *from*. Another Japanese structural word, mo, corresponds variously to *also, both . . . and, (n)either . . . (n)or, whether . . . or, even, if, though, -ever, as much as,* or prosodic emphasis. Japanese students can therefore be expected to have more trouble than Europeans in mastering the meaning and use of English conjunctions.

Japanese clause-conjunctions often double as postpositions or particles. Perhaps because of this, Japanese students do not always appreciate the clause-combining role of English conjunctions, and there is a strong tendency to use them with one-clause sentences:

*I am working very hard. Because I want to succeed an exam.
But I am afraid I can't succeed it. So I must be more diligence.

Vocabulary

Three factors aid the Japanese in learning the vocabulary of English.
1. Japanese itself has an enormous lexicon, much of it phonetically opaque, so that the meaning of an uncontextualised word becomes clear only when the word is seen – assuming that the learner knows the Chinese characters that constitute it. The Japanese are therefore accustomed to and skilled at learning vocabulary.
2. There are very few bad Japanese–English / English–Japanese dictionaries in Japan, and there are many excellent ones.
3. A surprising number of English words are used – though often in barely recognisable form – in everyday speech and especially in the blandishments of television commercials and in popular magazines. On the supermarket shelves only those products that are traditionally Japanese – sake, chopsticks, miso and so on – have Japanese trade names. 'Western' goods carry quasi-English names: Lion toothpaste, Pocari Sweat after-exercise drink. There are even a few false friends, like konsento (= *electric socket*), and telescopings like ensuto (= *stopping the engine*) and masukomi (= *mass communications*), which students use on the innocent assumption that they are current outside Japan.

Of the lexical pitfalls that yawn before the student, many lie on the border between vocabulary and grammar. Japanese distinguishes differently from English between state and action verbs, so that for instance okiru means *get up* and *be up*, kiru means *put on* and *wear*. The equivalent of *can* co-occurs with some verbs where English rejects it:

*If you come to Japan, I think you can enjoy.
Though Japanese has equivalents for *walk, fly* and *drive* it prefers *go (by) walking, go by plane* and *go by car* when reaching one's destination

is the main interest. *Come* and *go* are always seen from the *speaker's* viewpoint.

> *'Are you coming to my party?'* **'Yes, I'm going.'*

The same applies to *bring*, which has the added complication of corresponding to three Japanese forms according to whether it means *bring a thing*, *bring an inferior or equal being*, or *bring a superior being* – a feature shared by *take* in its sense of *accompany*, *bring with you*. *Receive* and *accept* can be confused, and *get* is no easier for the Japanese than for anyone else.

The verb yameru can mean *refrain*, *give up* . . . *-ing* or *give up the idea of*; hence such brave attempts as:

> **Please give up smoking on the coach.*
> **I've given up getting married.*

Itadakimasu – said before eating – and a large number of crystallised expressions have no neat English equivalent, which is the source of much embarrassment and perplexity. Many are subtle variants of *I'm sorry to . . . you* and *Thank you*. The Japanese, like the English, are embarrassed about giving and receiving compliments.

Hiroi and its opposite semai mean not only *wide* and *narrow* but also *spacious* and *cramped*.

> *England is very wide country.* (meaning that as England is fairly flat you can see a long way)

Translation problems may lead students to confuse *interesting* and *funny*, *funny* and *out of sorts*, *important* and *carefully*, *careful* and *dangerous*.

Japanese has adopted a large number of English words; however, their pronunciation has often been so modified that they are no longer recognisable to English speakers. Examples are:

> *emurushon (emulsion); torekkingu (trekking); ranchi (lunch); shiruba (silver); sabisu (service)*

Some of the 'English' words and expressions used in Japanese are home-grown, and unknown outside Japan:

> *beddo-taun (dormitory town); kanningu (cheating)*

Style

A problem with the written work of Japanese students is that though spelling, organisation and grammar may be faultless, over-use of abstract nouns and the invoking of unfamiliar images may result in incomprehensibility to the English reader. Abstraction is respected in Japan. There is a great tradition of poetry that uses simple concrete vocabulary to step outside itself, and a huge stock of abstract nouns, largely composed of two- or three-character compounds. Some of these have come into being during the last hundred years as equivalents to words current in Western European languages; some of them were born of a civilisation utterly remote from that of the West.

The language classroom

All Japanese nowadays do three years, 90% do six years and about 50% do at least eight years of English at school and college, but in addition a large number go to private schools in the evening and on Saturday afternoon – in addition to their regular studies – so as to do better in the subjects that will one day bring them success in the university entrance examination, where English looms large. Parents often insist that the private school should stick rigidly to the syllabus followed in the main school, so that listening, pronunciation, role play and language games sadly have no place. English-language broadcasts, newspapers and books are widely available, so that no-one need feel cut off from contact with English, but going abroad on holiday to a first-language, English-speaking country is expensive and – given the short Japanese annual holidays – impracticable for most people.

The traditional Japanese regard for authority and formality is in tune with teacher-dominated lessons where much heed is paid to the 'correct' answer, learning of grammar rules and item-by-item (rather than contextualised) vocabulary. The four performance skills are ranked as follows: writing, reading, speaking, listening; and what listening there is tends to be testing, where the student ticks off the approved answer in a multiple-choice set. Chokuyaku (word-for-word translation of real English into bizarre Japanese) is much favoured. At least in middle and high schools, covering the age-range twelve to eighteen, the foregoing still prevails; but in many universities and private language schools new methods are eagerly adopted – though some run counter to national temperament.

The Japanese do not care to be 'put on the spot' in public; getting it wrong can be a cause of real shame, especially in front of classmates who are younger or socially inferior (in the Japanese sense). A spontaneous answer is rare; long thought or a discreetly whispered conference with a compatriot usually precede the student's response. The Japanese tend not to air their private opinions in public, which means that 'What do you think of . . .?' topics of discussion can be full of long and painful silences. The non-Japanese teacher easily misinterprets embarrassment as inability to speak. The uninhibited, even aggressive participation in multi-national discussions by many Europeans may affront the Japanese sense of propriety, yet the student will often bottle up this unease for weeks, giving away no hint of it.

Chinese speakers

Jung Chang

Distribution

PEOPLE'S REPUBLIC OF CHINA, TAIWAN, SINGAPORE, Malaysia; there are also large communities of Chinese speakers throughout southeast Asia, Oceania and North and South America. About one fifth of the world's population are native speakers of Chinese.

Introduction

The Chinese language, or the Han language, as the Chinese call it, is a collection of numerous dialects which may be classified into eight dialect groups (sometimes referred to as different languages): Northern Chinese (also known as Mandarin), Wu, Hsiang, Kan, Hakka, Northern Min, Southern Min, and Yueh (i.e. Cantonese). While the last four dialects are the mother tongues of most Chinese speakers outside China, Northern Chinese is the native dialect of over 70 per cent of the Chinese population at large, and is the basis of modern standard Chinese, which is the accepted written language for all Chinese, and has been promoted as the national language.

The Chinese dialects share not only a written language but also important basic features at all structural levels. The problems discussed in this chapter are by and large common to speakers of all dialects.

Chinese and English belong to two different language families (Sino-Tibetan and Indo-European), and have many structural differences. Difficulties in various areas at all stages of English language learning may be expected.

Phonology

General

The phonological system of Chinese is very different from that of English. Some English phonemes do not have Chinese counterparts and are hard to learn. Others resemble Chinese phonemes but are not

310

identical to them in pronunciation, and thus cause confusion. Stress, intonation and juncture are all areas of difficulty. In general, Chinese speakers find English hard to pronounce, and have trouble learning to understand the spoken language.

Vowels

1. There are more vowel contrasts in English than in Chinese, so English vowels are closer to each other in terms of position of articulation than Chinese vowels. This means that more effort is required to distinguish them.
2. The contrast between /iː/ and /ɪ/ has no equivalent in Chinese. Learners confuse pairs such as *eat* and *it*, *bean* and *bin*.
3. The same applies to /uː/ and /ʊ/, leading to confusion, for instance, between *fool* and *full*, *Luke* and *look*.
4. /æ/ does not occur in Chinese. Learners tend to nasalise it. It may also be confused with /ɑː/, /ʌ/ or /e/, so that a word such as *cap* might be pronounced /kæp/, *carp*, *cup* or '*kep*'.
5. /ɒ/ has no equivalent in Chinese. Learners sometimes make it sound like /ɔː/, /aʊ/, /ʊ/ or a front vowel. So for instance *shot* might be pronounced *short*, *shout* or /ʃʊt/.
6. /ʌ/ is sometimes replaced by /a/, which is a close approximation to a Chinese phoneme.
7. Chinese diphthongs are usually pronounced with quicker and smaller tongue and lip movements than their English counterparts. Learners therefore make these sounds too short, with not enough distinction between the two component vowels.

Consonants

1. In the three pairs of stops /p/ and /b/, /t/ and /d/, /k/ and /g/, the unaspirated group /b/, /d/ and /g/ are voiced in English but are on the whole voiceless in Chinese. Chinese students tend to lose the voiced feature in speaking English.
2. /v/ is absent from most Chinese dialects. As a result, it is sometimes treated like /w/ or /f/: *invite* may be pronounced '*inwite*'; *live* pronounced '*lif*'.
3. Many Chinese dialects do not have /n/. Learners speaking these dialects find it difficult to distinguish, for instance, *night* from *light*.
4. /θ/ and /ð/ do not occur in Chinese. /θ/ is likely to be replaced by /t/, /f/ or /s/, and /ð/ by /d/ or /z/. So for example *thin* may be pronounced *tin*, *fin* or *sin*; *this* may be pronounced '*dis*' or '*zis*'.

5. /h/ tends to be pronounced as a heavily aspirated velar fricative (as in Scottish *loch*), which approximates to a Chinese consonant.
6. Most Chinese dialects do not have /z/. The usual error is to substitute /s/: *rise* may be pronounced *rice*.
7. /dʒ/, /tʃ/ and /ʃ/ are distantly similar to a group of three different Chinese consonants. Many learners' pronunciation of these is therefore heavily coloured and sounds foreign.
8. Some southern Chinese find /l/ and /r/ difficult to distinguish, leading to the kind of mistake caricatured in jokes about 'flied lice', etc.
9. Final consonants in general cause a serious problem. As there are few final consonants in Chinese, learners tend either to add an extra vowel at the end, or to drop the consonant and produce a slight glottal or unreleased stop: *duck*, for instance, may be pronounced /dʌkə/ or /dʌʔ/; *wife* may be pronounced /waɪfuː/ or /waɪʔ/.
10. /l/ in final position is particularly difficult: it may be replaced by /r/, or followed by /ə/, or simply dropped: *bill*, for instance, may be pronounced *beer*, /bɪlə/ or /bɪʔ/.

Consonant clusters

1. Initial consonant clusters are lacking in Chinese, and cause problems. The common error is to insert a slight vowel sound between the consonants, pronouncing *spoon*, for instance, as '*sipoon*'.
2. Final clusters are even more troublesome. Learners are likely to make additional syllables, or to simplify the cluster (for instance, by dropping the last consonant). So *dogs* may be pronounced /dɒgəz/ or /dɒg/; *crisps* may be pronounced /krɪsɪpuːsiː/ or /krɪsɪpuː/.

Rhythm and stress

Reduced syllables are far less frequent in Chinese than in English. Moreover, these syllables in Chinese are usually pronounced more prominently than in English, and undergo fewer phonetic changes. Thus learners tend to stress too many English syllables, and to give the weak syllables a full rather than reduced pronunciation:

'fish 'and 'chips (with *and* stressed and pronounced /ænd/)
'The 'capital 'of 'England 'is 'London. (with both *the* and *of* emphasised)

When students try to reduce the accent on the English weak forms, they sometimes find them so hard to pronounce that they omit them: 'fish 'chips.

Intonation

Pitch changes in Chinese (the 'tones') are mainly used to distinguish words whose pronunciation is otherwise the same; sentence intonation shows little variation. The English use of intonation patterns to affect the meaning of a whole utterance is therefore difficult for Chinese to grasp. Unfamiliar with these patterns, Chinese learners tend to find them strange and funny. Some add a tonic value (often a high falling tone) to individual syllables. Thus their speech may sound flat, jerky or 'sing-song' to English ears.

Juncture

The monosyllabicity of basic Chinese units leads to learners' separating English words rather than joining them smoothly into a 'stream of speech'. This contributes to the staccato effect of a Chinese accent. Learners need considerable practice in this area.

Orthography; reading and writing

Spelling

The writing system of Chinese is non-alphabetic. Chinese learners therefore have great difficulty in learning English spelling patterns, and are prone to all sorts of errors. Common mistakes include:
1. Failure to apply standard spelling conventions:
    dinner spelt **diner*   *eliminate* spelt **eliminat*
2. Problems arising from the lack of hard and fast spelling rules in English:
    *docter   **patten*   **liv*   **Wenesday*   **anser*
3. Mistakes arising from learners' incorrect pronunciation:
    campus spelt **compus*   *swollen* spelt **swallen*
    around spelt **aroud*   *sincerely* spelt **secerly*
4. Omission of syllables:
    *unfortually   **determing*   **studing*

Reading and writing

Alphabetic scripts present Chinese learners with quite new problems of visual decoding. The way the information is 'spread out' in each word seems cumbersome for a reader used to the compact ideograms of

Chinese speakers

Chinese. Individual words may take a relatively long time to identify, and (since words take up more space than in Chinese) the eye cannot take in so much text at a time. Chinese learners therefore tend initially to have slow reading speeds in English relative to their overall level of proficiency.

Alphabetic handwriting, on the other hand, presents no serious problems for Chinese learners.

Grammar

General

There are certain similarities between the syntactic structures of English and Chinese, yet the divergence is vast. It is advisable not to regard anything as a 'basic' point which students 'ought to know'.

Parts of speech

Parts of speech in Chinese are not always formally distinguished. There is no established comprehensive grammatical classification, and the same word may often serve different structural functions. As a result, learners have to try hard to remember the set classes of English words and their functions in a sentence. They may fail to distinguish related words such as *difficult* and *difficulty* in terms of their parts of speech, or to appreciate the fact that certain functions in a sentence can only be fulfilled by words from certain classes:

　*She likes walk.
　*I have not son.
　*He is not doubt about the correct of his argument.
　*It is very difficulty to convince him.

Sentence structure

Chinese sentences often start with a 'topicalised' subject or object which is grammatically detached from the rest of the sentence (as in English *That boy – I'm going to kill him one of these days*). This does not always transfer successfully to English, and can cause confusion, especially if a topicalised object is followed by a dropped subject pronoun (which makes the sentence look like a defective passive).

　*Old people must respect (meaning Old people – we must respect them).

Verb forms

Chinese is a non-inflected language. What English achieves by changing verb forms, Chinese expresses by means of adverbials, word order and context. English inflection seems generally confusing and causes frequent errors:

1. Subject–verb concord:
   > *Everybody are here.*
   > *Belong and Baoying has a shared kitchen.*
2. Irregular verb formation:
   > *strided   *hurted   *flied   *blewn*
3. Structure of complex verb forms:
   > *The window was breaking by the wind.*

Time, tense and aspect

1. Chinese expresses the concept of time very differently from English. It does not conjugate the verb to express time relations. Learners have serious difficulty in handling English tenses and aspects. Errors like these are common:
   > *I have seen her two days ago.*
   > *I found that the room is empty.*
   > *My brother left home since nine o'clock.*
   > *She will go by the time you get here.*
2. Some students have the false impression that the names of the tenses indicate time. For example, they think that the 'present tense' indicates 'present time'. They therefore find puzzling utterances like:
   > *There is a film tonight.*
   > *The play we just saw tells a tragic story.*
3. Progressive aspect causes difficulty:
   > *What do you read? (for What are you reading?)*
   > *I sit here for a long time.*
4. Certain conventions in using tenses cannot be explained semantically, which causes problems. In adverbial clauses indicating future time, for example, learners do not necessarily appreciate why the 'present' tense is required:
   > *We shall go to the country if it will be a nice day tomorrow.*
   > *She will submit the paper before she will leave the college.*

Verb complementation

1. Often transitive verbs are used as intransitives, and vice versa:
    He married with a charming girl.
    She talked a few words with one of the passengers.
2. Patterns of complementation cause difficulty even for advanced learners:
    I suggest to come earlier.
    The grass smells sweetly.
    Most people describe that he is handsome.
    She told that she'd be here.
3. It is particularly difficult for the Chinese to differentiate between the use of an infinitive (with or without *to*), a present participle, a past participle and a gerund. One frequently hears mistakes like:
    I was very exciting. (for *excited*)
    I'm sorry I forgot bringing your book.
    You'd better to come earlier.
    She's used to get up at seven.
4. Adjectives and verbs are frequently identical in Chinese. Thus the verb *to be* tends to be dropped when followed by predicative adjectives.
    I busy.
    She very happy.

Auxiliaries; questions and negatives

Chinese does not use auxiliaries to form questions and negatives. The insertion of *do/don't*, etc. presents problems:
    How many brothers you have?
    I did not finished my work yesterday.
Question tags meaning *Is that so?*, *Is that right?* are used very commonly in Chinese. These are often converted to an all-purpose *is it?/isn't it?* in English:
    He liked it, is it?
    You don't read that sort of books, isn't it?

Modals

Certain meanings of English modals have direct equivalents in Chinese modals and can be readily understood. But other meanings which have no Chinese counterparts are problematic. For instance, *should* as in *I think you should take up writing* is easy as it corresponds to a Chinese modal, yīnggāi. But *should* is more difficult in the utterances below since it has no straightforward Chinese translations:

It's strange that you should say this.
We should be grateful if you could do it.

On the whole, English modals indicate a wider range of meaning and feeling than their Chinese counterparts. Chinese learners therefore tend not to use them as frequently as they should, and may fail to express the nuances that English modals convey; they would for example be likely to say *This is definitely not true* in preference to *This can't be true*, or *I'm probably coming* rather than *I might come*.

One point needs particular mention here. Communication in English requires appropriate polite forms of instructions, invitations, requests and suggestions, in which modals play a central role. Not being able to use modals (and associated patterns) adequately, Chinese students often fail to comply with the English conventions, and may appear abrupt. For example, they may say such things as:

1. *Please read this article.*
2. *You come and sit here, please.*
3. *Can you do me a favour?*

when it would normally be more polite to say:

1. *You may like to read this article.*
2. *Would you come and sit here, please?*
3. *Could you do me a favour?*

Subjunctives

Chinese does not differentiate subjunctive from indicative mood. Learners are therefore likely to replace English subjunctives and 'unreal pasts' by ordinary present tenses or modals:

If I am you, I shan't go.
I suggest that this applicant may be considered at the next meeting.
I wish you can come.
It's time that we should leave.

Relatives

English relative structures are difficult for Chinese learners, who often simply avoid using them. Structures with zero pronoun (e.g. *The house we wanted was too expensive*) can cause comprehension problems. Typical mistakes with relative structures include the omission or addition of pronouns, and difficulty in using *whose*:

There are many people have that idea.
That's the shop that I told you about it.
It was a society which its rulers held absolute power.

Chinese speakers

Passives

Chinese learners often have trouble mastering English passive structures:
> *Both the burglars captured by the police.*
> *We were inviting to a party.*

Progressive and perfect passives are particularly difficult:
> *A new hotel is building in the centre.*
> *Tomorrow's meeting has cancelled.*

Articles

There are no articles in Chinese. Students find it hard to use them consistently correctly. They may omit necessary articles:
> *Let's make fire.*
> *I can play piano.*

or insert unnecessary ones:
> *He finished the school last year.*
> *He was in a pain.*

or confuse the use of definite and indefinite articles:
> *Xiao Ying is a tallest girl in the class.*
> *He smashed the vase in the rage.*

Gender

There is no gender distinction in the spoken form of the Chinese pronouns: for example, *he, she* and *it* share the same sound. Chinese learners often fail to differentiate them in spoken English:
> *I've a brother, and she's working in a factory.*
> *That is my aunt over there. Have you met him?*
> *Julie is a good director. His films are very engrossing.*

Number

Plurality is rarely expressed in Chinese. *-s* tends to be dropped:
> *I have visited some place around York.*
> *I've seen a lot of play lately.*

This is particularly true in speech, where there is already a problem with the pronunciation of final consonant clusters.

The countable/uncountable distinction

Chinese students sometimes find the English concept of countability hard to grasp. For example, *furniture, equipment, luggage, news*, etc. can all be counted in the Chinese mind. Hence such errors as:

Let me tell you an interesting news.
She's brought many luggages with her.

Pronouns

English uses pronouns much more than Chinese, which tends to drop them when they may be understood.

I bought the book before left the shop.
The teacher came in with a big book in right hand.

With personal pronouns, Chinese does not make a distinction between the subjective case (e.g. *I*) and the objective case (e.g. *me*). With possessives, it does not distinguish determiners (e.g. *my*) from non-determiners (e.g. *mine*). Students sometimes choose the wrong category of pronouns in English:

I am like she.
The book is my.

Word order

A. Questions

Chinese word order is identical in both statements and questions. Inversion in English interrogative sentences may be ignored or may be applied wrongly:

You and your family last summer visited where?
When she will be back?
What was called the film?
Would have she gone home?

B. Indirect questions

Chinese uses embedded direct questions in indirect questions. This sometimes leads to errors such as:

He asked me what does she like.
She wondered where is her father.

C. Inversion in general

Not only interrogatives, but also other sentences with inverted word order are error-prone:
>*Only by doing so they could succeed.*
>*He was unhappy, so I was.*

Postmodifiers

Noun modifiers in Chinese, no matter whether they are words, phrases or clauses, come before the nouns they modify. So English postmodifiers often hinder comprehension. In production, errors like these emerge:
>*This is important something.*
>*This is a very difficult to solve problem.*
>*That is the place where motion pictures are made there.*

Position of adverbials

Chinese adverbials usually come before verbs and adjectives in a sentence. A learner is very likely to say, for instance:
>(*)*Tomorrow morning I'll come.* (for *I'll come tomorrow morning.*)
>(*)*This evening at seven o'clock we are going to meet.* (for *We are going to meet this evening at seven o'clock.*)

Conjunctions and compound sentences

A common mistake is to duplicate conjunctions of concession and cause, as their Chinese equivalents usually appear in pairs:
>*Although she was tired, but she went on working.*
>*Because I didn't know him, so I didn't say anything.*

Prepositions

The use of English prepositions is highly idiomatic and difficult for learners. Errors of all kinds are common:
>*What are you going to do in this morning?*
>*I go York in May.*
>*He is suffering with cold.*
>*The text is too difficult to me.*

Vocabulary

False equivalents

English and Chinese words overlap a great deal in meaning. However, apart from some nouns, they rarely produce exact equivalents. The rough Chinese counterparts given to learners are therefore to a large extent false equivalents, which often lead to 'Chinglish' or even nonsensical errors. For example, the false equivalent of *until*, zhidao, leads to this sentence:

> *He took a rest until he had finished his work.*

when the intended sentence is:

> *He did not take a rest until he had finished his work.*

Phrasal and prepositional verbs

These verbs do not have equivalents in Chinese, and are very difficult to handle. Students tend to avoid using them. For instance, a Chinese learner is likely to say:

> *Please continue with your work* rather than *Please get on with your work.*
> *He finally yielded* rather than *He finally gave in.*

Lack of command of such items leads to various errors:

> *The plane takes up easily.* (for *takes off*)
> *They've worked forward this plan.* (for *worked out*)

Idiomatic expressions

Idioms are as difficult for the Chinese as for any other language learners. One area that needs special attention is that of social interaction, where Chinese and English typically employ different expressions to fulfil the same function. For instance, three common Chinese greetings translate directly as:

> *Have you eaten?*
> *Where are you going?*
> *You have come.*

(And Chinese students are indeed frequently heard to use these expressions in greeting English people!)

Other examples include:

> *Did you play very happy?* (for *Did you have a good time?*)
> *Don't be polite.* (for *Make yourself at home.*)
> *Please eat more.* (for *Would you like a little more?*)

Culture

Traditional Chinese culture places a very high value on learning. An English language teacher can expect to find his or her pupils admirably industrious and often in need of dissuasion from working too hard.

A related view in many Chinese students' minds is that learning needs serious and painstaking effort. Activities which are 'pleasurable' and 'fun' are rather suspect as not being conducive to proper learning. Teachers who have adopted an approach involving 'learning while having fun' should be prepared to show its validity.

Teachers are highly respected in Chinese culture, and are typically regarded as being knowledgeable and authoritative. Out of respect, Chinese students are usually not as ready to argue or to voice opinions in class as European students.

Regarding methods of learning, a salient feature of Chinese education is rote memorisation. One reason for this is that all the basic written units of Chinese, the characters, have to be learned by heart individually. This method plays a significant part in the way English is learned in China, and may predispose some Chinese students to spend considerable time on memorisation at the expense of practice.

Sample of written Chinese

Transliteration of Chinese text with a word-for-word translation

利戎：
　　来信收到了，谢谢你的问候。没有早些回信，
请原谅！

lirong:
lirong:

lai　xin　shou dao le, xiexie ni de wen hou. meiyou zaoxie
come letter receive,　thank your regard.　not　earlier

hui　xin,　qing　yuanliang!
return letter, please forgive!

ni　jinlai　shenti zenmeyang? xuexi shunli　ma?
you recently body how?　study smooth [interrogative]?

yiding　xiang wangchang yiyang guo de hen yukuai
certainly as　usual　same live　very happy

ba?
[particle inviting confirmation]?

wo hen hao, zuijin   you le
I   very well, recently have [particle indicating change of state]

nüpengyou, jiao shizhu, hen mei.
girl-friend, call shizhu, very beautiful.

zuotian   shi chuxi,   wo qu ta jia   li,
yesterday be new year's eve, I   go her home in,

he   ta quanjia   yikuair guo nian.   ta jia
with her whole family together spend new year. her home

keting   de tianhuaban, jiaju   he qiang shang
sitting-room of ceiling,   furniture and wall- on

daochu   gua zhe   ge zhong
everywhere hang [particle indicating state] all kind

zhihua,   lipin,   hai zhuang shang le
paper flower, present, also install- on   [particle indicating change of state]

caise dengpao. shizhu jianyi   zuo youxi,
coloured bulb. shizhu suggest play game,

ba   yanjing meng qilai
[particle introducing fronted object] eye   cover

mo liwu.   wo mo dao de hen hao, shizhu didi de
feel present. I   feel-get   very good, shizhu brother

ye   bucuo. wo wanr de hen kaixin, zhidao tian kuai liang
also not bad. I   play   very happy, until   sky soon light

cai zou. lin zou shi dajia yue hao xinnian   diertian   lai
only go. near leave time all   agree   new year second day come

wo jia.   zhen xiwang ni ye   neng lai!
my house. really wish   you also can come!

xiexie ni qing wo he didi   xiatian dao   ni   jia   zuoke.
thank you invite me and brother summer to   your home visit.

women yiding   lai.   wo zai guowai xuexi de jiejie neishihou
we   definitely come. my abroad   study   sister that time

ye   huilai le,   wo xiang
also return [particle indicating change of state], I   think

Chinese speakers

wenwen, ta nengbuneng gen women yikuair lai?
ask, she can-not-can with us together come?

bu duo xie le, qing daiwen quanjia
no more write, please on my behalf ask all family

hao. pan zaori huixin!
well. look forward to early return letter!

        zhu ni xinnian kuaile!
        wish you new year happy!

        cimin yijiubasi nian yuandan
        cimin 1984 year new year's day

An idiomatic translation

New Year's Day, 1984

Dear Lirong,

Thank you for your letter, and thanks for the regards. I'm sorry that I didn't write earlier. Please forgive me!

How have you been recently? Is everything going well with your studies? Are you enjoying life as usual?

I'm very well. I've got a girl-friend now. Her name is Shizhu. She's very beautiful. Yesterday was New Year's Eve. I went to her place and spent the evening with her family. The sitting-room of her house was decorated with all sorts of paper flowers, presents and coloured lights, hanging from the ceiling, the furniture and the walls. Shizhu suggested that we play a game. We were to take down presents with our eyes covered and to keep the first ones we got. The one I got was very good, so was the one Shizhu's brother got. I had a lovely time and didn't leave until nearly dawn. Before I left we all agreed to meet at my house on the second day of the New Year. I really wish you could be here!

Thank you for inviting my brother and me to stay with you in the summer. We would love to come. My sister who is studying abroad will be back by then. I wonder whether she could come with us?

I'll stop here for now. Please give my regards to your family. I'm looking forward very much to hearing from you soon.

A Happy New Year to you.

    Cimin

Korean speakers

Jung-Ae Lee

Distribution

KOREA, China, Japan, Kazakhstan and Uzbekistan; significant emigrant or student groups in the UK, the USA (including Hawaii), Canada, Australia, New Zealand.

Introduction

The Korean language is regarded by some scholars as belonging, like Turkish, to the Ural-Altaic language family. There are also some similarities between Korean and Japanese in that the syntax is similar, and both Korean and Japanese still use some Chinese characters, although the pronunciation is not as it is in China. However, it is important to emphasise that the Korean language, along with many Korean customs and ways of experiencing the world, is unique and unrelated to any other oriental languages.

Korean is now spoken by nearly 72 million people, 69 million living on the Korean peninsula and islands and the remaining three million abroad. It is the official language of both North Korea (Democratic People's Republic of Korea) and South Korea (Republic of Korea) but the separation of the two countries has resulted in minor differences in spelling and vocabulary choice. In South Korea there are seven dialects, including that spoken around the capital, Seoul, which is referred to as Standard Korean. There are differences of pronunciation from one dialect to another which can make them mutually incomprehensible. This also means that speakers of one dialect may have greater difficulties adapting to English than speakers of another, in that some dialects have sounds that more closely approximate to those of English than others.

Speakers of standard Korean – the pronunciation described in this chapter – have a slight advantage over speakers of other dialects.

Phonology

General

The Korean alphabet consists of 24 letters: ten vowels and 14 consonants. Singly and in combination, these represent the 40 distinctive basic sounds of the Korean language – eight simple vowels, 13 diphthongs and 19 consonants.

Vowels do not occur initially in Korean. Although some Korean words begin with a vowel in transliteration (place names such as Inchon and Ulsan, for example), none begins with a vowel *sound*. Such words are actually pronounced in Korean with a preceding consonant sound similar to the English /ŋ/. This, the eighth consonant in the Korean inventory, is known as the 'empty' or 'zero' consonant.

There is no long/short vowel distinction. Voiced and unvoiced consonants do not count as different sounds.

Vowels

Korean learners typically experience the following problems:
1. /ɔː/ and /əʊ/ are both pronounced as a pure /o/.
2. /ʌ/ is assimilated to the Korean /ɑ/ (which is not lengthened), so that the vowel in *cup* falls somewhere between /kʌp/ and /kɑːp/ (*carp*).
3. /æ/ (*hat*) is often assimilated to /e/.
4. There is no Korean equivalent for /ɜː/, which may be assimilated to /ɔː/ or /ə/. /wɜː/ is particularly problematic, so that even advanced students have difficulty distinguishing between *work* and *walk*. Other pronunciations of /ɜː/ arise from the Korean desire, shared with other nationalities, to distinguish vowel sounds where there is an orthographic distinction (cf. *her, heard, sir, journey, hurt, word*).
5. Instead of a long/short vowel distinction, Korean uses rising and falling intonation and the pause. This leads to confusion with vowel-length distinctions in English, for example that between /ɪ/ (sit) and /iː/ (seat).

Consonants

The following consonants are likely to cause problems:
1. A consonant may be voiced or unvoiced depending on the sounds that come before and after it. A voiced consonant does not therefore count, as it does in English, as a different sound from its unvoiced

equivalent, and distinctions like those between *writing* and *riding*, *lock* and *log* or *raced* and *raised* may be difficult for learners to grasp.

2. /r/ and /l/ are represented by the same character in Korean – with well-known consequences for Korean, as for Japanese, learner English. Pronunciation of /r/ is particularly difficult – or /belɪ belɪ dɪpɪkəlt/, as a Korean learner might say.
3. Since /v/ is assimilated to /b/ in end position, it often becomes /bə/.
4. /f/ is assimilated to /p/, so that learners studying abroad typically talk about their *host pamilies*, and *flay* becomes *pray*.
5. /z/ is often assimilated to /dʒ/. *Zoo*, for example, often becomes /dʒuː/.
6. /ʃ/: Although this sound is found in Korean, Koreans have difficulty in pronouncing it in many English environments, such as /ʃiː/ (she), and often assimilate it to /s/. Where it is found at the end of a word, Koreans typically add an additional vowel, so that *fish* becomes /pɪʃɪ/.
7. /tʃ/ is found in Korean, but not in final position, and as with /ʃ/, /dʒ/, /z/ and /t/, there is a tendency to add a completing /ɪ/ or /ə/ vowel, so *church* typically becomes /tʃɜtʃɪ/, as George becomes /dʒodʒɪ/, *noise* and *noisy* become interchangeable, and *mixed* becomes /mɪkstə/.
8. /θ/ is assimilated to /s/, and /ð/ to /d/. Korean students reading English aloud often simply ignore the definite article (because of their grammatical expectations), but where it is pronounced this assimilation is very obvious, as it is in the case of demonstratives.
9. /s/ and /z/ in final position, as in plurals, the third person singular of verbs, and possessives, are often not pronounced – but for reasons which have to do with Korean grammar rather than because these sounds do not exist in Korean. [See 'Nouns', below.] *Months* /mʌnθs/ and *clothes* /kləʊðz/, of course, do present genuine pronunciation difficulties.

Many of the above are exhibited in the transformation of English words that have been in Korean for a long time, especially those that became part of the language during the period of Japanese occupation.

Speech style, stress and intonation

It is extremely important that the English teacher should know that Korean employs neither syllable stress nor word stress. In almost all polysyllabic English words, one syllable is emphasised, whereas every Korean word sounds flat and regular. Furthermore, particular words in Korean sentences are not stressed in relation to other words in the sentence. (Emphasis is achieved by adding an emphasis-marking suffix, and by changing the position of the word in the sentence. See 'Sentence structure', below.) The differences that stressing one word can make to the meaning of a sentence are completely foreign to the Korean learner, and require concentrated attention to be perceived or produced.

To the Korean ear, the English native speaker speaking his or her own language sounds histrionic. Conversely, the Korean learner speaking English often sounds monotonous, bored, and therefore boring, to the English ear. This can make Korean English difficult to understand.

Korean intonation does share some characteristics with English intonation, however, in that it is conditioned by grammar, with falling intonation being characteristically used for statements and questions other than *yes/no* questions, and rising intonation for *yes/no* questions and requests. It can also add an emotional dimension – though it does so far less often than in English.

Orthography and writing

Korean letters are phonetic symbols, not ideograms. The individual letter has an independent form and phonetic values which depend upon its position in a word, its association with other letters, and whether or not it is doubled. Two or more letters are written together as syllables, but forming clusters, rather than rows, on the page.

Korean is transliterated into the Latin alphabet by means of the so-called McCune-Reischauer system. This is not used in Korean publications (except those written for foreigners), but is seen all over South Korea on signs and advertising billboards, so the Latin alphabet is familiar to Koreans, and they have little or no difficulty in becoming accustomed to its use in English. Obviously children need to be taught English handwriting, but this comes relatively easily to them, though variations on the style that all South Koreans are taught might initially present comprehension difficulties – a point of which teachers should be aware.

Punctuation

The Korean character cannot be capitalised.

The use of question marks, exclamation marks, full stops and quotation marks is more or less the same as in English. The use of the comma, semi-colon and colon can present difficulties, however: although the comma exists in Korean, it is rarely used. Generally the spaces between words fulfil all of these functions in Korean. There are no possessive apostrophes in Korean, the equivalent being a noun suffix.

Brevity is favoured in writing, and the Korean writer is encouraged to have no more than two consecutive lines of characters. This way of breaking up a text may be mistaken for paragraphing, which is only used in very formal documents in conventional Korean.

Grammar

Sentence structure

Unlike the subject–verb–object word order pattern of many languages, including English, Korean word order (along with Japanese, Turkish, Persian and others) is subject–object–verb. However, this order should not be taken too strictly.

Because of the agglutinative structure of the language, the pause is as important in defining grammatical structure to facilitate comprehension of spoken Korean as the space is in written Korean.

Verbs

There are no auxiliary verbs in Korean. The Korean verb is always expressed by one word. (See 'Questions and answers', below.) Furthermore, the verb is a more independent entity than in English, and as in Japanese, because of the complex system of suffixation, every verb except for the verb *to exist* can be a sentence in itself.

Korean verbs are divided into **Action verbs**, which usually have an equivalent English verb, and **Adjectival (Descriptive) verbs**, which describe the state or characteristics of things, and sometimes the speaker's or listener's feelings, and have no English equivalent. For example:

Action verbs

English	Korean (word-for-word translation)
A student *is going* to school.	Student to school *going-be*.
I *am learning* English.	English *learning-be*

Adjectival verbs

English	Korean
There *are a lot of* flowers here.	Here flower *many-be*.
This rose *is beautiful*.	This rose *beautiful-be*.
Don't you find Korean pottery *remarkable*?	Korean pottery *be-remarkable*?

It will be observed that Korean learners often omit the verb *to be* when using adjectives in English. This is because the copula function of the verb *to be* does not exist in Korean. The adjectival verb is in effect an adjective with the sense of *to be* incorporated into it. For this reason it is impossible to form a verb from an adjective in Korean. The transformation of *weak* into the English verb *weaken*, for example, is a surprising one for Koreans. (See 'Suffixes'.)

To be; there is *and* it is

The other sense of *to be* in English – *to exist* – is found in Korean, but there is no form corresponding to *there is/are*, or to the empty *it* subject as in *It will be hot tomorrow*, so that the Korean learner will produce sentences such as
   *Many foreigners exist in Seoul.
   *Tomorrow will hot.
Nor is there anything corresponding to the anticipatory *it* as in the English *It's a pleasure to do business with you*. The Korean equivalent of this corresponds to something like *With you do business a pleasure*. Note that the equivalent of *with you* is given prominence by being placed in *initial* position with an emphasis-marking suffix, rather than at the end of the sentence as in English.

   The verb corresponding to the English verb *to exist* also performs the function of *to have*:
   *In my house dog exist. (for I have a dog.)

Complex verbs

Complex verbs are formed by combining two verbs. These 'portmanteau' verbs, which may be active or adjectival, sometimes express a meaning which in English would require several words, for example, *I got up and . . .* in English, is expressed in one such verb in Korean, as is *to be black and blue.*

Conjugation of verbs

Korean verbs, like regular English verbs, consist of a 'verb stem' and a 'verb ending', and the stem stays the same, while the ending conjugates. The two levels of formality and politeness in Korean are distinguished not only by different forms of address (comparable to *tu* and *vous* in

French, and *du* and *Sie* in German), but also by different lexical verbs and different verb endings, so Koreans may be pleasantly surprised by the comparative simplicity of the English verb system.

The suffix may, like that of an English verb, indicate tense or aspect, and show whether the subject is singular or plural, but it does not conjugate according to person, resulting in frequent Korean omission in English of the third person *-s*. It can, however, nominalise the verb, fulfilling comparable functions to verb stem + *-ing, -ation, -al, -age* or *-ment* in English.

Tense and aspect

Both tense and the progressive aspect are conveyed by means of suffixes.

Aspect

There is no perfect aspect in Korean, and Korean learners share the difficulties other nationalities experience in learning to use this form. Thus, while the narrative use of the past simple in English, especially with a past time indicator (*last summer, in 1997*) presents no problems for Koreans, difficulties arise in distinguishing between the use of the past perfect and present perfect, and between the present perfect and simple past and present forms.

The progressive aspect is conveyed in Korean by a combination of the progressive suffix (which differs in the present, past and future tenses) with the word for *exist*, and can only be used with action (as opposed to adjectival) verbs. (See above.) In Korean this form is also used in the present to indicate repetitive actions or habits – where the present simple is used in English. In contrast, the use of the progressive form in English to indicate, for example, that an action is temporary rather than permanent, or (in combination with a future time reference) to refer to the planned future is alien to a Korean.

English	Korean
It has been raining since yesterday.	*From yesterday to now rain coming.*

Tense

Korean thus has six tense/aspect forms: future simple and progressive, present simple and progressive, past simple and progressive, but they are not necessarily used in the same way as in English.

If used with adverbs associated with a future time reference, the present form in Korean often indicates a future event (although the future form may also be used).

English	Korean
I am going to Pusan tomorrow.	*Tomorrow [I] to Pusan go.*
Tomorrow is my birthday.	*Tomorrow my birthday exists.*

Note that both of the above sentences translate with little alteration into English, thus facilitating a Korean learner's understanding of the use of present verb forms for the *scheduled future*. All the other forms of the future in English are expressed in Korean by the use of the same future suffix, and the teacher will find that Koreans, like other nationalities, have difficulty in distinguishing the uses of the various structures that English deploys to refer to the future, and use them indiscriminately.

Conditionals

There are only two conditional forms in Korean, expressing unreality and possibility respectively, so Koreans have the customary problems in discriminating among those in English, especially in view of the importance of the perfect form (as in *I would have been late*), which is non-existent in Korean.

Direct and indirect speech

Word-for-word reporting of what somebody says is indicated in Korean by quotation marks and a verb of saying (*answering, thinking, shouting*, etc.). Indirect speech does not give as precise a rendition of the original as is possible in English; it is best understood as giving the gist of an utterance in that certain information contained in the original is inevitably lost. As in English, in indirect speech, the subject of the quoted sentence and time and place references are changed from the original to the current speaker's point of view. There is no change of tense, however, so for example *When I saw her, she said she was happy* is usually rendered as . . . *she said she is happy* by a Korean learner.

Modal verbs

Korean has only three modal auxiliary verbs: the equivalents of *can*, *must*, and *should*, to which, in translation, the whole range of English modal verbs must be assimilated. Korean learners thus share with many other nationalities the problems of distinguishing among the full range of English modal verbs.

Passives

The passive in Korean is expressed by a suffix, rather than by an auxiliary verb + past participle as in English. Having grasped this principle, Korean learners have little difficulty with simple passives, although they are inclined to use *from* rather than *by*, for example.

> *I am taught from Dr Brown.*

The following cases do present problems, however.

1. The *to have something done* form does not exist in Korean, leading to such errors as:
   > *Have you cut your hair? (for Have you had your hair cut?)*
2. A verb + preposition, as compared with a transitive verb, is found difficult to manage, producing errors such as:
   > *These chopsticks difficult to eat.*
3. Also, since the perfective aspect does not exist in Korean, it is not surprising that passives employing this form, e.g. *The window has been broken*, present difficulties. In other cases, even when the available grammatical forms are comparable, there is no guarantee that the same forms will be used in the same contexts. A Korean will have difficulty in learning the conventional response *Thank you, I'm being served* (when offered assistance in a shop), simply because, although the passive may have progressive aspect in Korean, it is not employed in this case.
4. Finally, verbs with two objects, like *give*, are especially problematic in the passive, and will be avoided if possible.

Questions and answers

There are no auxiliary verbs in Korean, so questions are not formed as in English. There are, however, seven question words corresponding to the English *what, where, why, how, when, who*, and there is an interrogative verb suffix. Once the basic question forms in English are mastered, such embedded question forms as *I wonder where John is going* or *I asked him what he was doing / what to do* are understandably still found difficult.

Note that like Japanese and Turkish speakers, and unlike speakers of English, Koreans answer negative questions with '*Yes*' when they agree with the speaker, and '*No*' when they disagree, leading to such errors as:

> *'Don't you like mushrooms?'*
> ** 'Yes.'* – when the speaker doesn't like mushrooms.
> ** 'No.'* – when the speaker does like mushrooms.

The possibilities of misunderstanding are immediately apparent!

Tag questions and reply questions

Korean has two verbless forms which are used to prompt agreement with affirmative and negative statements respectively, and are used in both the tag question and reply question contexts. Thus *isn't it?* in both *'It's a nice day, isn't it?'* and *'It's a nice day!' 'Isn't it!'* would be translated by the same words in Korean, as would *hasn't he?, wouldn't she?, don't they?*, and so on. Similarly, there is one Korean expression corresponding to *has he?, would she?, do they?* and so on. Like other nationalities, Korean speakers are therefore bewildered by the tag question in English as a grammatical form. They usually understand its import, but avoid producing it whenever possible, not only because of its formal complexity, but also because the Korean equivalent suggests a lack of confidence in the addressee. (It is often used by teachers checking that small children understand something, for example!)

Short answers

These are also found difficult. Here, too, there is a very limited range of verbless possibilities in Korean. (Compare *Ich auch!* in German, *Moi aussi!* in French, *Jag också!* in Swedish, and watasimo in Japanese as translations of the various English expressions *So do I!, So am I!, So can I, So have I*, etc.)

Phrasal verbs

Phrasal verbs do not exist in Korean, and are in principle very difficult for Korean learners who, like those of other nationalities, find it hard to distinguish between prepositional verbs like *He turned on me!* and phrasal verbs like *He turns me on*. This leads to such familiar errors as:

> **If I don't know a word, I look up it.*

However, the Korean familiarity with rote learning and repetition may be exploited to make available to learners paradigms that will make phrasal verbs more acceptable:

Teacher: 'What do I do if I don't know a word?'
Pupils: 'Look it up!'

Teacher: 'What do I do if my jeans are too long?'
Pupils: 'Take them up!'

Relative clauses

The English-speaking learner of Korean will look in vain in a Korean grammar for this heading. The following literal translations will give some idea of how these functions are fulfilled in Korean. Note that the modifier precedes what is modified.

English	Korean
The dog, which was chained up, barked.	Chained-up dog barked.
Students who study in the library as well as in class do better.	Library-in-study-student + plural suffix class-in-student + plural suffix better do.

An awareness of this major difference will help the teacher to grasp the adjustment that a Korean learner has to make in becoming accustomed to the 'right-branching' structure of English. While Korean learners may appear to master these forms in the context of clearly focused grammatical exercises, their unfamiliarity typically inhibits the spontaneous use of them in both speech and writing.

Nouns

Korean nouns are not preceded by articles, have no grammatical gender, and do not normally have plural forms. Although nouns can be made plural by adding the suffix dŭl, this may be omitted when the meaning of plurality is obvious. Thus the word yunpil, for example, may mean *pen, the pen, a pen, some pens* or *the pens*. This sense of the 'irrelevance' of the plural ending is so deeply ingrained that Korean learners of English not only omit the plural -s in their own speech and writing, but also frequently fail to pronounce it when reading aloud. Terms such as *blue jeans* and *high heels*, which have been incorporated into Korean, are used without the -s by Koreans.

Koreans share with many other nationalities difficulty with the English ascription of the concept of uncountability to e.g. *news, advice, information, furniture* and *luggage*.

Two or more nouns are frequently combined in Korean to form a separate compound noun: a-chim-bab = morning + meal = *breakfast*; chaek-sang = book + table = *desk*; mul-gae = water + dog = *dolphin*. Korean students may be encouraged to discover that such compound nouns are also found in English (*breakfast* itself being an example, albeit of a verb + noun combination). The English distinction between *a company director* and *a company's director* is usually not a problem. Knowing when to use *of* rather than either a compound noun or the *'s* genitive is, so that such errors as **females' number* for *the number of females* and *only one sex's children* for *children of only one sex* (i.e. all boys or all girls) are common.

Suffixes after nouns

Korean has no prefixes – only suffixes. There are many of these, but their functions are usually very different from those of English suffixes. The only functions that English and Korean suffixes have in common are those of making the singular plural, and of indicating a numerical approximation (for example, 'How old is he?' 'I couldn't say exactly: *thirtyish.*') The latter function is a formal one, used in both speech and writing in Korean, however.

Students have problems with English suffixes which do not have equivalents in Korean: notably those used for negation (*colourful/ colourless*, for example), and for forming adjectives and adverbs. The concept of the 'word family' is quite alien to a Korean, but once grasped, is found very helpful as a way of organising the acquisition of English vocabulary.

Pronouns

Pronouns in Korean are divided into four types: personal, possessive (formed by the addition of a suffix to the personal pronoun), demonstrative and interrogative. Personal pronouns in Korean have three different levels of honorific forms – self-effacing, plain and honorific. These reflect the seniority of the people involved and the degree of respect to be shown. The much simpler English pronoun system presents few difficulties to Korean learners, although they will need reminding to use them in contexts in which the verb alone would be sufficient in Korean. The English word *Agree!*, for example, has been incorporated into modern Korean, complete with suffix, to express agreement – but is used without a subject pronoun.

The possessive pronoun is not used in Korean where the subject of the sentence makes it clear to whom something belongs. This results in English sentences such as:

*I must wash hair tonight.
*He was carrying briefcase and had raincoat over arm.

For the sake of emphasis (remembering that spoken Korean does not employ stress as English does) a pronoun may, however, be used in Korean which is redundant in English, resulting in sentences such as:
   Valerie, she is my teacher.
There are no impersonal pronouns corresponding to *it* or *they*: demonstratives are used instead. Korean demonstratives may correspond not only to *this*, *that*, *these* or *those*, but also, in the absence of a copula, to the English adverbs *here* or *over there*.

The teacher should also be aware that English personal pronouns are frequently represented in Korean as nouns. For example, teachers may find themselves being addressed as *teacher* rather than *you*:
   Has teacher corrected homework yet?

Adjectives

Korean adjectives either precede a noun or another adjective as in English, or they follow the subject and behave like a verb. (See 'Verbs', above.) In neither case is there the distinction between gradable and non-gradable adjectives that obtains in English, so that a Korean is likely to use adverbs of degree and emphasis inappropriately, for example:
   I am very exhausted.
   It's a bit impossible.

Adverbials

The difference between Korean and English adverbials which causes the Korean learner most difficulty is the fact that Korean adverbs (unlike many English ones) are not formed on the basis of adjectives. Otherwise Korean adverbials show many similarities with English ones. Thus the Korean schoolchild learns to classify the adverbials in Korean as adverbs of time, frequency, manner, place and degree.

Adverbials are usually positioned immediately before the word (whatever the part of speech), clause or sentence that is modified. Generalisation from Korean to English can therefore lead to incorrect positioning of adverbials in English, for example:
   I very well speak English.
It should be noted, however, that Korean has something very similar to the English adverb + adjective structure – except that what is modified in the case of Korean may be not only an adjective, as in:
   Extremely beautiful flowers bloom in that garden.
but also an adjectival verb, for example:
   Friday extraordinarily hot (was).

The Korean verbs corresponding to *look, sound, smell, feel* and *taste* are invariably followed by adverbs, not adjectives, leading to such errors as:
* * She looks sadly.
* * That violin sounds wonderfully.
* * These sausages taste deliciously.

Vocabulary

Korean has a large vocabulary, most of which finds an equivalent in English, although often what is one part of speech in English will be another in Korean. (For example, the range of words describing how water *runs, flows*, etc. is expressed by adverb + the adjectival verb *runs* in Korean.) This often makes vocabulary learning difficult for Koreans, who should be alerted from the outset to the importance of recording new vocabulary with an example showing how it functions grammatically. (School vocabulary learning inclines Korean students, like those of many other countries, to the context-free Korean/English word list.) Korean–English dictionaries are sometimes unreliable, and students should be encouraged to supplement them with English learners' dictionaries at the appropriate level.

Korean has an abundance of onomatopoeic and exclamatory words, and most Korean students take pleasure in discovering comparable words in English.

Both teachers and beginning learners will be pleasantly surprised to find that there are a large number of English words in Korean, many of which are today used with a recognisably English pronunciation. Indeed, allowing for the absence of syllabic stress, the pronunciation of these words is becoming more native-speaker-like with each generation, as more Koreans learn English, and are, to some extent, exposed to English language media. In view of the many grammatical and phonological differences between the two languages, Korean learners find it reassuring to be reminded how much English they already know.

However, as well as English words that have been imported into Korean and are used in the same way, there are others that constitute false friends: i.e. they are used with a different meaning in Korean, but are still pronounced in a recognisably English way. The following are in addition to those listed in *The Cambridge International Dictionary of English*:

cap (excellent)
chorus (*choir* is never used in Korean)
cutline (for the cut-off point below which candidates are not accepted for something)

close (for *closed*)
electric stander (standard lamp)
fine play (fair play)
form (an affected manner)
gag(man) (used for comedian)
give and take (for *to go Dutch*)
health centre (used for a health farm, or fitness centre)
highway (neither *motorway* nor *freeway* is used in Korean)
liner (used for the lining of a coat, but not of any other garment)
long leg and *short leg* (for a long-legged or short-legged person)
opener (used for all kinds of openers, such as corkscrews and
   can-openers)
over-eat (vomit)
politic (for politics)
rent car (for a hired car)
sailingboat (yacht)
sign (used for a signature)
stainless (for stainless steel)
tube (for any kind of swimming float)

Honorific vocabulary

Korean is rich in vocabulary used to convey respect on the one hand
and self-effacement on the other. Korean learners will, at first, be
embarrassed or confused as they try to find equivalent forms in English.
They are typically interested in and sensitive to a functional approach to
social interaction and questions of register. As in English, the speech
level in Korean is determined by the relationships between the speaker
and the listener and the subject being discussed, but the grammatical
consequences in Korean far exceed those in English. As the English
learner of Korean has to learn to match words and suffixes to achieve
consistency of expression, so the Korean learner of English has to
become aware of the possibility of inconsistencies of register in English.

Body language and gesture

It is important to understand the strong cultural pressure on Koreans to
speak in an unhurried way, and without facial mobility or gesture.
(Teachers of Korean academics and business people will find them
extremely reluctant to use gestures of any kind when giving a presentation, or speaking in public.) Koreans may appear unmoved, or may
smile. Anything more expressive is regarded as unacceptable. What may

be seen as woodenness or impassivity by native speakers of English is regarded as indicative of poise and composure by a Korean. Smiles which appear irrelevant to a European may in fact express agreement, embarrassment, shyness, incredulity or regret – but may also be rueful, sardonic or scornful. (Even to a Korean, a smile may be ambiguous, and may be questioned.) Because of the stress placed upon facial composure and a calmness of demeanour, an English teacher's didactically exaggerated expressiveness may initially be misunderstood and regarded as ludicrous – though perceptive students will come to appreciate it.

The meanings expressed in English by the words *please* and *thank you* are customarily expressed in Korean by tone of voice, a nod or bow. The translation of *please* is something like *I beg you*, and is regarded as ingratiating. *Thank you*, literally translated *I appreciate (something)*, is similarly regarded, so Koreans need to be made aware that it is courteous to be explicit in English in this context.

(See also 'Speech style', above, and 'The language classroom'.)

The language classroom

Koreans start to learn English, with a strong emphasis on grammar, at the age of thirteen and may continue through high school to university. The typical class size is 60 pupils, so they are not used to speaking in class. It is rare for a secondary school to have a language laboratory, and there are no foreign language assistants.

The pupils' study pattern is typically that of spoon-feeding followed by learning by heart, and there is still little development of their own arguments and ideas. The writing of essays rarely forms part of language instruction – or of any other subject – since the teacher would not have time to correct them. As a consequence, Korean students have little experience of such exercises as summarising evidence and presenting a rational argument. (Indeed, it is only very recently that training in logical argument, as a specific subject, has been incorporated into the school curriculum in an attempt to compensate for a cultural tendency to give priority to emotional rather than rational values.)

In this environment, it is almost impossible to learn foreign languages well, and most parents arrange some form of private instruction in English for their children. Regrettably, learners often derive little benefit from this, since the techniques used by many tutors are those of the traditional schoolroom. The many compulsory subjects and the heavy burden of the competition to get a place at a good university put a lot of pressure on pupils. As a result, they do not have time to read any books other than their textbooks, or to enjoy foreign language radio or television, so they lack cultural background and this affects their comprehension of English texts of any kind. If they are able to find the time to see a foreign film, it will be dubbed. These problems are well known, but the awareness of the need for change is purely theoretical and has not yet been translated into educational improvement.

In Korean schools, the teacher's authority is absolute, and if a teacher should make a mistake, pupils will not draw this to his or her attention. For their part, Korean learners, of whatever age, are extremely reluctant to speak without being certain that what they say will be correct. It is considered more polite by both sexes to leave unsaid what can be left unsaid than to speak in complete sentences, and tentativeness is valued. This also inevitably affects the Korean student's participation in class. Any form of exercise that encourages speaking will take some getting used to, but the teacher is likely to find that students (especially beginners) are more comfortable with role-play exercises (interacting with peers) than with self-revelatory tasks, especially those involving interaction with the teacher in a plenary situation. To be corrected by a teacher in front of one's Korean fellow students is humiliating. However, an impersonal treatment of an error, which turns it into a positive teaching point without reference to the person who made the mistake, is expected and valued. (Implicit correction is often not noticed.) In an international situation, in which the Korean does not feel that he or she is in competition with fellow students, this is usually not an issue.

Although pupils are expected to, and usually do, concentrate, they are not expected to show that they are paying attention by looking up at the teacher. On the contrary: eye contact is regarded as rude. (Compare 'staring at strangers', on which mothers place a taboo in bringing up young children in Western societies.)

The teacher may feel that Korean students should adapt to the mores of English-speaking societies – but this is not a process that can be rushed. The fluency of the native speaker language teacher, and, indeed, of many European non-native speakers of English, will be found over-whelming at first. Korean students value the considered pause – both because it gives them more time to process what they have heard, and because this is sympathetic to their own culture, in which a measured style of speech, with many pauses, is a sign of thoughtfulness, and of consideration for the interlocutor. What most English native speakers and Europeans see as openness, expressiveness and articulateness is censured as effusiveness and verbosity in the Korean cultural context, while authoritativeness may be interpreted as anger or the sign of an aggressive personality. The teacher may find it helpful to make such considerations explicit in a culturally heterogeneous class so that nationalities with conflicting speech styles are made more aware of areas of potential frustration. The differences that affect the group dynamics of the language class also influence interaction outside the classroom. The commercial world has already become aware of the importance of inter-cultural understanding. In a world in which English is for so many a *lingua franca*, communication will be much more effective if interlocutors are more sensitive to – perhaps even more appreciative of the values of – one another's speech styles.

A sample of written Korean

세종 대왕이 남긴 업적중 특히 중요한것은 훈민정음이다. 그때 까지 한국에는 한국 말은 따로 있었지만 문자가 없었기 때문에 오랫동안 한자를 빌어서 썼다.

Transliteration and word-for-word translation

se-jong dae wangi namgin upjuk   jung   tukhi Jungyohan
Se-Jong king   left   achievement among most important

gutun   hunminjongum   ida. kuttae kkaji hanguk enun hanguk
accomplishment hunminjongum is.   until   then korea   in   korean

malun   ttaro   itsut jiman guljaga   upsutgi ttaemune
language separately had but   writing system not   because

oledongan hanja   bilusu   ssutta.
long time chinese character borrowed used.

An idiomatic translation

Among the achievements left behind by the Great King Sejong, by far the most important is the Hunminjongum. Up to that point, although the Koreans had their own language, they used borrowed Chinese characters, because they did not have a writing system of their own.

Thai speakers

David Smyth

Distribution

THAILAND.

Introduction

Thai (formerly called 'Siamese') is a member of the Tai family of languages which are dispersed over a wide area of Asia, from northern Vietnam to northern India. Thai is the national language of Thailand and as such is spoken by over fifty million people. Distinct regional dialects of Thai are spoken in the north, northeast and south of the country, but the language of the Central Region is regarded as the standard and is used both in schools and for official purposes throughout the country.

Thai, like Chinese, is a tonal language, with the meaning of each syllable being determined by the pitch at which it is pronounced. Standard Thai has five tones – mid, low, high, rising and falling. It is a non-inflected language and much of its original lexicon is monosyllabic; a high percentage of polysyllabic words are foreign borrowings, particularly from the classical Indian languages, Sanskrit and Pali.

Thai is written in an alphabetic script that was originally derived from Indian sources. It is written across the page from left to right; words are not separated as in most European languages, and where spaces do occur, they very often correspond to some form of punctuation in English, such as a full stop or comma.

Phonology

General

There are significant differences between the phonological systems of Thai and English. In Thai, there are 21 consonant phonemes and 21 vowel phonemes. In the Thai consonant system, the aspirated voiceless stops /pʰ/, /tʰ/ and /kʰ/ are distinct phonemes and not simply allophones (varieties) of /p/, /t/ and /k/ as they are in English. English has more fricatives than Thai, and Thais tend to have difficulty in producing these (e.g. /θ/, /ð/, /v/, /z/, /ʃ/ and /ʒ/). Vowel length is significant in Thai, with a basic distinction made between long and short vowels.

Thais speak English with a 'Thai accent' because they try to fit every English word into the Thai phonological system. While this is to some extent true of every foreign accent, there does appear to be a peculiar reluctance among many Thai speakers to shed their accent. In Thailand, this can be explained perhaps by peer group pressure and not wanting to show off or be different in the classroom environment. But as numerous English loan words (including brand names of hundreds of consumer goods) have passed into everyday Thai, it has also become a perfectly normal and legitimate strategy to pronounce English words in a Thai way; to pronounce them any other way risks not being understood and sounding pretentious. This process is reinforced by teachers and English–Thai dictionaries providing transliterations of English words in Thai script in an attempt to clarify pronunciation. As a result, English consonants and vowels are widely pronounced as their nearest Thai equivalents.

Some of the more common features of a 'Thai accent' in English are:
– Stress on the final syllable of words.
– Problems in articulating certain final consonants and consonant clusters.
– A staccato effect, deriving from:
    a) a tendency to assign tones to syllables;
    b) a tendency to give equal weight and timing to each syllable;
    c) glottal stops before initial vowels;
    d) insertion of a short vowel /ə/ between certain initial consonant clusters;
    e) reduction of consonant clusters at the ends of words to single consonants.

Vowels

iː	ɪ	e	æ	eɪ	aɪ	ɔɪ
ɑː	ɒ	ɔː	ʊ	aʊ	əʊ	ɪə
uː	ʌ	ɜː	ə	eə	ʊə	aʊə / aʊə

Shaded phonemes have equivalents or near equivalents in Thai and should therefore be perceived and articulated without great difficulty, although some confusions may still arise. Unshaded phonemes may cause problems. For detailed comments, see below.

1. /æ/ is frequently pronounced as a long vowel /æː/.
2. Diphthongs /eɪ/, /əʊ/ and /eə/ are frequently pronounced as long pure vowels, /eː/, /oː/ and /æː/ respectively.
3. English words ending in a vowel frequently have the final vowel lengthened to accommodate the stress placed on the final syllable.

Consonants

p	b	f	v	θ	ð	t	d
s	z	ʃ	ʒ	tʃ	dʒ	k	g
m	n	ŋ	l	r	j	w	h

Shaded phonemes have equivalents or near equivalents in Thai and should therefore be perceived and articulated without great difficulty *when they occur as initial consonants*. Unshaded phonemes may cause problems. For detailed comments see below.

1. In pronouncing English initial consonants for which there is no rough equivalent in Thai, Thai speakers are likely to make the following substitutions:

English:	/v/	/θ/	/ð/	/ʃ/	/z/
Thai approximation:	/w/	/t/ /s/	/d/ /t/ /s/	/tʃ/	/s/

2. Many of the shaded consonants will cause great problems of articulation for Thai speakers when they occur as *final consonants*. Thai has only eight final consonant phonemes and no final clusters. As a result, English final consonants and consonant clusters are liable to undergo a radical change in pronunciation. Such transformations are not random, however; some typical changes undergone by single final consonants are:

English:	/d/ /θ/ /ð/ /s/ /z/ /ʃ/ /ʒ/ /tʃ/ /dʒ/	/v/ /f/	/l/
Thai approximation:	/t/	/p/	/n/

3. /g/ and /dʒ/ are often pronounced as unvoiced consonants by Thai speakers when they occur at the beginning of a word.
4. Although /r/ exists in Thai, it presents a problem to many Thai speakers even in their own language, where they may often substitute /l/. This strategy is then carried over when speaking English.
5. The glottal stop is a phoneme in Thai, and Thai speakers will often insert one at the beginning of English words that have an initial vowel sound; this tends to create a staccato effect and preclude juncture.

Consonant clusters

English has a much wider range of consonant clusters than Thai; consonant clusters never occur at the end of words in Thai. Among the initial two-segment clusters which do not occur in Thai are: /dr/, /fr/, /fl/, /fj/, /tw/, /sl/, /sw/, /sm/, /sp/, /sk/ and /st/. In pronouncing English words where such clusters occur, Thais tend to insert a short vowel, sometimes even creating another fully-stressed syllable:

>   *smoke* becomes '*sa-moke*'
>   *frown* becomes '*fa-rown*'

A similar process operates with English three-segment initial clusters:

>   *screw* becomes '*sa-crew*'
>   *strike* becomes '*sa-trike*'

There are, however, near Thai equivalents to initial /gr/, /gl/, /kr/, /kl/, /kw/, /pr/ and /pl/.

It is not uncommon, especially in Bangkok, for Thai speakers to drop the second segment of a two-segment consonant cluster at the beginning of a Thai word. Thus words like khray (= *who?*) and plaa (= *fish*) are frequently pronounced khay and paa. Thais who 'reduce' words like this in their own language may carry the process into English, and say '*bake*' for *brake* and '*fee*' for *free*; and '*fried rice*' is often pronounced as '*fide lice*'.

English final clusters present the Thai speaker with a problem and usually some way of 'reducing' them to a single manageable final consonant is sought. Generally, the first segment of the cluster is retained and the rest dropped.

>   *pump* becomes '*pum*'
>   *perfect* becomes '*perfec*'

Rhythm and stress

Every syllable in Thai carries a certain fixed tone. Thais tend to give equal weight and timing to each syllable and this, together with the fact that tonal pitch is located on single syllables (instead of groups of syllables, as it is in English) produces a rather staccato effect when transferred to English. The single most common mistake of Thai speakers is to stress the final syllable of polysyllabic English words, as in *but'ter, cof'fee, shop'ping*, and so on. More complex uses of stress, for example to alter meaning or to convey attitudinal meaning, are likely to present problems even to advanced learners.

Intonation

Intonation patterns in Thai are very different from those of English. Being a basically monosyllabic language, Thai has a sharp up-and-down pitch contour. Although questions in Thai are frequently marked by 'question words' at the end of a sentence which have an inherent rising tone, this does not automatically facilitate the reproduction of English question contours. Particular attention should be paid to the intonation of polite requests; Thai uses a whole series of untranslatable words or 'particles' at the ends of sentences to perform some of the functions fulfilled by intonation in English. When translating from Thai to English, the polite particles used in requests disappear, leaving a rather brusque imperative if the speaker has been too literal.

Juncture

In Thai it is impossible to produce new consonant clusters from the junctures of final and initial consonants; the glottal stop before initial vowels also tends to preclude a link between final consonant and initial vowel. Thai speakers are likely to be unaware of the phonetic changes that take place in English through juncture (e.g. *would you* /wʊdʒə/; *get back* /ge(p)bæk/) unless these are specifically pointed out.

Influence of spelling on pronunciation

Thais learning English obviously make numerous mistakes in pronouncing new words because of the considerable mismatch between spelling and pronunciation in English. Typical problems which persist even among fairly advanced learners are:

Thai speakers

1. Uncertainty as to when *th* is pronounced /θ/ and when /ð/ (assuming of course that the speaker can productively differentiate between the two sounds).
2. Uncertainty as to when *s* is pronounced /s/ and when /z/.
3. Failure to make a reduced pronunciation of the unstressed vowels in words such as *common, problem, police, possible, breakfast.*
4. Thais also tend to pronounce words such as *can, was, have* with their strong 'written' pronunciations instead of using weak forms.
5. The Thai spelling of common English loan words reinforces a non-English pronunciation, which then assumes a legitimacy which learners sometimes find hard to defy when dealing with the word in an English context.

Orthography and punctuation

Spelling and writing

Thai is written with an alphabetic system which runs across the page from left to right. There is no distinction between upper and lower case. The position of the vowel symbols varies, with some written above the consonant, some below, some to the left and some following on the right – and some surrounding the consonant on three sides. Thai words are not separated by spaces; the spaces that do occur occasionally in Thai writing generally correspond to punctuation marks in English. Most Thais are exposed to the Roman alphabet at an early age and spend a considerable amount of time at the initial stage copying out letters and words; even those with little or no knowledge of English may be sufficiently familiar with the Roman alphabet to decipher words in isolation.

Punctuation

Essentially, there are no punctuation marks in Thai, although spaces between groups of words are used to indicate pauses. In the past there has been some experimentation with western punctuation marks, and question marks, exclamation marks and inverted commas can often be found in old books; they are, however, redundant and less common nowadays. Punctuation presents quite a problem to Thai learners; errors of omission are frequent, while the concept of what constitutes a sentence may prove an obstacle.

Grammar

General

The grammatical structure of Thai is very different from that of English. Plurals of nouns and verb tenses are normally unmarked; when it is necessary to distinguish between singular and plural or the time an action takes place, this is done by the addition of structural words rather than by inflection. Thai adjectives and adverbs can also function as verbs, while the Thai pronominal system is more complex, with different sets of pronouns reflecting different degrees of intimacy and hierarchy. One of the few broad areas of similarity is the order of words in a sentence, namely, 'subject + verb + object'; however, the subject is commonly omitted in Thai when it is clearly understood who or what is referred to.

Auxiliaries; questions and negatives

There are no auxiliary verbs in Thai.

1. In Thai, a sentence is transformed into a question by the addition of a question word which is placed at the end of the sentence. Since the question word has no equivalent in English, Thai speakers will often simply substitute a rising intonation in an otherwise literal translation:
   He go? (Note also the uninflected verb.)
2. Negative questions – and answers – frequently cause confusion, Thais typically answering 'yes' where English requires 'no'.
   'You're not going, are you?' '*Yes (I'm not).*'
3. More specific questions such as *When?*, *Why?* and *How?* have direct equivalents in Thai, but since the first two can occur at either the beginning or the end of the sentence, the learner may produce sentences like:
   When he go?
   He go when?
   How many? is frequently used to the exclusion of *How much?* and the verb is often omitted also:
   How many the price that shirt?
4. Negatives in Thai are formed by putting the negative word mây in front of the verb. Confusion sometimes arises as to whether this word should be translated as *no* or *not*, resulting in sentences like:
   He not go.
   He no go.

Time, tense and aspect

The Thai verb has no inflected forms; a single word pay (= *go*) covers not simply *go* and *goes*, but also *went, was going, has gone, is going, will go, would go* and so on. Usually situation and context preclude any ambiguity, but where there is a possibility of misunderstanding arising, structural words are added, usually immediately in front of the verb, to clarify the time-reference. In normal narrative, it is usually quite enough to use the verb without any pre-verb modifier.

Verb inflections and complex verb phrases present a formidable obstacle to Thai learners, and many prefer to use the unmarked base form of the English verb rather than attempt a more difficult form which they feel will more than likely be incorrect.

> *Yesterday we visit London.*
> *She pay already.*
> *I leave him since ten o'clock.*

Note, however, that a Thai who appears to be using the base form of a verb in speech may actually be having problems with pronunciation rather than grammar. He or she may be trying to say, for instance, *cooked* or *arranged*, but failing to pronounce the *-ed* at the end of the cluster. This is obviously a major area in which Thai speakers are at a disadvantage compared with European learners of English, and this should be borne in mind when teaching classes of mixed nationalities.

Articles

There are no articles in Thai, and errors of confusion between indefinite and definite articles, as well as when to omit articles, occur frequently:

> *He is very nice man.*
> *What the food you like?*
> *The buffaloes are the important animals in Thailand.*

Adjectives and adverbs

Adjectives and adverbs in Thai occur after the noun or verb which they modify. They also function as verbs meaning *to be* (the Thai equivalent of *to be* is not used as a copula with adjectives). Thus the expression rót dii (= *car-good*) can be considered as either a phrase (*a good car*) or a sentence (*the car is good*). As a result, the verb is often omitted in English sentences:

> *This car not good.*
> *This food very tasty.*

In Thai, there is no distinction between adjective/adverb pairs as there is in English (e.g. *good/well, clear/clearly*). Thai learners tend to overuse the adjectival form in English:

*You speak Thai very good.

The comparative and superlative degrees of adjectives and adverbs in Thai are formed by the addition of the equivalent of *more than* and *(the) most* respectively, immediately after the base word. As a result, the English suffixes *-er* and *-est* are frequently disregarded by Thai learners:

*This dress is beautiful more than that one.
*I work the most hard of my brothers.

Nouns

Thai nouns have neither gender nor case, nor is there any distinction between singular and plural forms. Context is generally sufficient to indicate whether a noun has singular or plural reference, but in instances where it is important to be more precise, Thai employs 'pluraliser words' which occupy a fixed position in relation to the noun, or exact numerical descriptions. Thai learners make frequent errors in using the singular form of an English noun (the unmarked form) where a plural should be used:

*I have many friend.

Again, however, it must be borne in mind that the Thai sound system has no final *-s*, nor final consonant clusters; some learners may have problems in oral production yet reproduce correct written forms.

Numerical expressions in Thai are more complex than in English, and involve the use of a special 'noun classifier'. *Two cars* and *five girls* would be expressed in Thai as:

car	two	vehicle
girl	five	person
(noun) +	(number) +	(classifier)

The Thai pattern seldom causes interference, but failure to pluralise a noun after a number is very common:

*I have five brother.

Pronouns

The pronoun system of Thai is considerably more complex than that of most European languages, with a wide range of words to indicate relationships of both hierarchy and intimacy. Kin terms and personal names are widely used as first and second person pronouns to signal intimacy. English pronouns present problems for the Thai learner, because the two languages make different distinctions in both gender and number. Thus, there are masculine and feminine first-person pronouns in Thai, while the most commonly used third-person pronoun makes no distinction between gender, with the result that Thai learners frequently use *he* and *she* interchangeably in English:

> *My girlfriend, he is very nice.*
> *The policeman she chase me.*

(Note also the duplication of noun and pronoun which occurs commonly in spoken Thai.)

The same third-person pronoun not only does not differentiate gender – it does not distinguish number either, resulting in confusing statements like:

> *My American friends are in Thailand. He stay at the hotel.*
> *My sisters study at the university. He work very hard.*

Thai pronouns do not have separate forms to indicate subject or object functions; nor is there a possessive pronoun in Thai. Possession in Thai is expressed in the terms 'noun + of + noun/pronoun', although the Thai word for *of* is optional and frequently omitted. This can lead to mistakes like:

> *house of my father* or *house of father*

It is very common in Thai to omit the subject from a sentence if it is perfectly clear who or what is being talked about. This means that pronouns are frequently discarded in Thai sentences, a pattern sometimes carried over into English:

> *My brother was angry when came home.*

Prepositions

Most English prepositions have near Thai equivalents and are relatively easy for Thai learners to grasp. More difficult are English 'verb + preposition' or 'adjective + preposition' combinations which have a single-word Thai verb equivalent. This leads to errors such as:

> *I angry you.*
> *We interest / are interested it.*
> *He frighten / is frightened you.*

Subordinate clauses

Thai learners inevitably experience difficulty in producing the correct verb tenses in complex sentences with subordinate clauses; again the most common strategy is to opt for the unmarked form. Relative clauses present a further problem in that Thai has only one relative pronoun, and *who* and *which* in particular are frequently confused:

*My friend which I met . . .

Conditional clauses in Thai frequently omit the word for *if*, and this is sometimes carried over into English. Other typical sentence constructions arising from a literal translation from Thai include:

*Although . . . but . . .
*Because . . . therefore . . .

Vocabulary

Traditionally, Sanskrit and Pali have been used for coining new words in Thai; however, the influx of western technology and consumer goods has resulted in a considerable number of English loanwords being adopted into the Thai lexicon. Such borrowings are given a Thai pronunciation which some Thai learners find difficult to shed when using the word in English, for example:

plastic	pát-tik
style	sa-taay
strike	sa-tráy
football	fút-bɔɔn
pump	pám
alcohol	ʔɛn-kɔ-hɔɔ

Apart from these loanwords, there is no similarity between the Thai and English lexicons, and the Thai learner has none of the advantages of the Western European learner who can draw on some familiarity with Latin and Germanic roots to guess vocabulary. The fact that many Thais with limited communicative competence in English nevertheless seem to have an extensive English vocabulary is largely due to traditional methods of education, which put great emphasis on rote learning at the expense of developing communication skills.

Culture

Generally speaking, Thais have a very positive attitude towards learning English. Competence in the language is seen as both a mark of sophistication and a passport to a more prosperous life. Most top jobs require a sound knowledge of the language, and tens of thousands of parents make considerable financial sacrifices each year so that their offspring can move from the provinces to the big cities, or from the big cities to overseas, in order to gain a better facility in the language. There even appears to be a certain social prestige attached to simply attending

English classes, for many people with little need for English and little real interest appear to be willing to part with considerable sums of money to register for courses from which they will gain little benefit and to which they feel even less commitment.

English has been regarded as essential for national development and has therefore been a compulsory element in the secondary school curriculum for many years. However, the quality of language education provided varies enormously; in Bangkok, expensive private schools often provide English at the primary level, and with competent teachers and sometimes native speakers on their staffs, their pupils can be very fluent speakers by the time they leave school. Children from a rural background face a severe handicap by comparison, for the best teachers have traditionally gravitated towards the capital, where the pay and conditions are better; it is there, too, that most of the opportunities open to foreigners wanting to teach English in Thailand are to be found.

The teacher is traditionally a highly respected and respectable figure, and a class in Thailand is likely to have definite ideas about what is and what is not appropriate 'teacher behaviour'. Most things are a matter of common sense, although the Thailand-bound teacher would be well-advised to find out something about cultural *faux pas* from the numerous culture and etiquette guides now available. One area where Westerners do sometimes offend is in the matter of dress: appearance is very important in Thai society and a failure to adapt to this (and other cultural values) can seriously undermine the effectiveness of the teacher and even create latent hostility. When it comes to actual teaching, engaging pupils' active participation can be a problem. More used to receiving knowledge passively, they may feel threatened by a more active communication-oriented approach; alternatively, they may feel that they are learning nothing once the blackboard examples of grammar rules give way to apparently chaotic conversation classes. The Western teacher should also bear in mind that Thai society is a very hierarchical one; older learners should be treated with respect at all times. 'Face' is also important and any attempt to humiliate a student (e.g. by leaving a long pause after a question which the learner cannot answer, brushing aside pedantic questions too quickly, etc.) may rebound on the teacher, with the class withdrawing cooperation in sympathy with the victim. Similarly, showing anger and impatience, no matter how justified it may seem, is as culturally inappropriate and counter-productive in the classroom as anywhere in Thailand and will invariably alienate a class.

A sample of written Thai

Type-written Thai

ประชากรทางภาคใต้มีลักษณะแตกต่างจากประชากรทางภาคอื่นบ้างในทางผิว
พรรณและรูปร่างหน้าตากับสำเนียงภาษา ส่วนความเป็นอยู่และอาชีพนั้นส่วนใหญ่ก็คือ
การกสิกรรม แต่มีข้าวน้อยกว่าภาคกลาง มีผลไม้มากซึ่งพอจะเป็นรายได้ดีถ้าการขน
ส่งสะดวก หาตลาดได้ไกล ๆ ผลิตผลที่เป็นรายได้ขึ้นหน้าขึ้นตากว่าผลไม้คือยางพารา
ซึ่งปลูกกันมากในจังหวัดตอนใต้และเหมืองแร่ดีบุกในบางท้องที่

A direct transliteration

prachaakɔɔn thaaŋ phâak tâay mii láksanà tɛ̀ɛktàaŋ càak prachaakɔɔn
thaaŋ phâak ɯ̀ɯn bâaŋ nay thaaŋ phĭwphan lɛ́? rûuprâaŋ nâataa kàp
sămniaŋ phaasăa sùan khwaam pen yùu lɛ́? aachíip nán sùan yày kô khɯɯ
kaan kasikam tɛ̀ɛ mii khâaw nɔ́ɔy kwàa phâak klaaŋ mii phŏnlamáay
mâak sɯ̂ŋ phɔɔ ca pen raaydâay dii thâa kaan khŏn sòŋ saduàk hăa talàat
dâay klay klay phalìtphŏn thîi pen raaydâay khɯ̂n nâa khɯ̂n taa kwàa
phŏnlamáay khɯɯ yaaŋ phaaraa sɯ̂ŋ plùuk kan mâak nay caŋwàt tɔɔn
tâay lɛ́? mŭaŋrɛ̂ɛ diibùk nay baaŋ thɔ́ɔŋthîi

A word-for-word translation

person way region south have characteristic different from person way
region other somewhat in way of complexion and shape face eye with
sound language. as for living and profession part big is agriculture but
have rice few than region middle. have fruit much which sufficient will
be income good if carry send convenient find market can far far.
product which is income rise face rise eye more than fruit is rubber para
which grow together much in province part south and mine tin in some
area.

An idiomatic translation

The people of the South differ somewhat from the people of other
regions in their complexion and physical appearance and in their
language. As far as their way of living and occupations are concerned,
they are mainly involved in agriculture. But there is less rice than in the

Thai speakers

Central Region. There is a lot of fruit, sufficient to bring in a good income if transportation is convenient and markets can be found over a wide area. A product which brings in a more noticeable income than fruit is the para rubber tree, which is grown in the southern provinces, and the tin mines in some areas.

The CD

On the accompanying CD, speakers of the various languages referred to in the book were recorded:

1. reading the introduction to the story shown in the picture strip below;
2. continuing this story in their own words;
3. reading aloud the shopping list which follows;
4. giving brief details of their nationality, place of birth and first language.

In this way they produced samples of controlled and semi-controlled speech, in which common characteristic phonological and syntactic difficulties may be exemplified. The reading texts are briefly annotated to indicate areas of difficulty some speakers may have.

The interviews are in the order of the chapters but, for the benefit of those readers who enjoy a challenge, the nationality and first language of the speakers are not revealed until their closing remarks.

The introduction to the picture story

My uncle, John Smith, has a very good job. He's a university professor, actually, and very intelligent. But the strange thing is, he's always losing things. It's quite extraordinary. Last Thursday, for example, during a trip to London on business, he accidentally left his umbrella on the train. It must be the sixth time he's lost that same umbrella. It's a rather special one, with red and yellow stripes, a present from his youngest daughter for his birthday one year. Anyway, the next day, as soon as he was free, he called at the Lost Property Office to ask about it. Fortunately, it's in the next street to his house. He's no stranger to the people there. They know him quite well.

In addition to the general rhythm, intonation, phrasing and tone of the reading, the discrete points listed may illustrate specific L1 problems.

my uncle . . . link with /j/ (also *very intelligent, he accidentally, Property Office*)

John . . . initial /dʒ/ (also *job*)

John . . . final /n/ after a vowel (also *London, train, one, soon*)

Smith . . . initial cluster (also *strange, special, stripes, stranger*)

job . . . final voiced consonant(s) (also *strange, things, called*)

very intelligent . . . pronunciation of /l/ and /r/ (also *lost, umbrella, red and yellow stripes, present, free, Lost Property, stranger*)

the strange thing . . . pronunciation of /ð/ and /θ/ (also *Smith, Thursday, sixth, that, rather, with, birthday, there, they*)

extraordinary . . . pronunciation and initial cluster /kstr/

Thursday . . . pronunciation of /ɜː/ (also *university, birthday*)

accidentally . . . pronunciation of initial cluster /æks/

for example . . . linking *r*

the sixth time . . . cluster /ksθt/

special . . . pronunciation of /ci/ > /ʃ/

red and yellow . . . weak form of *and*

stripes . . . pronunciation of final cluster (also *intelligent, left, must, lost, present, called*)

youngest . . . pronunciation of medial /ŋg/

daughter . . . pronunciation of /ɔː/ (also *always, extraordinary, called, fortunately*)

one year . . . initial /j/

as soon as he was free . . . rhythm, junctures and weak forms of *as* and *was*

to ask . . . link with /w/

about it . . . unstressed final pronoun

fortunately . . . pronunciation of /tu/ > /tʃ/ (also *actually*) and syllable stress

the next street . . . a cluster of six consecutive consonant phonemes to cope with

to his house . . . while the /h/ may be elided on *his*, it should not be on *house*

quite well . . . pronunciation of /w/ sounds

The conclusion of the story to be told in the speaker's own words

At the Lost Property Office

1

2

3

4

5

Artwork by Joseph McEwan

The Shopping List reading passage

This list contains examples of the 44 English phonemes; in addition to the overall rhythm and tone, the way the phonemes and junctures are realised may indicate common L1 interference. The words *some, of, for, and* and *to* would normally have their weak, unstressed pronunciations (/səm/, /əv/, /fə/, /ən/ and /tə/).

	phonemes	clusters and junctures
If you're going shopping, John,	/j/ /g/ /ŋ/ /ʃ/ /dʒ/	ŋʃ ŋdʒ
could you get me these few things, please?	/ð/ /z/	d-j (/dʒ/) ŋz pl
Three kilos of beans,	/iː/ /θ/ /b/	θr nz
six fillets of fish	/ɪ/ /f/ /ʃ/	ks ts
some red and yellow peppers,	/e/ /r/ /j/ /p/	
a bag of apples,	/æ/ /b/ /g/	plz
half a kilo of large tomatoes,	/aː/ /h/ /f/ /k/ /dʒ/	dʒt
a coffee pot,	/ɒ/ /f/ /p/ /t/	
some corned beef and a pork pie,	/ɔː/ /b/ /p/	ndb kp
a cookery book,	/ʊ/ /k/ /b/	
one tub of butter,	/ʌ/ /b/ /t/	nt vb
two tubes of glue,	/uː/ /g/	bz gl
the turkey for Thursday,	/ɜː/ /ð/ /θ/ /i/	zd
eight paper plates,	/eɪ/ /p/	pl ts
a Dover sole,	/əʊ/ /d/ /v/ /s/	
a light white wine,	/aɪ/ /l/ /w/ /n/	tw
some brown flour,	/aʊ/ /m/ /n/ /aʊə/	mbr fl
some pure olive oil,	/ʊə/ /ɔɪ/ /v/	mpj
some beer, not too dear,	/ɪə/ /b/ /d/	mb t-t
a pair of jeans to wear,	/eə/ /dʒ/ /w/	nzt
six packets of crisps	/s/ /p/ /k/	ksp ts kr sps
a television magazine	/v/ /ʒ/ /g/ /z/	nm
some orange juice	/ɒ/ /dʒ/ /uː/	ndʒ dʒ-dʒ
and some Dutch cheese,	/tʃ/ /d/ /z/	tʃ-tʃ
cut thick or thin	/θ/ /k/ /n/	tθ
Thanks very much for your help, John.	/θ/ /v/ /tʃ/ /h/ /dʒ/	ŋksv lpdʒ

Note: The compounds *corned beef, pork pie* and *olive oil* should have two equal stresses, while *coffee pot, cookery book, television magazine* and *orange juice* should have the main stress on the first element.

Contents of the CD

Duration 71 mins 30 sec approx.